Glenveagh Mystery

Mystery

The Life, Work and Disappearance of Arthur Kingsley Porter

Lucy Costigan

MERRION

Dublin • Portland, Oregon

First published in 2013 by Merrion
an imprint of Irish Academic Press

8 Chapel Lane   920 NE 58th Avenue, Suite 300
Sallins   Portland, Oregon,
Co. Kildare Ireland   97213–3786, USA

British Library Cataloguing-in-Publication Data

Costigan, Lucy.
Glenveagh mystery : the life, work and disappearance of
Arthur Kingsley Porter.
1. Porter, Arthur Kingsley, 1883-1933. 2. Missing persons--
Ireland--Inishbofin. 3. Donegal (Ireland : County)--
Intellectual life--20th century.
I. Title
941.6'930822'092-dc23

978-1-908928-10-8 (cloth)
978-1-908928-11-5 (paper)
978-1-908928-16-0 (Ebook)

Library of Congress Cataloging in Publication Data
An entry can be found on request

Typeset by FiSH Books Ltd, Enfield, London
Printed and bound by CPI Group (UK) Ltd, Croydon, CR0 4YY

For Mike and Kathleen Costigan
In love and light, always

Contents

List of Illustrations ix

Acknowledgements xiii

Glossary xvii

Introduction 3

1.   The Search: Inishbofin, Co. Donegal, 8 July 1933 7

2.   Early Life: The Scandal that Shook Darien 13

3.   Coming of Age: Freedom and Vocation 36

4.   Establishing Roots: Marriage and Yale 47

5.   War and Separation 69

6.   Travels in France 78

7.   European Travels 91

8.   Elmwood, Harvard and Further Travels.............................108

9.   Accolades and New Horizons 131

10.   Depression and Confession..143

11.   Glenveagh Castle and Inishbofin.......................................159

12.   Ellis and the Ménage à Trois 177

13.   Harvard Witch-Hunt 194

14.   Rendezvous on Inishbofin...204

15.   Disappearance and Inquest 213

16. Verdict 226

17. Aftermath 232

18. Legend and Legacy 242

Notes 249

Bibliography 286

Index 309

Illustrations

1. Glenveagh Castle, Co. Donegal. Michael Cullen.
2. Lucy and A.K. Porter at Elmwood, photograph, c. 1920. Harvard University Archives, HUG 1706.125 (15).
3. Inishbofin Island, Co. Donegal. Michael Cullen.
4. Arthur Kingsley Porter in a canoe, Lake George, New York, 1912. Harvard University Archives, HUG 1706.125 (2).
5. Clockwise (left to right): Blachley Lodge, Noroton, Darien, CT; Timothy H. Porter; Schuyler Merritt; Interior of Blachley Lodge. Stamford Historical Society, from 'Gracious Living in Stamford, Late 19th and 20th Early Centuries', c. 1892.
6. Letter from Timothy H. Porter to Kingsley Porter, dated 15 July 1886. Harvard University Archives, HUG 1706.110, Family correspondence and papers of Porter Family 1885–86, Folder 1892–93.
7. Kingsley and fish at Boat House, Saranac Club, and guide, photograph, c. 1895. Harvard University Archives, HUG 1706.125 (14).
8. Arthur Kingsley Porter's room at Yale College, photograph, c. 1904. Harvard University Archives, HUG 1706.194.
9. Coutances Cathedral, France. Stanley Parry.
10. Kingsley aged 25 in 1908. Courtesy of Brooklyn Museum Archives. Goodyear Archival Collection. General correspondence (1.1.066): Porter (1910). Location unknown, 1908.
11. Letter from Lucy Bryant Wallace to Kingsley Porter, dated 26 December 1911. Harvard University Archives, HUG 1706.114, Correspondence of Arthur Kingsley Porter and Lucy W. Porter, 1911–25; 1911–12: After engagement.

12. Arthur Kingsley Porter, leaning on railing, Lake George, New York, 1912. Harvard University Archives, HUG 1706.125 (8).

13. Lucy Porter on honeymoon at Lake George, New York, 1912. Harvard University Archives.

14. Harkness Tower, Yale, New Haven, CT. Michael Cullen.

15. Soldiers removing art works from Cathedral in Reims, c. 1918. From *Rheims and the Battles for its Possession*, Illustrated Michelin Guides to the Battle-Fields (1914–1918) (Clermont-Ferrand: Michelin & Cie, 1919; published in eBook format by Project Gutenberg, 2011), p.23.

16. Letter from Kingsley Porter in Rome to Lucy Porter in Paris, dated 13 November 1918. Harvard University Archives, HUG 1706.114, Correspondence of Arthur Kingsley Porter and Lucy W. Porter 1911–25, 1918.

17. Cormicy Church (c. 1918). From *Rheims and the Battles for its Possession*, Illustrated Michelin Guides to the Battle-Fields (1914–1918) (Clermont-Ferrand: Michelin & Cie, 1919); published in ebook format by Project Gutenberg, 2011, p.145.

18. Notre Dame, Pontorson, France, taken by A. Kingsley Porter. Courtesy of Brooklyn Museum Archives, Goodyear Archival Collection, General correspondence (1.1.066): Porter (1910).

19. Photograph of Spanish monument, Santillana del Mar, Santander, Spain, taken by the Porters, n.d. Courtesy of Brooklyn Museum Archives, Goodyear Archival Collection, Visual materials (6.1.012): miscellaneous photographs.

20. Porters in car with chauffeur. Harvard University Archives, HUG 1706.125, Box 1, folder 1.

21. Bernard Berenson and I Tatti. Courtesy of Wikipedia Commons.

22. Elmwood, Cambridge, MA. Courtesy of Wikipedia Commons.

23. Arthur Kingsley Porter in Spain, c. 1924. Harvard University Archives, HUG 1706.125p (Folder 13), W272203_1.

24. Faculty members of Harvard's Fine Arts Department in the courtyard of the new Fogg Art Museum, January 1927. Standing (left to right): Meyric R. Rogers, Langdon Warner, George H.

Edgell, Arthur Kingsley Porter, Chandler R. Post, Martin Mower, Kenneth Conant; seated (left to right): Paul J. Sachs, George H. Chase, Denman W. Ross, Edward W. Forbes, Arthur Pope. Harvard University Archives, HUG 1706.125, Box 1, folder 11.

25. Sarcophagus of Alfonso Ansúrez, son of Count Pedro Ansúrez. From the monastery of San Benito, Sahagún, León, Spain. Courtesy of Wikimedia Commons.

26. Lucy and Kingsley Porter at Elmwood, Cambridge, MA, photograph, c. 1920. Harvard University Archives, HUG 1706.125p, Hollis No: olvwork272201; Photo no: W272201_1.

27. Passport photograph of Arthur Kingsley and Lucy Porter. Harvard University Archives, HUG 1706.125, Box 1, folder 4.

28. Kingsley sitting on the steps at Elmwood, Cambridge, MA. Harvard University Archives.

29. High Crosses at Clonmacnoise, Co. Offaly. Michael Cullen.

30. Signature of Arthur Kingsley Porter on the frontispiece of *Psychoanalysis and Aesthetics* (1924) by Charles Baudouin in Glenveagh Castle Library. Michael Cullen.

31. Glenveagh Castle, set amid the spectacular lakes and Derryveagh Mountains in Donegal; Glenveagh Castle exterior. Both Michael Cullen.

32. View of Lake George, Adirondacks Region, New York, 1912. Harvard University Archives, HUG 1706.125 (3).

33. Repairs to ruined cottage on Inishbofin, photograph, c. 1929. Harvard University Archives, HUG 1706.125 (10).

34. Library in Glenveagh Castle. Michael Cullen.

35. Æ (George Russell). Courtesy of Wikipedia Commons. Paintings by Æ in Glenveagh Castle library. Michael Cullen.

36. Master bedroom in Glenveagh Castle. Michael Cullen.

37. Havelock Ellis, from Stefano Bolognini, *Havelock Ellis: Philosopher of Love* (Cambridge: Riverside Press, 1928), photograph by Houston Peterson.

38. Porter holding pages of a newspaper or photographs. Harvard University Archives, HUG 1706.125, Box 1.

39. Lowell House at night, Harvard, Cambridge, MA. Michael Cullen.

40. Map of Donegal coastline and Inishbofin Island, from a mural in Falcarragh, Co. Donegal. Photograph by Michael Cullen.

41. Cliffs on Inishbofin. Michael Cullen.

42. Man wading and man in rowboat, Inishbofin shore, photograph, c. 1929. Harvard University Archives, HUG 1706.125 (12).

43. Woodland Cemetery, Stamford, CT, USA. Michael Cullen.

44. Inishbofin Island showing ruined hut. Michael Cullen.

45. Arthur Kingsley Porter, Courtesy of Glenveagh Castle Archives.

Acknowledgements

There are so many people to thank for their time and assistance during the researching and writing of *Glenveagh Mystery*, and for supporting the Arthur Kingsley Porter Project. A huge thank you to everyone involved, especially to each of the following:

Thomas Williams, without your original idea and persistent belief that this story was worth investigating, there would never have been such a book;

Theresa Cullen, for helping with all the research in Pusey Library in Harvard, in the British Library in London, in the National Archives of Ireland and National Museum in Dublin, and for trolling through so many archaic American newspapers and digital archives;

Michael Cullen, for adding such beauty and depth by the inclusion of your superb photos of Co. Donegal; of the High Crosses; of Cambridge, MA, and Connecticut, and for all the great graphic design suggestions;

Anthony Costigan, for the sharing of your brilliant ideas for the development of the story;

Robert Marburg, for your guided tour of Massachusetts and Connecticut, and for all your support and enthusiasm;

Raymond McGovern, for your help with the research of documents at the National Archives of Ireland, the National Museum of Ireland, and the Garda Museum at Dublin Castle, and for your constant support;

Lisa Hyde from the Irish Academic Press and Merrion, for your faith in the story and for all your brilliant editing and production;

Seamus Heaney, for your generous permission to allow me to quote from your beautiful poem, *Lovers on Aran*, and for all your kindness and support;

Loïc Jourdain and Cliodhna Kennedy of Lugh Films, for your support and guidance with the entire Arthur Kingsley Porter Project;

Pauline Sweeney and Donegal Airport for your generous sponsorship of the Arthur Kingsley Porter Project and website;

David Duggan, Regional Manager at Glenveagh Castle, and Tres Connaghan, Events Manager, for your kind use of the castle for photography and the use of material in the Glenveagh Archives;

James Laidlaw Dickson, Sales Executive at Execflyer Charter Helicopter Flights, for coming on board as part of the team;

Patrick Hogan, for sharing your photography skills and for all your support;

Dick Walsh, General Manager of the Talbot Hotel, Wexford Town, and all the wonderful staff there who have looked after the Arthur Kingsley Porter team over many years during our project meetings;

Michael Heaney, Director of Community, Culture and Planning with Donegal County Council;

Charles Sweeney, Donegal Community and Enterprise Administrative Officer;

Joeleen McDermot, of Donegal County Council for all your great ideas and enthusiasm to promote the Project in Donegal;

Noel McBride, Councillor in Donegal;

Padraig Doherty, Councillor in Donegal;

Helena McClafferty and Paddy McHugh from An TSean Bheairic, Falcarragh, Co. Donegal;

Tony Walsh, Media Spokesperson for the Arthur Kingsley Porter Project, for your invaluable support, your infectious enthusiasm and for your kindness and friendship;

Margo Doyle, Principal Dealer and Marketing Manager for Slaney View Motors, Honda stockists, and for sponsorship of the Arthur Kingsley Porter Project;

Elaine McIntyre, Director of Sales, at the Radisson Blu Hotel, Letterkenny;

Martha Conover, from *Martha's Travel Corner* in Illinois, USA, for developing unique tours based on *Glenveagh Mystery*;

Seán McElwee, General Manager of Óstán Loch Altan, Gortahork, Co. Donegal, for creating the Arthur Kingsley Porter lounge and library, and for your incredible vision;

Patrick Gallagher Travel, Churchill, Co. Donegal, and Gavin Boyce of Boyce Coach Travel, Letterkenny, Co. Donegal, for courtesy coach services;

The Shelbourne Hotel, Dublin, for generous sponsorship;

Dinny McGinley, Minister of State for Gaeltacht and the Islands;

The wonderful artists who have created unique collections of various exquisite artworks, inspired by the story of Lucy and Kingsley Porter, including Brendan McGloin, Lisa Mullin, Patsy Flood O'Connor, Carmel Grant, Liam Logue, Rónán and Conor McGarvey of Donegal Pens, Pauline Murphy, Kerstin Gronvall;

Helen McCleary, a poet of rare talent, for creating a collection of poetry in honour of the Porters;

Gearoidín Breathnach, a traditional storyteller or Seanchaí, for creating a collection of stories based on *Glenveagh Mystery*;

Ann Tuite, official harpist for the Porter project, for composing a remarkable musical piece to commemoration Kingsley Porter;

Melanie Porter Torres, Great Grand Niece of Kingsley and Lucy Porter;

Danny and Annie McIntyre;

Pusey Library in Harvard, Cambridge, MA;

The British Library, London;

The Brooklyn Museum Archives, New York;

The Director of the National Archives of Ireland and the staff at the National Museum of Ireland, Kildare Street, Dublin;

Orla Fitzpatrick, Librarian at the National Museum of Ireland;

Sean O'Gaoithin, Head Gardener at Glenveagh Castle;

Fr Ferry, for your generous help and support with the project;

John O'Brien, for sharing stories about Kingsley Porter on Inishbofin;

Ann Shields from Cumann Amaitéarach Drámaíochta;

Cormac O'Kane, Head of Design and Creative Media, at Letterkenny Institute of Technology;

Edmund Cassidy, for sponsorship of Elmwood Downs, Letterkenny;

Carmel Barron and the library staff throughout Co. Donegal;

Kathleen Hinds, creator of 'Murder Mystery', based on the inquest of Kingsley Porter, and the members of the Omagh Players' drama group;

Noel McGinley, for your help and enthusiasm in promoting tourism in Donegal and Ireland based on the Kingsley Porter story;

Maura Aine Gardener and Joan Crawford, from Failte Ireland in Letterkenny;

Charlie McGinley, the Donegal Association, Dublin;

Nial Gibbons, Chief Executive of Tourism Ireland;

Siobhan McManamy, Head of Co-operation Marketing, Tourism Ireland, Dublin;

Theresa Farrell, Glendown Bed and Breakfast, Co. Donegal;

Una McGarrigle, Secretary of the Donegal Historical Society (DHS), for your help and wonderful contacts;

Barbara Kaye of the Stamford Historical Society, CT, for your helpful information on the Porters of Darien and Woodland Cemetery;

Steve Marburg, for your kind hospitality when we stayed with you in Maine during our East Coast tour;

Carol and Larry Williams, for all your generosity and kindness when you opened your Stamford home to us;

All of the Costigan and Cullen families for your love and support: Sharon, Paul, Damien, Sean, Kathleen, Lisa and Antoinette;

The special friends who are always so supportive of every project: Isabel MacMahon, Clara Martin, Carmel Larkin, Maura O'Connor, Rita and Jimmy Murphy;

And finally, a big hug for my royal companions, Lynsey, Sophie and Kila, and also for Tiger, for sharing all those early morning and midnight vigils.

Glossary

Altarpiece: A picture or relief representing a religious subject suspended in a frame behind the altar of a church.

Apse: A semicircular recess covered with a hemispherical vault or semi-dome.

Barocco: A picturesque, exalted, architectural style that prevailed in ecclesiastical architecture for two centuries and is most associated with Michelangelo, its creator, and with the architects, Bernini and Borromini.

Capital: Forms the top-most member of a column.

Caryatid: A sculpted female figure serving as an architectural support taking the place of a column or pillar, supporting an entablature on her head.

Cloister: A covered walk in a convent, monastery, college or cathedral on one side and a colonnade open to a quadrangle on the other.

Fresco: Any type of mural painting executed on plastered walls or ceilings.

Gothic: Architectural style that flourished during the twelfth century, and is characterized by pointed arches. The dates associated with the Gothic style are between the twelfth and the sixteenth centuries.

Medieval: A period in history that can broadly refer to the period between the fifth and the fifteenth centuries.

Mosaic: Art of creating images using an assemblage of small pieces of coloured stone, glass or other material.

Moulding: Process of manufacturing by shaping pliable raw material using a rigid frame or model called a pattern.

Portal: Opening in the walls of a building, such as a door or gate.

Relief: Sculpture where the sculpted material has been raised above the background plane.

Renaissance: Cultural movement that began in Italy and spread to Western Europe, spanning the fourteenth to the seventeenth centuries.

Romanesque: Architectural style developed in Italy and western medieval Europe, characterized by semi-circular arches and vaults and by profuse ornamentation. There is no definite period for its development, but it usually refers to monuments built between the sixth and eleventh centuries; between the Roman and Gothic architectural styles.

Sacristy: A room in a church where vestments, sacred vessels and church records are stored.

Sarcophagus: Funeral receptacle for a corpse.

Sepulchral: Relating to a tomb or interment.

Tracery: The stonework elements that support the glass in a Gothic window.

Triptych: A set of three pictures or panels usually hinged together so that the two winged panels fold over the central one.

Tympanum (Tympana): The triangular space or pediment above a portico, door or window.

Vault: An arched form, used to provide a space with a ceiling or roof.

The timeless waves, bright, sifting, broken glass,
Came dazzling around, into the rocks,
Came glinting, sifting from the Americas

From 'Lovers on Aran', in *Death of a Naturalist*
(Faber & Faber, 1966)
By kind courtesy of Seamus Heaney.

Introduction

My visit to Glenveagh Castle in October 2005 was even more thrilling than I could ever have imagined. I had been travelling around Co. Donegal for the past five days accompanied by my nephew, Michael, our friend, Thomas, and my beloved King Charles spaniel, Kila. We had traversed the county, revelling in the wild, unspoilt beauty that uniquely belongs to this remote, north-west county. I can still vividly recall driving through Glenveagh National Park, surrounded by the glorious Derryveagh Mountains, entranced by the soft sunlight as it danced across a series of pristine lakes. Then finally our first glimpse of Glenveagh Castle: a granite fortress, sitting perched, overlooking its solitary kingdom. Luckily we were just in time for the castle tour. I urged Thomas to take the first tour, while Michael and I brought Kila for a well-deserved walk, exploring the Victorian walled garden, the exquisite Italian and Tuscan gardens, and the Gothic Orangery.

After a lovely walk, Michael went off to photograph the gardens while I was happy to loll in the fading sunlight and breathe in the pure air. I closed my eyes for a few moments. I could hardly imagine how wonderful it would be to own Glenveagh Castle, to sit in these gardens in midsummer and to order afternoon tea for my guests. I could almost smell the freshly baked scones, the dainty sandwiches and slices of fruitcake, complete with full cream and home-made jam, all served on a silver salver.

I was awakened from my reverie by the reappearance of Thomas who was beside himself with excitement.

1. Glenveagh Castle, Co. Donegal.
Michael Cullen.

'That was really amazing! I couldn't believe what happened to one of the owners – Arthur Kingsley Porter. He was an American professor – from Harvard, I think – and a famous archaeologist and author, a multimillionaire who bought Glenveagh in the twenties and came to live here with his wife...'.

He was speaking so fast it was hard to keep up. But there was no doubting his exhilaration.

'It's incredible! He went out for a walk during a storm on a nearby island and he vanished, he simply disappeared without trace. But he was very athletic and a strong swimmer, and for years afterwards people swore that they saw him as far away as India. Then there was talk that he used to come back to visit his wife in the castle at night. There was a rumour too that locals had done away with him. But no one seems to have bothered to investigate all this. Isn't that incredible? A wealthy American professor and the owner of all this!' He gestured towards the sweeping castle grounds and gardens. 'He disappeared into thin air and no one has a clue what happened to him or why he might have disappeared. Now *that* is a fantastic story.'

The fate of Professor Porter was indeed intriguing to contemplate. I had already fallen under the spell of Glenveagh and this mystery just added another layer to the exquisite ambience of this enchanted place. In time, the life of Arthur Kingsley Porter and that of his devoted wife, Lucy, would become my full-time pursuit over several years, as I read the professor's academic books and plays; perused Lucy's diaries; read through their copious correspondence located in Pusey Library in Harvard University, and the British Library in London; strolled through the district of Noroton, in Stamford, Connecticut, where Kingsley was reared; visited their mansion, Elmwood, in Cambridge, Massachusetts; said a silent prayer for all the Porters and Hoyts who were finally at rest beneath my feet in Woodland Cemetery, Connecticut; walked the last

known route that Kingsley Porter trod on Inishbofin island, before his sudden disappearance.

I took the final tour that day in Glenveagh Castle. The tour guide brought us through several rooms that had been decorated by the Porters and had never been altered. The pale-gold library still contains the four paintings presented by the poet Æ (George Russell) to his friend, Kingsley. The sumptuous master bedroom is

2. Lucy and A.K. Porter at Elmwood, photograph, c. 1920.

Harvard University Archives, HUG 1706.125 (15).

dominated by the mahogany four-poster bed that Lucy Porter brought with her to Glenveagh. Walking through the shadowy corridors I began to feel that Professor Porter wanted the truth of his life and disappearance to be finally told. And so it is that this most singular tale of a brilliant but complex man is here unravelled and transcribed. For only then can all concerned be set free.

Lucy Costigan, 12 March 2012

Chapter one

The Search: Inishbofin, Co. Donegal, 8 July 1933

Lucy Porter hurried towards the cottage. The storm was beginning to rage now, tugging at her coat, threatening to pull off her hat and scatter her grey-speckled hair to the four winds. She leaned in close to the window and anxiously peered inside, her stomach lurching as she surveyed the empty chairs still arranged around the kitchen table. Nothing stirred within. So he hadn't had a change of heart. He hadn't put off his plan to write outdoors and instead come back early for another cup of coffee or to share some idea that had suddenly flashed across his mind. She stood staring for several moments, then slowly turned to face the full blast of the wind. She glanced furtively up and down the beach but it was deserted.

The wind had risen considerably in the past hour since Kingsley and Owen McGee had gone out to secure the curragh. If the weather had stayed fine they'd be rowing back by now or perhaps they'd already have reached Magheraroarty. They might even have been on the road to Glenveagh, where they could have spent a leisurely afternoon doing some weeding or maybe a little reading, waiting for the arrival of their dear friend, Æ.

In the distance, the dark mass of Inishdooey momentarily caught her gaze. The sea was turning silver grey and the angry currents were whipping the waves wildly towards the shore. It was no weather to row a curragh across the sea. The mere thought of it sent a shiver down her spine and she pulled her coat tighter, crossing her arms to shield her body from the relentless wind.

3. Inishbofin Island, Co. Donegal.
Michael Cullen.

A sudden thought gripped her and she began to half-walk, half-run away from the cottage. Maybe Kingsley had passed the hut and gone towards Meenlara? Lucy was breathing hard now as she struggled to keep her footing. Boulders were strewn across the rough, uneven terrain. The makeshift path would have been easier going but crossing the hillock would ultimately save more time.

It seemed to take ages to reach Cave Arch. Lucy fretfully surveyed the craggy coastline but it was deserted. She searched in vain, desperately trying to discern the tall, stately figure of her husband amid the rocks and waves and sky.

Lucy's heart was thumping now. Where was Kingsley? She tried to piece together the events of that morning, searching for some clue that she might have missed, just before he had left the cottage with Owen McGee. They had sat down to breakfast at 9.30. Then Owen had arrived at 10 and she had made breakfast for him. Kingsley had decided that it was too rough to cross back to Magheraroarty and that, instead, they could spend some time writing. He had chosen to stay indoors while she went for a short walk with Owen. When they returned, Kingsley told Owen he'd give him a hand securing the curragh since there was a high tide expected.

She turned her back on Meenlara. An enormous gust of wind hit her a fierce blow. The last words he'd spoken were something like: 'Here are your pencil and paper if you start first.'[1] She could feel the tears of panic and frustration begin to trickle from her eyes, blown sideways by the force of the wind. That parting phrase had been so mundane for a man who was brilliant with words. He hadn't called her 'My Bobbie',[2] or spoken of all they'd meant to each other for the past twenty-one years, through the spectacular heights of passionate love and sparkling success, to the seeping despair of lonely nights and shattered dreams. But there was no time for crying. Kingsley had to be found.

It was around 10.30 when he'd left the cottage with Owen. She had spent a short while tidying up after breakfast and by the time she'd gone out to join him it must have been 10.40. She had walked to the Head side of the island where they often went to sit and write, close to the cliffs.

As the sight of those treacherous cliffs came into clear view in her mind's eye, a cold shudder ran through her. He was always stepping too close to the edge, seemingly oblivious to any mortal danger. His need for adventure was never far from the surface, his restless spirit demanded constant travel and exploration. Freedom! Perhaps for the first time many small pieces began to form themselves into a giant jigsaw, with Kingsley's lifelong search to be whole, to be free, to be true to himself becoming illuminated at the core. For Kingsley had been tethered all his life. A brilliant mind shackled, even by Harvard, by dear friends, by the need to always conform. Even bound by the love of his devoted wife. But surely he wouldn't have left the island without her?

Lucy picked up her pace again, retracing her steps to the cottage. Even some distance away she knew that the approaching figure was Owen and not Kingsley. He hadn't seen Kingsley either. Almost dazed now, she left Owen and walked back towards Meenlara. This time she walked nearer to the caves and began to call out: 'Kingsley! Are you there, Kingsley?'

As she called, the faces of friends and foe began to assail her: Her sister, Ruth; Kingsley's brother, Louis; the dear smiling eyes of Æ; the shadow of a young man who was sadly lost; the stern countenance of President Lowell. A bout of anxiety assailed her and she ran, almost stumbling, back towards the cottage. Owen was still working where she'd left him.

'Owen!' she panted, struggling to catch her breath. 'I'm uneasy about Mr Porter. Come with me at once and we'll look for him.' Thus began their search of the island. It was almost noon by the time they'd searched the Meenlara side of the Peninsula. Lucy had gone out to Gobrinatroirk, sending Owen towards Ilannamara. She continued to search along the Tory side, marking the point she had reached with her handkerchief. The two of them criss-crossed the island, going as far as Horn Head.

Exhausted, Lucy sat down on a rock to take a minute's rest. It was now 3 p.m. and the thunderstorm was beginning to team down in torrents. She closed her eyes and let the elements soak her. Kingsley's handsome face materialized before her. It was a snapshot, a moment when Kingsley sat in his rowing boat, smiling, happy to be back on his beloved lake. The words he had once written to her also formed in her mind: 'I love you more than the seven worlds or the nine heavens. I only live because of you and when I am beside you. Every moment when I am separated from you is a moment of living lost from my life. I love you.'[3]

All morning she had been pushing the terror down low and deep, swallowing the rising fears. She closed her eyes tightly and clung to the granite rock, willing her strength not to fail her in this her greatest trial. She breathed in the cool sea air and listened to the screeching gulls, their cries muffled by the rising wind.

She looked up and Owen was beside her. His face was pale and there was worry in his eyes. 'Owen!' She suddenly awakened from her reverie. 'Run down to Pat Coll and ask him to help us.' Owen nodded, and ran towards the thin scattering of houses. Lucy hurried back to the cottage to get the waterproofs. When Owen and Pat returned they

4. Arthur Kingsley Porter in a canoe, Lake George, New York, 1912.
Harvard University Archives, HU6 1706.125(2).

donned the jackets and the three of them set out to search the entire island. The rain had softened the earth now and Lucy half-ran, half-stumbled over tufts of grass and clambered over large, slippery boulders.

'Kingsley! Can you hear me, Kingsley?'

'Mr Porter! Mr Porter!'

The thunderstorm raged unabated. The search continued along the Glenveagh Bay side. Then back to Meenlara while Pat searched the Tory Island side. Lucy began to run blindly back towards the cliffs, tripping, half-falling, seized by a mounting dread as the hours ticked by and there was still no trace of her beloved Kingsley.

At 5.30 p.m. the storm began to subside. The threesome searched on while the islanders also streamed out to join in the search. The Porters had been good to the locals and they were genuinely well liked. It would be a catastrophe if anything happened to the wealthy American, the owner of Glenveagh Castle. It would even be worse if any aspersions were ever cast on the locals, that in some way they had been involved. No islander would want that kind of infamy.

It was now evening but the search continued. There was no sign whatever of the husband she had loved, assisted, protected and adored. By 8 p.m. Lucy, Owen and Pat were exhausted. The whole island had been thoroughly searched.

The wind and sea were much calmer now. Lucy knew she couldn't bear to spend another night on the island. Owen offered to row her back to Magheraroarty. The islanders still had hope that he would be found. But Lucy's hope had long since been extinguished during her nightmarish, eight-hour ordeal.

When Lucy reached the pier at Magheraroarty, her dear friend Æ took her hand and helped her ashore. Having faced the worst in the midst of the search on Inishbofin, her demeanour was now stiff and composed. On the drive back to Glenveagh Lucy broke the silence as she turned to Æ.[4]

'Kingsley will not return tonight,' she said. 'Kingsley will never return.'

Chapter two

Early Life: The Scandal That Shook Darien

Arthur Kingsley Porter was born on 6 February 1883 in Darien (pronounced Dari-ann), a small community on Connecticut's 'Gold Coast', situated between Norwalk and Stamford.[1] Even in the Porters' time it was considered an affluent town where wealthy businessmen chose to set up home, while commuting to work in New York City. The early Puritans, known as the New Haven Colony, had travelled from England during the 1630s to 1660s and had settled in the area.[2] They bought land from the Siwanoy, a peaceful Indian tribe. These early settlers applied their staunch Protestant beliefs, conservative values and strict work ethic to gradually establish prosperous communities throughout Connecticut. In 1848 the New Haven railroad's first scheduled line was built through Darien, and this created even greater wealth and affluence for the town.

Published accounts of the early life of Arthur Kingsley Porter have been, until now, extremely scant and brief. One typical report stated that 'fortune seemed to favour him from the beginning'.[3] In fact, all the literature consulted converged on one main point: the Porters of Connecticut combined economic privilege with the finest pedigrees in education. This, however, is merely the surface veneer: the true story of the formative years of Arthur Kingsley Porter reads more like a modern-day soap opera, involving a series of tragedies and sensational public scandals that were played out in the full glare of the national press.

Timothy Hopkins Porter was almost 57 years old, and on the verge of retirement from a successful banking career, when his youngest son, Arthur Kingsley, was born.[4] Timothy H, as he was known, was the son of Deacon Timothy and Annie (Todd) Porter. He was born on 16 February 1826, at Waterbury, Connecticut. Both Timothy H and his brother, David Gustavus, studied at Yale University in New Haven. Both brothers were studious and applied themselves diligently to their work. David G went on to become a Professor of Latin at Rochester University and a renowned scholar of theology.

In 1852 Timothy H entered Yale Theological Seminary, but remained only a short time before completing his studies at the Union Theological Seminary.[5] The newly ordained Reverend Porter then spent three years studying in Germany and France before returning home to Waterbury in 1859. He continued to preach occasionally at the Baptist Church in Stamford but his travels in Europe had brought about a change of heart, and his earlier plans to settle for a religious career were abruptly overturned. Timothy H suddenly turned his attention to more worldly matters and set about carving out a lucrative career in finance. Opportunities materialized when he was offered a position with the banking house of Soutter & Company in New York. By all accounts he made rapid progress and his ambitions for a comfortable lifestyle quickly came to fruition. In 1859 he married Agnes K. Soutter, daughter of his business partner, James. T. Soutter. The marriage did not last long, however, as his wife died two years later, on 27 December 1861, at the age of 27.[6]

Timothy H continued to work at Soutter's and in 1866 he was promoted to senior partner with the firm.[7] He then began to court the affections of another young socialite, Miss Maria Louisa Hoyt, the eldest daughter of the Stamford multimillionaire Joseph B. Hoyt. The Hoyt clan held a family gathering in June 1866 at Stamford that was attended by affluent members from all over the US.[8] At this prestigious event, Louisa's father was selected to represent the prosperous Connecticut branch of the family.

The Hoyts of Connecticut had long established their position at the top of the social pecking order over centuries of diligent work and

5. Clockwise (left to right): Blachley Lodge, Noroton, Darien, CT;
Timothy H. Porter; Schuyler Merritt; Interior of Blachley Lodge.

Stamford Historical Society, from 'Gracious Living in Stamford,
Late 19th and 20th Early Centuries', c. 1892.

astute investment. In the late nineteenth century, the United States was admitting large numbers of Europeans who sought to make their fortune in the land of opportunity. It was therefore paramount to the survival of the oldest families that wealth was not the only requirement for admittance to the highest social strata. The Hoyts fulfilled all the criteria for being one of the most influential families in Connecticut, by possessing great wealth but also having an old family tradition that no amount of money could buy.

Louisa was not only wealthy but was also highly educated, being one of the first women to study at Vassar College in New York.[9] Louisa possessed every social grace and economic advantage that Timothy H could ever have dreamed of and, by wielding his considerable charm, he somehow secured the affections of both Louisa and her esteemed family. On 3 November 1870, Timothy H married Maria Louisa Hoyt at her parents' residence.[10] At the time of the wedding Louisa was aged 23 while her husband was 44, over twenty years her senior.

The Porters began married life at Blachley Lodge, located in the fashionable district on Noroton Hill, in Darien. Louisa's sister, Frances, married the successful Stamford industrialist, Schuyler Merritt, in October 1879.[11] The Merritts were neighbours of the Porters, also residing in a fine house on Noroton Hill. The Porters' large timber-framed mansion occupied a superb location on a large estate.[12] The interior photo taken at Blachley Lodge shows a cluttered room with a panelled ceiling, a large window, an ornate stairway, Victorian-style furniture, drapes, statues, paintings and hanging lamps.

The Porter's first son, Louis Hopkins, was born on 10 March 1874, and Blachley Hoyt followed on 27 February 1876.[13] When Arthur Kingsley was born on 6 February 1883, his father was preparing to retire from business. The family had no financial worries as Timothy H had had a lucrative banking career, while his wife, Louisa, possessed great wealth from the Hoyt family's vast fortune.

Much of the correspondence between the young Kingsley, his parents and his brothers still remains. The letters show a surprising outpouring of love and affection between all of the family members. There was constant correspondence between the brothers, telling of school experiences and trips undertaken, and describing various leisure pursuits that included sports and hunting. The tone of the letters is one of intimacy and deep caring, conjuring up scenes of the brothers enjoying every moment outdoors during school holidays: searching for birds' nests in springtime, swimming and boating in summer, and snow sledding during winter.

This feeling of affection is also present in the letters frequently exchanged between the parents. Louisa, in much of her correspondence, addresses Timothy H as 'My Precious Husband'.[14] As Timothy H spent weekdays residing in New York, there was usually daily correspondence between husband and wife, both relaying anecdotes about work and home. Louisa gave constant reports on how the children were progressing at home and school and of how she had spent her day. The following is a snippet of a typical letter that she sent to her husband each day: 'I have washed and dressed the baby [Kingsley], settled the housekeeping for the day and am now waiting for Aunt Frank to come to lunch with us.'[15]

In the same letter, Louisa wrote that Louis was taking dancing lessons and learning deportment.[16] She had just returned from visiting her sister, Fanny, and they had spent a pleasant time together. Louisa had even managed to make some free time to read Bradley's lectures on Dean Stanley, recommended reading by Timothy H. Her letter is signed: 'With fondest love, Your Louise'.

Timothy H was particularly imaginative and playful when writing to his children. In a letter to Blachley, he wrote: 'This old Papa cat is feeling very lonesome to-night and he wants to see his little white kitty very much indeed. If he were only here the old papa cat would purr and sing to him and tell him ever so many stories.'[17]

In a letter to Kingsley, when Timothy H and Louisa were holidaying in California, the devoted father wrote:

> Mine dear little Kingsley,
> Papa wants to see his brave little boy very much, because papa and mama love him ever so much. And we are coming home on Saturday to see him and give him a tight hug and a kiss. We have not had any little boy to kiss and sleep with since we went far away in the cars.[18]

Timothy H also displayed great interest in the older boys' education and was already setting high standards for his eldest son, Louis: 'I was agreeably disappointed in Louis' school report. It is no comparison with what his report will be this term, but I noticed that it was better – that it showed a higher term mark average than any one of the Hill boys.'[19]

STEVENS HOUSE,
J A N G A STEVENS.
PROPRIETORS

Lake Placid, N. Y. July 15 1886.

My Dear Kingsley:

I wrote you a letter when we were in Saratoga. Since then, we left Saratoga and came to this place which is called Lake Placid. We did not come to this place in the Cars, because there is no Railroad here. We came here in a great Coach or Carriage drawn by four horses. These

was a little frightened, because it was so high and she was afraid she might fall off. But very soon she did not mind it at all. And the driver made the four horses go as fast as they could go — gallop - to gallop - to gallop. It was very exciting & great fun. We both of us wished you had been with us so as to enjoy the ride too. —

Where we are now, is a beautiful Lake that people sail upon in row boats. But the Lake is all surrounded by

Coaches are very large & very high & will hold a great many people. The one we came in would hold all our family & all Grandpa's family and all Aunt Fannie's family at the same time. People ride away up on the top of it and on the outside just as well as in the inside. Mama & I and Grandma rode on the top outside. It was so high that Mama had to climb very hard & I had to help her to get up on top. And at first she

great tall mountains. You never saw such very high mountains. The tops of them are sometimes higher than the clouds. This morning, we could not see the tops of the highest mountains, because they were all out of sight & covered up in the clouds. Next time, we must have you come with us to see the mountains. You would enjoy seeing them very much, they are so grand and impressive. I am sure, you are a very good boy & Mama & I want to see you very much. A kiss & a hug & ever so much love from.

Your dear Papa.

6. Letter from Timothy H. Porter to Kingsley Porter, dated 15 July 1886. Harvard University Archives, HUG 1706.114, Family corresponndence and papers of Porter Family 1885–86, Folder 1892–93.

This regard for excellence must have rubbed off on Louis as, in a letter to Kingsley, he praised his younger brother's fine handwriting: 'Dear King, I was very glad to get your letter and especially to see how well it was written. I wish you would always write as well as that. Between you and me the writing in your letter was better than that which either Blach or I write, and I hope you will keep on writing carefully like that.'[20]

It is also clear from the brothers' early correspondence that Kingsley had a particular interest in drama. On 17 April 1892, Blachley wrote to the 9-year-old Kingsley, asking how his play was progressing and hoping that he and his classmates had mastered their parts.[21]

The entire family displayed a fascination with nature. While on holiday in California, Timothy H wrote to Kingsley, telling him of the impressive lakes and mountains that he had seen during a stagecoach drive to Saratoga.[22] Blachley delighted in telling Kingsley about a host of creatures he had recently encountered, such as crows, squirrels and blue jays.[23] This love of nature and the outdoors became a central facet in Kingsley's development.

Timothy H's deep regard for his wife, Louise, is apparent throughout the entire correspondence but most particularly in the poems he wrote to commemorate each of her birthdays. On her twentieth birthday he wrote:

> To my darling
> On her 20th Birthday
> Twelve months ago with trembling hand,
> Upon this sixth of May
> I greeted thee, as maiden fair,
> In timid, sacred lay...[24]

Louisa's sister, Frances, gave birth to two daughters: Louisa Hoyt, on 7 September 1880, and Katherine Krom, on 9 January 1886.[25] Both Merritt daughters were close in age to their cousin Kingsley and they attended many childhood events together. The happy Porter household, however, was struck with a major calamity soon after Kingsley's birth, when Timothy H suffered a stroke of apoplexy.[26] In 1887 he was stricken by a second stroke that completely paralysed his left side.

The Porters, Hoyts and Merritts continued to be on genial terms. On 27 December 1888, Louisa's father, Joseph B. Hoyt, died at the age of 75.[27] The Stamford leather merchant left a vast fortune of approximately three million dollars that was to be administered by his executors: his widow; his sons-in-law, Timothy H. Porter and Schuyler Merritt; and his intimate friend and associate Thomas Ritch.[28] The main beneficiaries of the will were family members, including Louisa Porter, but there were also bequests of large sums to religious and educational institutions. Bitter disagreements as to the administration of the will developed between the executors and were subsequently fought out in a seven-year battle in the Court of Probate, the Superior and Supreme Courts.[29]

As the 1890s dawned, a series of tragedies of catastrophic proportions was about to befall the Porter family. Louisa became ill with pneumonia and died just three days later, on 13 December 1891, at the age of 44.[30] Timothy H always believed that his wife's death was hastened when she was persuaded to add a codicil to her will, making Schuyler Merritt co-executor.[31]

All three sons had been particularly close to their mother. Kingsley, aged just 8 years, must have felt a deep sense of loss and bewilderment at her sudden death. Also, his father was greatly weakened from his own illness, while Kingsley's older brothers, Louis, aged 17, and Blachley, aged 15, were preoccupied with their studies. A young governess, Miss Mabel Hastings Earle, was employed by Kingsley's father to provide the young boy with care, companionship and tutoring.

Mabel was born in Massachusetts in 1866, the daughter of Oscar T. and Katherine S. Earle.[32] Her father was an inventor who filed several patents, including improvements to the rotary engine, with the United States Patent Office.[33] The Earles had five children and soon after Mabel's birth they moved to Connecticut, finally settling at 504 State Street, Bridgeport.[34] Oscar T's business was quite successful so the family employed two servants.[35]

Mabel's mother died on 1 October 1891.[36] Mabel then took up residence with Reverend R.G.S. McNeille in Bridgeport. Rev. McNeille was a colourful character by all accounts and was particularly popular with female churchgoers.[37] Later in his career he was forced to resign because he insisted on wearing a 'dress suit and patent-leather pumps' when he preached on Sundays.[38] Mabel finally left Rev. McNeille's premises and obtained the position of governess with the Porters.

Contemporary accounts suggest that Mabel was a rare beauty, possessing style, charm and grace. There is no report of the extent to which Kingsley bonded with his new governess or whether he ever came to regard her as a maternal figure. What is clear is that Blachley Lodge must have been a bleak place for a child to live, without the devotion of his mother or the companionship of his brothers, left alone with a sick and aged father. The presence of a young, charming governess must have at least lightened Kingsley's drab existence.

Timothy H may have been ill but he was still very much involved in the affairs of his late wife's will. Louisa's large fortune was to be administered by her brother-in-law, Schuyler Merritt, and Thomas E. Ritch, of the New York law firm Arnoux, Ritch & Woodford. Louisa left her husband a life income of $100,000.[39] The remainder of Mrs Porter's vast estate, valued at over four million dollars, was to be held in trust for her three sons until they reached the age of 25.[40]

At the time of his wife's death, Timothy H was aged 65 and partially paralysed. After having a successful career in finance and having built up a reputation as a respectable member of the community, his sons might have been forgiven for believing that their father would be well pleased to live out his twilight years in a comfortable, dignified and uneventful manner. This, however, was far from Timothy H's plans. Now that he found himself freed from the constraints of work, no longer in need of marrying for financial security, and perhaps as a late revolt against his repressed Baptist upbringing, Timothy H turned his attention to securing the affections of various young women of his acquaintance.

Between December 1892 and June 1893, Timothy H corresponded with at least a dozen young women in the locality.[41] He seemed to have had a particular fetish for schoolteachers, aged between 30 and 33. The first of his letters was written to Miss Clark of Stamford, whom he called Zora:

Oh! if Zora was only here! How ineffably sweet it would be for me to lie here on the lounge while Zora should sit in a chair by my side and read to me Longfellow's 'The day is done.' Or if somebody should occupy the sofa with me and let me feel somebody's soft hand smoothing and soothing my anxious weary brow. What a perfect divine thorough happiness this! While I was in the village this morning I saw a piece of jewellery that quite took my fancy. It was Venus greeting the new May moon. The ornament was set in genuine diamonds and gold and I at once bought it. I thought the conception was worthy of a much richer setting, but then I remembered that this was much better as it was, since this could be worn without attracting particular attention or inquiry, whereas the one I had in mind, particularly of the locket inclosed by miniature, would almost surely betray our mutual secret. So I decided to send you this in the same form in which I found and bought it, and inclose it to you in this note, and later I will some time write you a verse of poetry upon the Goddess of love throwing her unvarying and effulgent breasts upon the rising new moon of love!

A letter to Miss Clark, dated 20 January 1893, mentioned Timothy H's young son, Kingsley: 'I have been at home this whole day lying upon the lounge and entirely alone excepting the few minutes Kingsley spent with me.'[42]

The letter goes on to report how much he missed Zora:

How I wished you could have been seated beside me, holding my hand with that soft dainty hand of yours, and reading or talking to me with that soft sweet beautifully modulated voice of yours! That would have made a day of rest indeed! I have spent a great many

Sundays of this character. It was our favourite way of passing the day when either of us did not feel like going to church.

As this is Sunday why should I not close with quoting a verse – a modified version from your Sunday School hymn:
'My Zora, I love thee. I know thou art mine.
For thee all other lesser pledges of life I gladly resign;
My hope, trust, and fastness, and guerdon art thou.
If o'er I had love, my Zora, 'tis now.'

Between February and April 1893, Timothy H began to log details of a selection of precious and semi-precious jewels that he was planning to have specially made for Miss Clark:

CONTENTS OF JEWEL CASKET SELECTED FOR Z.
1. One large 3½-carat solitaire diamond ring.
2. A large Hungarian opal.
3. A large ruby ring with beautiful diamond setting.
4. A large sapphire ring richly set with beautiful diamonds.
5. A very beautiful emerald ring, tastefully mounted with diamonds.
6. A superb Marquise diamond ring.
7. A very large Alexandrian ring, mounted with fine large diamonds.
8. An amethyst brooch, consisting of a large magnificent amethyst, mounted in a diamond setting of thirty-two first water, old-mine stones.[43]

During April he sent the jewellery list to Miss Clark, along with the following note:

All of the above stones have been chosen and selected by me personally, even to every small diamond used in the mounting, and have been mounted under my direction and under my personal supervision.

I will deliver to you to-morrow only a part of the above list, for I do not wish to suddenly so shock you by my extravagance as to give you the impression that I have lost my head. Besides, you will not be able to wear the jewels in the present state of affairs without disclosing the secret of our relations. For there is not a single jewel on the list but that would indicate to any intelligent person who should see it that it came from me. You will therefore have to enjoy them by yourself for the present, or till we are ready to let others know what we alone know now.

In selecting the above casket of jewels I have had in my mind the certain following ideas, which I felt like embodying in a permanent form and as souvenirs of facts and incidents which have made an abiding impression:

1. Intended as a conventional engagement ring.
2. As a souvenir of our first meeting after our first separation.
3. As a souvenir of a first nameless confidence between us.
4. A coming Easter present.
5. A souvenir of a zealous heart's pledge of fidelity and love.
6. A souvenir of our honeymoon.
7. An emblem of married life.
8. Your next birthday present; the 32 diamonds and the large amethyst, making 33 stones, corresponding to the years of your life.[44]

Timothy H appears to have written his final letter to Miss Clark on 24 April lamenting the end of their relationship:[45]

During the few last terrible weeks how gladly would I have purchased a single daily hour of your presence at the cost of $100 per visit had it been possible, so that sitting by my bedside I might have had the comfort of your presence, the sweetness of your guileless spirit, the tenderness of your true loyal heart and the deep pathos of your tender unfeigned sympathy.

If you prefer our intercourse and relations should not be renewed, I will acquiesce regretfully, but subserviently and uncomplainingly. Yours ever.

T.H. Porter.

Within five days, however, on 29 April, Timothy H was writing to Kingsley's governess, Miss Mabel Earle, requesting a meeting of a confidential nature: 'I feel I must have a leisurely long personal interview with you. There are many, many things that are vital to my happiness if not to my life that I feel sorely in need of, I must advise and confer about. And you are the only person living to whom I could confide them.'[46]

Between May and June of the same year, several letters were written to a number of women, including a friend of his late wife's on 16 May, asking her to consider marriage and outlining the esteem in which ladies in general held him:

> Perhaps I ought to say that I have and have always had the most exalted opinion and admiration for women. I most firmly believe that in every point of comparison they are not only the equal of men but vastly superior to us men in every desirable respect, except alone in the matter of physical strength. As a consequence of this belief, I have always had such a feeling of respect, deference and reverential regard for ladies as has always made me a favourite with them, and they give me their love because they soon see that I appreciate it and prove myself worthy of it. In this way only can I analyse the esteem in which my lady friends have always held me.[47]

Sometime during the latter months of 1893, Porter's sons, Louis and Blachley, became aware of their father's correspondence. Not only were they deeply shocked by their elderly, paralytic father's pursuit of women almost forty years his junior, they were also enraged that their mother's fortune was being whittled away on jewels and other gifts for his various female acquaintances. Blachley, now aged 17, began to take copies of his father's love letters whenever he could obtain access to his personal journals.[48] The situation was brought to a head in January 1894 when Timothy H informed his family that he was engaged to Kingsley's former governess, 28-year-old Mabel Hastings Earle.

This was the final straw for the family. The eldest sons, in consultation with the executors of their mother's will, Schuyler Merritt and Thomas Ritch, ruminated that Timothy H had completely lost his sanity.[49] This was an era when raw sexual desire, particularly in an ailing, elderly widower who was deemed to hold a respectable position within the community, was totally unacceptable. Freud's theories of sexual development and repression were as yet unknown. The prevailing medical model viewed sexual deviation from an accepted norm as a symptom of mental illness that needed to be controlled and treated, often by committing the patient to an asylum.

In January 1894 the first of a series of lengthy lawsuits and counter suits commenced, amid much prurient interest. In the Probate Court in Stamford, Porter's sons and co-executors began legal proceedings to have Timothy H declared insane. This dispute coincided with the legal battle already being pursued in the courts to settle the will of J.B. Hoyt.[50]

Fearing an immense sexual and financial scandal, the family confined Timothy H to his home, under restraint of two Stamford officers, Bolster and Shoeck.[51] Timothy H's brother, David, his sister, Mrs Walton, and a nephew were also advised of the situation. They arrived at Blachley Lodge and took up residence to care for their relative while the Probate Court decided his fate.[52]

Timothy H was held captive in his own home for several weeks. This bizarre situation, of having his father's authority superseded by that of his brothers and uncle, must have been highly traumatic for the 11-year-old Kingsley. There must also have been a torrent of emotions erupting when he discovered that his pretty governess had suddenly been transformed into his elderly father's fiancée. After the happy, idyllic years of his early childhood, Kingsley was now a reluctant witness to the destruction of his family. The press set about humiliating every aspect of his father's previously impeccable reputation as, one by one, his love letters were read out in court and printed in newspapers each day for all the world to savour. The coverage of the case in *The Sun* (New York) was typical of the blend of sensationalism and humour that was employed by reporters to fascinate and amuse their readers. The edition of 11 January 1894 described Timothy H as 'a model old gentleman, and he used to carry himself with a full realization of the dignity of his character. He was tall and erect and his beard and hair were quite white.'[53]

The next day's edition lampooned the romantic exploits of the eccentric millionaire:

> The epistolary part of the love making which seems to have occupied the leisure time of the paralytic millionaire, Timothy H. Porter, since the death of his wife three years ago, and which is presumably the main excuse for the application recently brought to have him adjudged insane, was produced in court through his son Blacheley[sic], who copied them from a book in which his father first wrote them. It is largely upon these letters that the case of the sons rests. It is insisted on Mr Porter's side of the controversy that they allow evidence not of mental weakness or aberration, but the contrary. In the absence of a standard for love making at various ages, this may be a matter of opinion; but his sons think that any one who could write such letters and send them should certainly have someone to guide him in his affairs.[54]

In court, Timothy H swore that his brother-in-law, the wealthy manufacturing magnate Schuyler Merritt, along with Thomas Ritch, had conspired to destroy his character and dismantle his estate.[55] Porter's sons gave evidence that they began to question their father's sanity, not only when he began writing love letters and giving lavish presents to a series of women, but also when his spelling deteriorated, as this was a sign of his failing powers. Further revelations followed. Louis testified that his father believed his paralysis could be cured by the installation of an electric plant, consisting of a four-horsepower engine and a dynamo. Louis had been put to work in the cellar to operate the plant. He also testified that Mr Porter insisted on maintaining a temperature of eighty degrees in the house, while he continued to wear a huge cape overcoat.

The strain and complexity of the whole situation must have been enormous as Kingsley was forced to choose sides between his father and the rest of the family. It was at this time that Kingsley's uncle, Schuyler Merritt, became a surrogate father to his young nephew. The close relationship between Kingsley, his uncle and his Merritt cousins, particularly Katherine, continued throughout his life.

During the ensuing scandal, Kingsley attended King's Academy, a private school for boys located in Stamford.[56] At 11 years old and on the cusp of puberty, there is little doubt that he had to endure a constant barrage of bawdy repartee from his schoolmates concerning his father's sexual transgressions. Kingsley, sensitive and imbued with an artistic nature, must have been deeply humiliated by this relentless onslaught of lewd jokes and jibes, while struggling to come to terms with his own awakening sexuality. It was probably at this time that Kingsley began to withdraw from his peers and to spend as much time as possible alone, either buried in his beloved books or roaming the countryside, marvelling at the many wonders to be found in nature.

Timothy H was only released from house arrest when he agreed, under strong duress, to sign over control of his property and estate to his wife's executors, Merritt and Ritch.[57] Once control of Timothy H's assets had been secured, the family agreed to drop all accusations. On 26 March, attorney Samuel Fessenden appeared before Judge Finch in the Probate Court in Stamford and, on behalf of his clients, withdrew their original application to have Mr Porter declared insane.[58]

Timothy H had already married Miss Mabel Earle the previous week. The wedding was solemnized at the rectory of the Episcopal Church at Barrington, Massachusetts, on Friday 16 March 1894.[59] The wedding reception took place on 29 March 1894 at the home of Miss Earle's aunt, Mrs Kellog, of West Avenue in New York.[60]

The third Mrs Porter was described in several New York newspapers as being accomplished, pretty, well known in society[61] and possessing an attractive figure that fascinated Timothy H.[62] Mabel's marriage portion was said to be $25,000 in cash, and she was also given a contract for an undisclosed annual allowance.[63] None of the groom's family was present at the ceremony. The newly wedded couple spent their honeymoon in Boston. One newspaper reported that the couple returned to their new home in Bridgeport, Connecticut, to begin married life,[64] but later reports confirmed that they had set up home in Blachley Lodge, much to the consternation of the eldest son, Louis.[65]

The marriage, however, was not the greatest misfortune that the family had to face. Even greater disaster came to pass when, in July 1894, Timothy H sued his late wife's executors and the officers who restrained him for $200,000 in damages, for unlawfully imprisoning him and forcing him to sign over the vast bulk of his fortune.[66] Thus ensued a legal battle and family feud of a kind that the ultra-conservative citizens of Connecticut had rarely witnessed.

'The Conspiracy Case', as it became known, contained layers of sexual intrigue, financial scandal and family hostility that soon made headline news in local and national papers all over the East Coast. The case was tried in the Superior Court in Bridgeport, Connecticut, between January 1895 and March 1897.[67] The case made by Samuel Fessenden, attorney for the defendants, was described as 'the most voluminous document ever filed in the Superior Court in this county'.[68] Crowds jostled for seats as Timothy H gave evidence against Schuyler Merritt, Thomas Ritch, the officers who restrained him, and his sons who were party to his house arrest.

On 12 January, the greatest thrill of all for the spectators who filled the courtroom was the testimony given by Timothy H. Porter's young wife, Mabel.[69] She was questioned at length about the time she was employed as governess at Blachley Lodge.[70] Louis's accusations were put to her that, instead of tutoring Kingsley, she was spending most of her time 'cutting up with Mr Porter'. Mabel declared this to be untrue.

'Is it true,' she was asked by Mr Fessenden, 'that you were frequently alone with Mr Porter in his study, with the shades drawn down?'[71]

Mabel, without hesitation, replied:

> There was no truth whatever, to such a statement. The only times that I remember being alone with Mr Porter in his study were when he outlined the plan for Kingsley's education. I think I was with him about fifteen minutes. On another occasion, when I was about to leave the Lodge, I went to him and saw him in his study. I did not tell him of the shameful treatment accorded me by his sons because I did not wish to create a feeling between them and the father. While we were conversing Louis walked up and down the veranda adjoining the room. I never attempted to screen the room.[72]

At this point there was a heated exchange between Mr Fessenden, who acted on behalf of the Porter sons, and Judge De Forest, with Mr Fessenden shouting, 'You act like a wild hyena.'[73] Judge De Forest replied: 'Well, it's enough to make any man excited to be compelled to listen to such heartless threats by a son against his father.'[74]

Mabel was then questioned at length about her courtship by Timothy H:

> I believe a period of more than two years elapsed between the time I left the Lodge and the occasion of the first proposal. I refused the offer. He repeated it, and I accepted. He wrote me a letter stating that a plan was on foot to have him placed in an insane retreat. Up to that time I had never written endearing letters to him, and what letters I had written were signed by my full name. The letters were simple, and perhaps sympathetic. He had proposed marriage to me, and of course I had more than a friendly interest in him. Before the marriage Mr Porter and I discussed the matter of a marriage settlement. He said he did not wish to have my marriage to him criticized, and he did not want

people to say that I had married him for his money. Therefore, to protect me and himself as well, he submitted the ante-nuptial agreement. I was to receive $25,000 and release all claim on his estate. The agreement was drawn up on December 14 1893 and signed by Mr Porter and myself.[75]

Mabel was also asked about her reception at Blachley Lodge when she arrived there after the marriage ceremony.[76] She said that when they arrived they found the doors had been locked against them. They finally found a window open at the rear of the house and they had to scramble in. There was no food for them anywhere in the house and Timothy H finally sent to the village and obtained food that the maid prepared. Mabel then said that she met Louis Porter and he addressed her in an insulting way.

Next morning, when Mabel came down to breakfast with her new husband, Louis was already seated at the table.[77] She said he was sitting in his father's chair and had his arms spread out. There were no chairs set for herself or Mr Porter. She then detailed how Mr Porter had put some bread and cake on a plate but that Louis tried to snatch it from him. During the ensuing struggle Mr Porter fell down and lay on the floor.

The ante-nuptial contract was then produced in court and offered in evidence. It stated that Mrs Porter was to relinquish all dowry rights in her husband's property for the sum of $25,000.[78]

Before a verdict on the case had been reached, yet another appalling tragedy struck the Porter family. On 1 August 1895, Blachley Hoyt Porter was killed outright in a bizarre accident when on holiday with his brother, Louis, in Arizona.[79] He was just 18 years old. Louis and Blachley had set out two weeks earlier to visit Alaska, via California. By some zany quirk of fate they missed the steamer that would have taken them from San Francisco to Alaska, and instead they joined an exploring group that was on route to the Grand Canyon in Arizona.[80] The party and their guides became caught in a thunderstorm in the canyon and sought shelter under a jutting rock. A bolt of lightning struck the rock, shattering it completely and instantly killing Blachley. Louis and the guide were also struck by lightning and were badly burned. The family physician, Dr Lelb, travelled to Arizona to treat Louis and to bring Blachley's body back to Darien.

The effect on Kingsley and the whole family after such a bizarre and shocking incident can only be conjectured. Kingsley must have been deeply traumatized by his brother's sudden death. The loss of Blachley, in many ways his closest friend, with whom he had spent countless happy days roaming the countryside, must have been an excruciating blow. As for his father, a former minister and the son of a Baptist preacher, Timothy H must have been acutely aware of the irony that the son who had dragged his name through the courts, and in every manner disobeyed him, had suddenly and inexplicably been smitten down by a bolt of lightning.

As a young teenager, Kingsley began to attend Browning School for boys in New York.[81] A rare photo of Kingsley at this age shows him smiling beside a guide, waving his cap in the air and holding up several fish he has just caught. The photo was taken at the boathouse at Saranac Lake, in the heart of the Adirondacks wilderness area, north-east of New York State. The awesome power of nature had captivated Kingsley since childhood. The sea in particular held a fascination for him. Here he could escape from mediocrity by immersing himself in its unfathomable depths. Within the ever-changing sea he discovered a refuge, away from dry land with its complex customs, beliefs and tribulations. The wilderness held its own perils and mysteries but these only added to Kingsley's feelings of exhilaration when exploring remote mountains and forests, or swimming and fishing in nearby lakes.

It may have been a blessing for Kingsley to gain some distance from the continuing legal disputes that were waged within the family. On 29 July 1896, the contest over the will of Kingsley's grandfather, J.B. Hoyt, was finally settled.[82] Timothy H withdrew his petition for the removal of Schuyler Merritt and Thomas Ritch as executors. Accountants then examined the assets of J.B. Hoyt so that the bequests of the will could finally be administered.

7. Kingsley and fish at Boat House, Saranac Club,
and guide, photograph, c. 1895.

Harvard University Archives, HUG 1706.125 (14).

On 9 December 1896, Timothy H was yet again on the stand as plaintiff in the conspiracy case, giving evidence that his son, Louis, had become enraged when he heard of his engagement to Miss Earle. He testified that Louis had shouted: 'That woman, Miss Earle, will never be permitted to enter this house. I will send you both to hell if you marry her.'[83]

When his father remonstrated with Louis for his rashness of temper, Louis replied: 'This is not a rashness of temper, but a feeling of hate, undying hate. Three times every day we will pray to God to curse you, and will teach Kingsley to do so. We will consent to your marriage to Louise Plumbley [his mother's school friend]. Now if you want war. You can have it.'[84]

On 13 March 1897, Judge Prentice of Fairfield Superior Court handed down a verdict on Mr Porter's conspiracy case.[85] The judge concluded that no conspiracy had been perpetrated against Mr Porter and that all actions had been taken in good faith. Mr Ritch was completely exonerated from having had any part in what transpired. Mr Merritt, although responsible for Mr Porter's restraint, was deemed to have performed his duty to protect his sister's estate that had been left in his charge. Constable Schock and Sheriff Bolster, the officers who had kept Mr Porter in confinement in his own home, were also exonerated.

Timothy H was outraged by the verdict and appealed the case to the Supreme Court. On 5 January 1898 the Supreme Court gave its verdict, confirming the decision made by Judge Prentice.[86] Timothy H. Porter had lost the case, the goodwill of his family and his once respected position within the community.

The quality of marital relations between the aged and paralytic Timothy H and his pretty young bride can only be imagined. In an era when women had little chance of finding a comfortable living unless they married into wealth, Mabel clearly saw a glorious opportunity in marrying Mr Porter to secure her financial future. Mrs T.H. Porter, as Mabel was now known, continued teaching at Sunday school where she instructed young girls in sewing and crafts. In the winter of 1898 she helped her students to prepare Christmas boxes for the less fortunate, that were then sent to New York.[87]

Timothy H was most eager to escort his pretty wife to many of the leading social events in Connecticut, including attendance at Governor George E. Lounsbury's inaugural ball in Hartford, on the evening of 4 January 1899. A spectator at the event described the lavish ball: 'Major Cheney presented the guests to Governor Lounsbury and led the grand march with Mrs Lounsbury. Governor Lounsbury followed with Mrs Cheney, and the dancing continued almost without interruption for many hours. Supper was served by Besse and the music from Beenian and Hatch's Orchestra and Colt's Band was exceptionally good.'[88]

The beautiful Mrs Mabel Porter was truly the belle of the ball. *The Bridgeport Herald* waxed lyrical on the portrait that was later painted of Mabel, attired in the same ballgown that she had worn at the governor's ball: 'It is a full-length figure of Mrs Timothy H. Porter of Stamford attired in the exquisite costume in which she appeared at Gov. Lounsbury's inaugural ball. The predominating feature in this painting is its strength and it is said to be an excellent likeness of the charming woman.'[89]

Mabel's portrait was exhibited in Connecticut for several months in the spring of 1900.[90] This must have been a bitter pill for Kingsley and Louis to swallow, as they must have been reminded of their once happy home life, when their father had commissioned a portrait of their mother from the distinguished artist Henry Augustus Loop.[91]

In less than a decade, Kingsley had suffered two family bereavements: the loss of his beloved mother, and the sudden, inexplicable death of his 18-year-old brother in a freak thunderstorm. He had witnessed the desecration of his family's once respected name through legal battles and public scandal. The role of his young governess had been irrevocably altered into that of stepmother, while his elderly, paralytic father was parodied as a petulant, extravagant lover. Far from being favoured by fortune and on the cusp of a new century, Kingsley Porter had to dig deep indeed to surmount the disasters of his early traumatic life.

Chapter three

Coming of Age: Freedom and Vocation

In 1900, at the age of 17, Kingsley followed in the footsteps of his father and brothers and enrolled in Yale University, located in New Haven, Connecticut. In many ways it must have been a relief to spend time away from his feuding family and to become engrossed in his studies. Louis spent most of his time in New York, where he pursued a legal career. His offices were located at 45 Broadway.[1]

Timothy H had been living with Mabel in Blachley Lodge since their marriage. It was here that Timothy H died just before 8 p.m. on the evening of 1 January 1901.[2] He was 74 years old. A private funeral was held the following Friday and the infamous patriarch was finally laid to rest in Woodland Cemetery, beside his second wife, Louisa.

Within days of the burial, the estate of Timothy H. Porter was again at centre stage in the Stamford courts. The will was filed in the probate courts on 13 January.[3] Timothy H's will was described as 'one of the most tangled estates that ever came before a Connecticut Probate Court'.[4] His estate was estimated to be worth between one and three million dollars.[5] When the will was read, it emerged that Timothy H had left the bulk of his estate to his young widow, Mabel. An amount of $10,000 was left to Louis, a similar amount to his cousin, Joseph A. Porter, and the remainder was willed to his youngest son, Kingsley.[6] However, the estate also included a number of lucrative bonds and railroad securities belonging to his late wife, Louisa. These valuable commodities had been transferred to the Union Trust Company of New Haven when Timothy H was forced to sign them over to Merritt and Ritch, in order to secure his freedom from house arrest in 1894.[7]

Louis Porter was beside himself with rage at the thought that Mabel, the former governess, would get a cent of his late mother's estate. Also, Mabel had signed an ante-nuptial agreement, stating that she would receive no more than $25,000 of her late husband's estate. Louis immediately contested the will and swore to continue the legal battle for as long as it took to prevent the young widow from getting a share in the estate.[8] Louis contended that the stocks administered by the Union Trust Company of New Haven should also form part of the estate to be inherited by Kingsley. A large legal team from Stamford represented Louis and Kingsley, including Samuel Fessenden, Hart & Keller, Homer Cummings and Clarence I. Reld. Mabel was represented by Goodwin Stoddard of Bridgeport.[9]

On 12 April 1901 the estate of Timothy H. Porter was finally settled. The remaining value of stocks from the Union Trust Company of $3,900 was paid into the estate.[10] The existence of the ante-nuptial agreement denied Mabel any further claim on her late husband's estate, though she had prospered greatly during her years of marriage. Mabel went to live in New York before joining her father in Talbot County, Maryland, where he had developed a large oyster business.[11] In 1906, Mabel paid $1,250 for Lambdin House, a modest one-and-a half-storey frame dwelling in Water Street, St Michaels, Maryland, where she continued to live.[12] Mabel had secured her financial future through her marriage and subsequently had no further contact with the Porter family.

The finalizing of his father's will insured that Kingsley, now aged 18, became an enormously wealthy man. Finally he was free from the peculiarities of his father's lifestyle, from the stress of legal battles and the shame of family scandal. Louis, as the eldest son, inherited the family home at Blachley Lodge that had been part of Louisa's estate, as well as $10,000 that had been willed to him. Throughout their lives the brothers maintained a strong bond of unity and affection. When Louis married Miss Ellen Marion Hatch of New York, on 3 October 1901,

Kingsley was best man.[13] The newlyweds moved into Blachley Lodge to begin married life.

The effect on Louis after years of litigation against his father finally caught up with him. In December 1901 he became seriously ill with appendicitis,[14] and an emergency operation had to be performed by Dr Bull of New York. Louis was then allowed to convalesce at home, under the care of doctors Bull, Tiffany and Hurlbut.[15]

Louis's illness had seriously weakened him and he was unfit for some time to return to work. Although Kingsley was in his second year at Yale, he proposed that they take a cruise around the world so that Louis could recover his health. On 8 January 1902, Kingsley applied for a US passport, stating that he planned to return to the US in September. On his passport application, Kingsley stated that he was six feet one inch in height; he had blue eyes, light hair and a fair complexion; he had a high forehead, a long face, a small mouth and chin, and he possessed a Greek nose.[16]

At the age of 18, Kingsley possessed many advantages, including a strong, slender physique. His love of the outdoors was insatiable and he went on frequent hunting expeditions to Canada and Newfoundland.[17] He was shy and reserved with the look of a poet,[18] but he was also friendly and modest which brought him a close circle of friends.[19] For the handsome young millionaire with the keenest intellect and a congenial though sensitive disposition, the world was indeed his oyster.

On 22 January 1902, Kingsley and Louis boarded the twin-screw express SS *Auguste Victoria* in New York.[20] The luxury seventy-three-day world cruise to the Orient had recently been introduced by the Hamburg–American Line. The cruise itinerary included stops at Funchal (Madeira), Gibraltar, Granada and Malaga (Spain), Tangiers (Morocco), Algiers (Algeria), Genoa (Italy), Villefranche and Nice (France), Monte Carlo (Monaco), Malta, Alexandria, Cairo, Luxor and Assouan (Egypt), Beirut and Baalbek (Lebanon), Damascus (Syria), Jaffa (Palestine), Jerusalem, Constantinople (now Istanbul), the Bosphorus, the Black Sea, Piraeus and Athens (Greece), Taormina, Messina, Palermo, Naples and Genoa (Italy). The cruise was to return to New York from Genoa. However, the Porters continued their travels to India and the Far East.[21] They re-entered the US via the West Coast and travelled across the Rockies, before reaching the East Coast.

Kingsley, now aged 19, must have been incurably infected with the yearning for travel and adventure after witnessing all the delights, tastes, sights and experiences that a world tour provided. It certainly opened him to the richness and diversity of art and culture and to the incredible marvels of nature across continents and oceans.

8. Arthur Kingsley Porter's room at Yale College, photograph, c. 1904.
Harvard University Archives, HUG 1706.194.

Kingsley finally returned to Yale in September 1902 and continued his studies, graduating with a degree of Bachelor of Arts on 27 June 1904.[22] Out of a total of 195 men who graduated that year, Kingsley was one of the twelve who received the highest award of philosophical oration.[23] This elite group also included William Pickens from Little Rock, Arkansas, an African-American who later became an author and civil-rights campaigner.[24] Overall, Kingsley finished fourth in his class.[25]

Although Kingsley possessed a fortune, he immediately set about finding a suitable career. Men who had inherited their wealth from the old families of New England were reared with a work ethic that life was only meaningful if they had a vocation to nurture. This was unlike the ethos of rich European aristocrats or the young American nouveau riche who were happy to spend their lives indulging all the sensual pleasures that money could buy. It had always been his mother's wish that Kingsley would study law and work in his brother's firm. Finally, though, Kingsley had gained a positive legacy from his family and this great wealth allowed him to carve out a life of his own choosing. During the summer of 1904 he postponed a decision about further studies and instead sailed to France.[26]

It was during his tour of Normandy that Kingsley experienced a mystical conversion at Coutances Cathedral.[27] While staring up at the Gothic turrets and superb ornamentation on the cathedral's facade, Kingsley was enveloped in a shining light and fell into a trance, totally enraptured by the structure's exquisite symmetry.[28] This mystical experience convinced the 21-year-old Kingsley Porter that his path lay in the study of architecture.[29]

There is little doubt that Kingsley, after the extraordinary family misfortunes he had suffered, was ripe for spiritual transformation and in great need of a meaningful vocation. In architecture, Kingsley had found a marvellous escape from the cares and the ugliness of a chaotic world. The study of architecture meant he could revel in beauty, design and symmetry, each based on eternal principles. As with all great art, Kingsley could admire the romantic aspirations of the artist and the inner passion and spirit of the craftsman that had given the work its power. The simple truth was that Kingsley loved architecture: the way it made him feel when he visited a magnificent cathedral; the sense of freedom he found in travelling to foreign lands to explore ancient monuments; the joy he derived from imaging the lives of artists who crafted such glorious structures. All of these elements converged and clearly surfaced on that momentous day in Coutances.

9. Coutances Cathedral, France.

Stanley Parry.

On his return to New York, Kingsley enrolled at the Columbia Architectural School.[30] Initially he began studying beaux-arts with a view to becoming a practising architect but midway through the course he switched to the study of architectural history.[31] While at Columbia he began researching medieval architecture. After graduating in 1906, Kingsley immediately set sail for Europe to continue his research of medieval architecture in France and Italy.[32]

By December, Kingsley was back in New York. On 4 December 1906 he attended the wedding of Blakeman Quintard Meyer,[33] a friend from his days at Yale,[34] and on 6 February 1907 he celebrated his twenty-fourth birthday. Although he continued to remain on friendly terms with his old college mates, Kingsley was a serious, studious scholar who had little interest in gaiety or frivolity. His greatest excitement derived from travel abroad where he could indulge his fascination with the origins of stone monuments. He also loved going on frequent expeditions to the mountains and lakes, particularly the Adirondacks, where he could be alone to ponder and reflect.

Throughout 1907, Kingsley's sole occupation was the research and writing of his mammoth book, entitled *Medieval Architecture: Its Origins and Development*.[35] Although he had little formal training to write such a book, he had a deep inner confidence and conviction that his personal travels, studies and observations would lead him to discover significant, previously unexplored medieval monuments.

The 1,000-page book was completed at Kingsley's apartment at 320 Central Park West, New York City, on 24 September 1908.[36] In the preface, Kingsley stated that *Medieval Architecture* was written for the general reader who had little or no training in architecture. Its main purpose was to inform travellers who visited these masterpieces in Europe to gain the greatest appreciation and enjoyment of Gothic architecture. Although Kingsley was largely self-taught and inexperienced, he still managed to create the first book on medieval architecture written by an American.[37] Quite simply, it was an immense achievement. The bibliographies were testament to the staggering breadth and depth of the reading he had undertaken before attempting this mammoth work.[38]

10. Kingsley aged 25 in 1908.
Courtesy of Brooklyn Museum Archives. Goodyear
Archival Collection. General correspondence
(1.1.066): Porter (1910).
Location unknown, 1908.

Although the book mainly dealt with
the Gothic architecture of France, it also
encompassed a history of architecture from
Greek and Roman times. Kingsley was just
26 years old when the book was published
in two volumes in 1909, by Baker & Taylor
of New York. It contained over 300 illustrations that Kingsley had commissioned.
The work was considered groundbreaking,
as Kingsley used documents to ascribe dates
to monuments as the means for tracing the evolution of Romanesque
and Gothic architecture. This revolutionized the rather careless method
employed by previous researchers, of deducing the chronology of
development from conjectured theories.[39]

To attempt such an enormous work at a young age shows an inner
confidence in his research, analytical and literary abilities. His writing
style was clear and fluid, displaying an incredible knowledge of his
chosen subject but also showing a deep passion for the planning,
construction and ornamentation of architectural wonders, including
Roman temples, Gothic cathedrals and Norman towers. The actual
writing of the book must have taken him many thousands of hours,
spent alone at his desk, constantly refining and editing every sentence.

The work also shows Kingsley's love for medieval monuments and,
in particular, the mystical delight he derived from the beauty of a
Gothic cathedral that could transport him to another realm:

But the Gothic Cathedral alone possesses the power to lift the
mind entirely from the cares and thoughts of the world, de
materialibus ad immaterialia transferendo, the power to call forth

within the soul a more than mortal joy, until for the moment the material world is forgotten, and the mind is carried captive to that strange shore of the universe which is more of the mould of Heaven than of Earth.[40]

The book was widely acclaimed. A reviewer for *The Sun* (New York) described the work as a 'stupendous undertaking. The bibliography of the subjects of the first volumes embraces 2,500 separate entries and is in itself a remarkable contribution to the study of a single art.'[41]

According to *The Washington Times*, 'For six years, Mr Porter, who is a young man, has constantly applied himself to the production of this monumental history of architecture, making several Asiatic and European trips required by the book since his graduation from Yale and working on the subject daily for years.'[42]

Even after his great success, Kingsley had no time to rest. He travelled to Italy during the winter of 1908, spending January 1909 in Naples.[43] Here he conducted further research into Italian architecture that would form the basis of his second book, *The Construction of Lombard and Gothic Vaults*. At this stage of his career Kingsley was not affiliated with any university. He must have incurred enormous expense in conducting independent research in Europe but his considerable wealth allowed him to pursue any quest that captured his interest. Kingsley had found an area in which he excelled and which provided him with meaning and purpose. He was therefore more than content to throw himself, body and soul, into the study of his chosen subject.

Kingsley needed no justification for spending money in the pursuit of art. In fact, he abhorred art that was made for commercial reasons. In later writings he made this abundantly clear:

There are two kinds of architecture, as there are two kinds of painting, of sculpture, and of literature. One is artistic, created for the joy of bringing into the world a beautiful thing – material compensation may or may not be given, but is secondary; the other is commercial, made primarily for expediency, for money, for fame. Roman art is of the commercial variety... They were opportunist structures, lacking intellectual and emotional content.[44]

When it came to commercialism in art, Kingsley took a high moral stand. There was no allowance made for struggling artists who had to feed themselves and their families. Even in Kingsley's time, there were very few artists who could indulge their art to their heart's content. Poverty would certainly concentrate the mind to dwell on more physical and mundane matters. Whatever emotional turmoil that Kingsley had so far faced in his life, the lack of finance had never been a factor.

For Kingsley, the joy and delight he experienced when researching ancient monuments in Rome was adequate compensation. His descriptions of his Roman travels after the publication of *Medieval Architecture* reveal a man who has indeed found a vocation that is all-consuming: 'the opportunity has come to linger long in Rome; to draw and photograph among the ruins of the Agro, to poetize with Carducci on the Aventine or in the Baths of Caracalla. Often as I have stood in the august presence of the Roman Forum, it has never been without emotion.'[45]

While in Italy, Kingsley's good friend and mentor William Henry Goodyear, the curator of the Brooklyn Institute of Arts and Sciences, wrote to him, advising him to take accurate photographs of the churches and monuments he visited: 'In my own experience, I have often undervalued the great importance of photographic record and have very frequently been obliged, on account of necessary haste, to omit observations which have involved sometimes revisiting a monument at great cost in some other year, and on many occasions I have never been able to make good.'[46]

Goodyear's advice was to stand Kingsley in good stead over his many years of productive research. He quickly became very proficient as a photographer and never went anywhere without his camera. From 1909 onwards, Kingsley no longer needed to buy book illustrations, as he was quite capable of producing his own photographic images.

In April 1909, at the age of 26, Kingsley was elected a member of the prestigious Société Française d'Archéologie, a rare honour for an American scholar. His election was in honour of his unique contribution to the study of medieval architecture.[47] During the remainder of 1909 and the whole of 1910, Kingsley continued his studies of Lombard architecture.

The Construction of Lombard and Gothic Vaults was completed in 1911 and published by Yale University Press. In this work, Kingsley discovered the earliest examples of rib vaults to have been created in Lombardy, in northern Italy. He then logically described the vault's evolution from Roman architecture to French Gothic.[48] In the opening chapter Kingsley summarized his findings: 'Rib vaults therefore were invented in Lombardy as a simple device to economize wood. They were adopted by the French builders for the same purpose. The same desire to dispense with temporary wooden substructures governed the development of architecture during the entire transitional period, and eventually lead to the birth of Gothic.'[49]

In the decade following his father's death, Kingsley had largely reversed the scandal and public lampooning of his family. Arthur Kingsley Porter had established himself as a brilliant scholar, an author of international acclaim and an authority on medieval architecture. Having immense wealth at his disposal and being surrounded by like-minded friends in New York, Kingsley was now living the good life. There was just one final element to be fitted into place: it was time for Kingsley to fall in love.

Chapter four

Establishing Roots: Marriage and Yale

Kingsley met Lucy Bryant Wallace at a social gathering that took place in early 1911. When they were introduced and began to chat about Italy, art and monuments, both immediately felt a deep, comfortable connection. Beside Lucy, Kingsley could feel himself thawing out, relaxing and forgetting his usual self-consciousness. Kingsley may have been somewhat of a loner but he had always enjoyed the company of intelligent, cultured and literary peers. It was most unusual, though, to meet a woman who possessed Lucy's knowledge of art and architecture, an undoubted intelligence and an innate charm. Even Kingsley's shyness could not prevent him from chatting all evening with the bright, dark-haired woman who exuded such confidence and social grace. He agreed to loan Lucy some photographs of Italian architecture and so another meeting was arranged.[1]

When they first met, Kingsley was 28 while Lucy was 35. The fact that Kingsley was seven years Lucy's junior was no deterrent. Kingsley failed to notice that Lucy's hair was dappled with tiny grey streaks. He had never been interested in pretty, painted girls who giggled and flaunted their physical attributes. From the moment that Kingsley set eyes on Lucy Bryant Wallace there was only one woman he wanted in his life. A series of meetings resulted and their relationship quickly flourished.

Lucy was much smaller than Kingsley, slightly plump and broad-faced. Lucy was of practical disposition and was a great organizer, whereas Kingsley was a romantic, a poet and a dreamer. Lucy had been educated at Miss Porter's School in Farmington, Connecticut. She had later studied at Yale and Columbia Universities.[2] Her pedigree was exemplary: well educated, highly intelligent and independently wealthy. Lucy was almost a carbon copy of Kingsley's beloved mother, Louisa.

Lucy admired Kingsley's abilities as a scholar and a writer. She was drawn to his quiet charm, his steady, honourable character and to all the attributes he possessed that made him a gentleman. Although Kingsley was reserved and shy among strangers, he was kind, sensitive and articulate among close friends. Lucy worked as a schoolteacher by choice and her financial status gave her great freedom, placing her on an equal social footing with Kingsley.

Lucy was the youngest daughter of Thomas and Ellen (née Bryant) Wallace.[3] Thomas was born in England and immigrated to America in 1832, aged 6 years. His family moved to Derby in New Haven County, Connecticut, in 1841. He worked at various trades before establishing Wallace & Sons in Ansonia, Connecticut, specializing in rolling metal and drawing wire. Thomas married Ellen Bryant from Massachusetts in 1857 and they had seven children. Their sixth child, Lucy Bryant, was born on 23 January 1876 in Ansonia, Connecticut.[4]

By 1880, Wallace & Sons had become the largest brass plant in the Naugatuck Valley, elevating the Wallace family to great wealth and social standing.[5] When Thomas Wallace retired from business the family moved to 346 West 71st Street, New York. Lucy's eldest sister, Elizabeth, married James B. Waller, a member of the prosperous real-estate family in Chicago.[6] The Wallers' attendance at society functions and events was frequently reported in Chicago newspapers. They mingled with the rich and famous, including the young beauty Miss Hazel Martyn, later to become the wife of Irish artist Sir John Lavery.[7] This further elevated the Wallaces' social position, as the Wallers were ranked among Chicago's elite for their lavish hospitality and generous patronage.[8]

Kingsley corresponded with Lucy frequently during 1911. In the early months of their courtship, Kingsley addressed her as 'Dear Miss

Wallace'.[9] They wrote about journeys undertaken, cultural events attended, art and books. During June 1911, Kingsley reported that he had been playing tennis and had also attended a Russian ballet in the Winter Garden in New York.[10] By July the letters had become less formal and Kingsley addressed his lady friend as 'My Dear Lucy'.[11] He also began to escort Lucy to her school each morning.[12]

On 24 July he sent Lucy a copy of *Medieval Architecture*. In the same letter he chatted about various events he had attended, including a yachting race that 'made my hair curl with excitement'.[13]

Even in these early letters to Lucy, Kingsley's love of adventure surfaces. While Lucy was touring the West Coast, Kingsley was at home reading but very much envying Lucy's own adventures: 'I thoroughly envy you the experience. I hate hard climbs while I am doing them – always get as scared as a kitten and never fail to vow to myself that if I get down safely I shall never no never try a mountain again – and yet one always does.'[14]

Later that year Lucy was introduced to Kingsley's uncle, Schuyler Merritt, and his cousins. Kingsley wrote to her from Pittsburg, apologizing for their lack of warmth at that first meeting: 'sorry the Merritt's call was stiff. I foresaw it would be however. The Hoyt blood is always that way, but I am sure you will find that they warm up when you get to know them better.'[15]

Kingsley also confided in Lucy that, despite his closeness with his brother, Louis, there was a sense of formality whenever he dined with his family:

> Occasionally, I go to dine with my family and occasionally my family comes to our house to dine. There is no one I ever see at Stamford except relatives. When one dines with relatives everyone tries to make conversation, but nobody ever quite succeeds. Usually for the first ten minutes (immediately after the cocktails) ... everybody talks at once as at a suffragette meeting. Then half the people stop to listen to the other half. Then everybody listens. At long intervals some valiant soul makes a

banal remark, which some other equally valiant soul tries to answer... And at nine-thirty everyone goes home to bed. It's a merry town.[16]

It was during December 1911 that Kingsley and Lucy became engaged. Lucy was beside herself with delight and appears to have been taken completely by surprise when Kingsley asked her to become his wife:

Dear, dear Kingsley,

.   My first engaged letter must be to him who caused it –must it not? I am so stunned, dear, I do not know what I am saying, so perhaps it is as well I am beginning with you.
My family are surprised chiefly at the suddenness of it.
Father was so sweet. He said 'I liked that young man's face the moment I saw him. He is a gentleman and he is alright.' I am so happy about it.[17]

After the engagement, Lucy's natural spontaneity and openness began to flow freely throughout the pages of her letters. Many happy afternoons were spent in her garden, sitting close to Kingsley, stealing hugs and kisses that set her heart racing. She simply rejoiced in the depth of her love for Kingsley: 'Sweet adorable Kingsley... I must wait forty-four hours before you can hold me in your arms again.'[18]

Lucy's letters are full of playfulness and sheer exuberance. She can hardly believe that, at the age of 35, she has finally found love. Her endearments are full of sweetness and light, more like the sentiments of a young girl than the expressions of a mature, sophisticated woman. On 26 December she wrote again to Kingsley: 'Sweetheart (How will you address me, I wonder!) Did you enjoy the trip out with your good friend? Did your attention never waver for one second as he discoursed upon the significance of the lotus in Egyptian art? Ah, Kingsley, dear, how I wish you might have been talking to me instead.'[19]

346 West 71 Street

December 26, 1911.

Sweetheart:

(How will you address me
I wonder!) Did you enjoy the trip out
with your good friend? Did your attention
never waver for one second as he
discoursed upon the significance of the
lotus in Egyptian art! Oh, Kingsleydear,
how I wish you might have been talking
to me instead. A telegram, *from Henrietta* I found this
morning on my return begging
me to come on "with" Mr. Porter to
stay as long as possible with her
So dear of her. Please thank her and
please like her awfully. I do Ned
neergaard so you ought to. By the way,
a fine, bully letter from him to
show you. And more ofte. I really must

11. Letter from Lucy Bryant Wallace to Kingsley Porter,
dated 26 December 1911.

Harvard University Archives, HUG 1706.114, Correspondence of Arthur Kingsley
Porter and Lucy W. Porter, 1911–25; 1911–12: After engagement.

The shy and reserved Kingsley appears to have gone through his own transformation. Much of the stiff formality seems to have fallen away and, instead, Kingsley's romantic and poetic side begins to emerge:

> A good hug and kiss and a heartful of love to you darling. And remember to take care of yourself and to think of me once in a while. I wish you knew how constantly you are in my thoughts, and how I am anticipating the time when we can travel together. I am always imagining what fun these trips would be were you along.[20]

In the following months the couple attended all the main social and cultural events in New York, including theatrical productions and concerts. In January 1912, Kingsley wrote to Lucy after one such social engagement, worried in case his lack of social tact had upset her. He was obviously aware that, in the highly conservative society in which they lived, every move was open to scrutiny and discussion:

> I wonder, darling, whether you minded my sitting on the arm of Katherine's chair this afternoon as I should have minded it had the case been reversed. Under the circumstances I think it was very poor taste and soon realized it, when she asked me to, I accepted it without thinking. I am afraid you have in hand a wild and wayward nature that has so afterwards occurred to me that it might give you pain. Forgive me dearie, won't you?[21]

Amid all their joyous plans for a June wedding, a tragedy struck the western world on 15 April when the RMS *Titanic* sank on its maiden voyage from Cobh, Ireland, to New York, with a loss of life of over 1,500.[22] Many of the wealthiest Americans were on board, including multimillionaires John Jacob Astor and Benjamin Guggenheim, both of whom perished.[23] It is likely that both Kingsley and Lucy knew some of the first-class passengers who had to endure this ordeal. It must also have been a great shock to Kingsley, who was a frequent traveller to

Europe and could easily have been crossing back on the *Titanic* if he had been researching abroad that April.

In May 1912, Kingsley sent Lucy an exquisite bouquet of roses, and Lucy wrote to him in a great outpouring of love:

> Darling I adore them. Their very fragrance takes me back to the first roses you sent me. How they excited me by breathing to me in their mysterious way that you were interested in me! How I hung over their deep enfolded beauty dreaming as much as I dared of you.
>
> How these, their sister, come with such a different message. They tell me the finest, noblest, most thoughtful man of all the peoples of the earth loves me. I am dippy at the thought darling, how did it come about? [24]

The pair married on 1 June 1912 at the residence of Lucy's parents. The ceremony was performed at 4 p.m. by Rev. George H. Buck, rector of St James Church, Derby, Connecticut.[25] Only relatives and intimate friends were present. The bride's only attendant was her sister, Ruth. The best man was Kingsley's brother, Louis. Lucy's sister Elizabeth, her husband James B. Waller and their daughter Ellen, wife of John Borden, travelled from Chicago to spend the week before the wedding in New York.[26] The ushers were William L. Peltz of Albany, Franklin J. Walls of New York, and Kingsley's friend from his student days at Yale, Dr Arthur Neergard. Lucy's youngest brother, Harold, also travelled from Chicago to attend the wedding.[27] On their wedding day, Kingsley was 29 years old while Lucy was 36.

Kingsley and 'Queensley', as Kingsley affectionately called his new wife, became inseparable. They travelled to Lake George, set in Kingsley's beloved Adirondack region of New York State. The photos taken on their honeymoon reveal a smiling Kingsley, leaning against the ship's railing, wearing suit and tie and carrying a hat. Lucy looks radiant in white, wearing a cloche hat and leaning on her parasol. She is smiling and looking off to the side, a spectacular lake and low hills visible behind her. On their return to New York, Kingsley was in no hurry to buy a house so the couple moved into an apartment at 450 West End Avenue.[28]

12. Arthur Kingsley Porter, leaning on railing, Lake George, New York, 1912.
Harvard University Archives, HUG 1706.125 (8).

13. Lucy Porter on honeymoon at Lake George, New York, 1912.
Harvard University Archives.

In a letter written to Kingsley just four months after her marriage, Lucy's deep happiness is still boundless: 'Dearest, such a lovely day to write you. It seemed to me quite the most delightful one since we were married. But then so many are the very nicest one – just as it is with our good times.'[29]

In the latter months of 1912, the Porters extended their honeymoon with a lengthy trip to Italy. For those who were lucky enough to afford first-class tickets, these enormous ships possessed every luxury. Amenities on board included a gymnasium, a saltwater swimming pool, electric and Turkish baths, a barber's shop, cafés, a sumptuous dining room, opulent cabins with private bathrooms, elevators, and both open and enclosed promenades.[30] The time taken to cross the Atlantic in 1912 varied, depending on many factors including weather conditions, but would have taken an average of seven days.[31] The Porters enjoyed the best of cuisine, nightly entertainment provided by resident musicians and the privacy of their staterooms where they could write, read or rest. In fine weather they spent time on deck, walking along the promenade and enjoying the sea air or sitting in deckchairs, reading, chatting or sleeping.

The Porters would have shared these journeys in first class with some of the wealthiest American families, such as Vanderbilt, Rockefeller and Carnegie. They would also have encountered the nouveau riche who travelled to Europe annually, indulging in every frivolity imaginable. A member of Caroline Astor's millionaire set described her life in the era before 1914 as 'Breathless rushes across continents – One country blending into another – journeys by car, by train – Paris – Newport – New York. Paris again – London –Vienna – Berlin – the Riviera – Italy. Champagne years, colourful, sparkling, ephemeral . . . Always entertaining, being entertained, the same scene in a new setting.'[32]

'Ritzonia' was the word coined by Bernard Berenson, American art historian and collector, to describe the false, dull, tedious world inhabited by listless millionaires.[33] The American novelist Edith Wharton admitted to Berenson: 'Yes, it's nice to be petted & feasted – but I don't see how you can stand more than two or three weeks of that queer rootless life.'[34] The majority of the ladies who frequently sailed first class from New York to Europe were overdressed in furs, wore large hats with huge plumes, and dresses of thin, pale silks.[35] They travelled with several maids and an array of trunks, suitcases, crates, a medicine chest and a special pouch for their jewels. The men smoked, drank to excess and played poker for high stakes. The majority were spoiled and conceited, always expecting to be served and pampered.[36]

There is little doubt that the Porters would have given these revellers a wide berth. Kingsley's New England work ethic would have abhorred idleness, believing that a worthy occupation and a meaningful purpose were necessary to maintain one's dignity and contentment. Neither Kingsley nor Lucy had any time for ostentation. Both were happy to spend time reading, taking pleasant walks on deck, and staring out to sea, observing its changing colour and mood.

In Italy, the Porters did so much sightseeing that Kingsley developed an illness and Lucy became exhausted. On 3 February 1913, Lucy was so tired that she went to bed early while Kingsley completed her correspondence. He wrote to Lucy's mother, telling her of their plans to travel from Florence to Sicily, via Rome and Naples. He also praised Lucy's ability to take such good care of him: 'Lucy has developed into a most wonderful travel nurse, and has taken care of me intensely during the first part of the sickness and at nights always I think myself that it was she rather than the doctor that pulled me through so nicely.'[37]

Their time in Italy was full of happiness for Lucy. She loved walking arm in arm with her beloved Kingsley, strolling through glorious piazzas in Florence or along sunny country roads, breathing in the sweet scents of vineyards. She cherished their visits to medieval churches, with their fine stone statues and magnificent murals. Many years later she recalled their visit to St Monty Chiavenna in northern Italy, where she first fell in love with the church of St Fidelis of Como.[38] There was nothing Lucy enjoyed more than standing beside Kingsley and being part of his world, discussing his latest theories, inspecting a particular symbol that had caught his attention, and sharing her own views on favourite artworks. Both Kingsley and Lucy had spent a great deal of their adult lives alone. Now, finally, they had each found a special companion with whom to share all their thoughts, feelings and dreams. Life had simply never been sweeter.

Later that year the Porters returned to Europe. Life had become a wild, colourful adventure for Lucy as her new husband had an insatiable desire for travelling. Lucy became his beloved companion and indispensable assistant, photographing sculptures and architectural wonders during their many years of research and travel together. On 8 December they travelled home via Lapland and disembarked in New York.[39]

On 5 April 1914, Kingsley's review of the research undertaken by his friend and colleague William Henry Goodyear was published in *The New York Times*.[40] Goodyear, the curator of the Brooklyn Museum, had been conducting a series of studies involving the photographing and measuring of European buildings. Kingsley corresponded with Goodyear until his friend's death in 1923. In the review, Kingsley gave Goodyear the accolade of 'the first American art historian'.

The Porters had to curtail their travels when, on 28 June 1914, Archduke Franz Ferdinand of Austria, the heir to the Austria-Hungary throne, was assassinated. Thus began the First World War that lasted for over four years. Civilian travel to Europe was far too dangerous and Kingsley had to content himself with excursions within the States.

Kingsley's brother Louis had become a successful lawyer in New York. By January 1915 he had four children: Louise Hoyt, called after his beloved mother was aged 11; Louis Hopkins Junior was aged 10; Joyce was aged 6 and Beatrice was aged 4. Their fifth child, christened Arthur Kingsley Porter, had died shortly after birth.[41]

On 31 March 1915, the misfortune that had dogged the Porters during Kingsley's early life resurfaced. Louis's home at Noroton Hill was destroyed by fire, entailing a loss of over $100,000.[42] The fire had started on a porch roof when a spark from a plumber's torch ignited. A fifty-mile-an-hour north-west gale fanned the flames and created an inferno. Luckily, none of the family was hurt in the ensuing blaze. Louis's wife, Marion, had to be restrained from entering the blazing house to save her jewellery. However, her jewellery collection that was valued at several thousand dollars was destroyed. Louis and Kingsley lost their collection of native birds that was considered the most valuable and rare in America.

In April 1915 the danger of travelling across the Atlantic became abundantly clear when the German Embassy issued a warning that was printed in fifty American newspapers, advising passengers who intended to travel on British ships to do so at their peril.[43] On 7 May 1915 the threat became an appalling reality when RMS *Lusitania*, en route from New York to Liverpool, was torpedoed by a German U-boat, just eleven miles from the Irish coast at Kinsale, Co. Cork. The ship sank within eighteen minutes with a loss of life totalling 1,198 passengers and crew.[44] Unknown to the passengers, the ship had been carrying arms and munitions. The casualties included eminent industrialists, politicians, authors, architects, professors and newspaper tycoons, from the United States, Canada and Britain. The Irish art collector Sir Hugh Lane was also a victim, and the priceless case of paintings he was transporting was lost.[45] The sinking of the *Lusitania* and the subsequent outrage at the fact that innocent civilians had been ruthlessly killed by a German military operation was a major contribution to the United States' entry into the First World War.[46]

In the circumstances, Kingsley had to be content to remain on home soil. During 1915 he began teaching at Yale, his alma mater, where his family had studied since the 1840s.[47] Although noted for his shyness, Kingsley's students always gave glowing accounts of him. They absorbed his passion for art and blossomed under his original tutoring style. While at Yale, he also began working towards a Bachelor of Fine Arts. Kingsley had fond memories of his undergraduate years at Yale and he quickly threw himself into the university's stimulating social life. At the Art School he taught five courses that dealt with medieval and Renaissance painting, architecture and sculpture. He also expounded the cultural riches that were on offer at Yale, not only in the subject matter covered in its art and history courses, but also the artistic treasures that were exhibited at the Jarves Gallery.[48]

During Kingsley's time at Yale he commuted to college while Lucy remained in New York. Lucy always enjoyed a rich and varied social life, meeting with friends for luncheon in some of the best hotels, dining out in the evening and then taking in a play or a concert.

14. Harkness Tower, Yale, New Haven, CT.
Michael Cullen.

Kingsley's research and writing always took precedence, and period-ically he needed time alone to work on his latest project.

The first day of January 1916 was the dawning of a sad day for Lucy when her father, Thomas Wallace, died in his eighty-ninth year.[49] Perhaps being reminded of his own mortality, Kingsley began formulating a new will. On 28 January he wrote to the President of Yale, Arthur Twining Hadley, stating that he wished to leave a bequest to the university, to establish a Faculty of Art History.[50] Kingsley was aware that the setting up of an Art History department at Yale would meet with stiff opposition from some quarters, and he stated: 'I understand the powers of darkness are strongly entrenched in certain quarters of New Haven.' The bequest he proposed was the sum of half-a-million dollars that would be used:

1. To provide salaries for professors or instructors in the history of art in the academic department, as might be required.

2. To provide for the running and overhead expenses of such a department, the purchases of equipment, slides, photographs, books, etc.

3. Any residue to be used for the purchase of additional works of art to add to the collection of the Art School, and for the proper maintenance and housing of the same.

Kingsley also offered to bequeath to the university his Italian paint-ings and other art objects.[51] It was indeed a grave disappointment when the university declined his offer. These years at Yale had been some of Kingsley's happiest, but the refusal to accept his bequest proved that he had little power to influence the university's authorities. It was a bitter pill to swallow, reminding him of his insignificance within the greater academic circle. For the moment Kingsley bided his time and remained at Yale.

On 1 March 1916, Kingsley wrote to his brother Louis, instructing him to make changes to the draft of both his and Lucy's wills that were being drawn up. Lucy bequeathed a selection of her jewellery and ornaments to each of Louis's children: Louis Junior, Louise, Joyce and Beatrice.[52]

Throughout 1916, Kingsley rekindled his childhood interest in drama by joining the Yale Dramatic Society.[53] He took part in *Cupid and Psyche* that was performed in the magnificent Woolsey Hall on 20 October 1916. This was a glittering occasion in which the Hollywood actress Lorraine Huling, who had recently appeared in the silent motion picture *The Fall of a Nation*, played the heroine's role. Kingsley played the Archbishop of Florence, one of the characters from the court scene.

In November, the Porters attended the Davanzati Palace auction held at the Plaza in New York.[54] This was yet another interest that the couple enjoyed, browsing around galleries and antique auctions in search of a priceless piece of medieval art. It was also quite a social occasion, where art collector and investor mingled with New York's elite society. Kingsley couldn't miss the opportunity of adding further Italian artworks to his valuable collection. He purchased several items, including a panel of St Michael the Archangel by the Venetian artist Il Guariento, at a cost of $425; a Crucifixion panel from a primitive school of Florence for $850; a Madonna and Child panel by Tommaso di Cristoforo Fini for $725; and a painted wooden cross from the Tuscan school for $310. On the afternoon of 4 December, Kingsley gave an illustrated lecture on French medieval art in the ballroom of the Colony Club in New York.[55]

The year 1917 was a particularly fruitful period for Kingsley. On 20 March he was promoted to Assistant Professor of the History of Art at Yale.[56] He also received his Bachelor Degree in Fine Arts from Yale. In July, Kingsley's third book, *Lombard Architecture*, was published in four volumes by Yale University Press.[57]

Kingsley had been fascinated by Lombard architecture since his early travels in northern Italy. The task of writing an architectural study of the remaining monuments and churches in the Lombard region was colossal, as most of the original buildings had been destroyed during renovations and reconstructions. This, however, was no deterrent to Kingsley. In the first volume he painstakingly traced the development of Lombard architecture from its Byzantine beginnings in the sixth century, through its Romanesque, Gothic and Cistercian epochs,[58] using documentary evidence and comparative masonry analysis.[59] He also discussed the use of ornament, in particular the grotesque. He described the personal inscriptions left by craftsmen, often of a humorous nature, such as the carving of an old man who rubs his beard, accompanied by the caption: 'I am here to amuse fools.'[60]

The book was undoubtedly original and inherently courageous. Kingsley challenged many cherished theories postulated by contemporaries and shattered the misconceptions of previous authorities. Through his findings he argued that the authentic Lombard style began to emerge as 'more interesting, more worthy of study, and certainly more beautiful'.[61]

The second and third volumes were devoted to the discussion of individual monuments, while the fourth contained 1,000 fine plates that illustrated the chronological development of the style. Kingsley brilliantly captured the beauty and character of Lombard architecture, with its broken straight lines, its incredible colours, mosaic pavements and marvellous frescoes. *The New York Times* reviewed the book in glowing terms: 'the clarity of the author's thought and expression makes his description and comment extremely interesting to the moderately informed reader. The form of the work reaches the high standard set by the Yale University Press for its important publications.'[62]

The book, however, met with severe rebuke in certain circles. The proof proffered by Kingsley that the ribbed vault, on which Gothic architecture depends, was first created in Lombardy before travelling to France[63] was met with caustic criticism by French art historians. Émile Mâle, the celebrated French medieval art historian, wrote a hostile review of *Lombard Architecture* in 1918. Mâle severely criticized Kingsley's dating of Italian Romanesque monuments and his suggestion that sculpture from the Emelia-Romagna region exerted influence on artistic developments in France.[64] Mâle postulated that all major artistic developments began in France and that Lombard architecture was always derived from French design. He refuted Kingsley's assertion that significant building and sculpture had occurred between the eighth and tenth centuries and he strongly criticized Kingsley's theory that sculpture had been created in Europe before 1100.[65]

Although Kingsley may have presented a withdrawn and diffident exterior at social gatherings or to passing acquaintances, when it came to defending his archaeological theories he did so with great passion, eloquence and self-belief. He immediately responded to Mâle's rebuff in an article, 'The Rise of Romanesque Sculpture'.[66] He challenged Mâle's Franco-centric views and theorized that artistic exchange occurred during the pilgrimage to Santiago de Compostela, in northern Spain. He postulated that Lombard craftsmen travelled the pilgrim route to Santiago, stopping at Languedoc before travelling to Spain. He argued that international artistic exchange was how medieval craftsmen learned and shared their artistic secrets, without regional boundaries.[67] In defence of his work, Kingsley displayed the full gamut of his brilliance as a researcher, an author and a tactician. Thus an infamous battle raged between the two scholars, as to the origins of Romanesque sculpture in Christian Spain, that continued well into the next decade.[68]

Despite Mâle's criticism, the work catapulted Kingsley to international acclaim. Bernard Berenson, renowned art historian and specialist in Renaissance art, was full of praise for *Lombard Architecture*.[69] Berenson sent Kingsley a very flattering letter, telling him that they were indeed kindred spirits. Kingsley replied with great appreciation: 'I have read and reread and admired your works so intensely, that an autograph from you carries with it the romance of a relic. I wish I dared believe you that there is kinship between my method and yours. I think it may be so in the sense that your scholarship has been my inspiration.'[70]

The stream of correspondence with art historians and museum curators in the US, including Kingsley's friend William Goodyear, Brooklyn Museum's Curator of Fine Arts,[71] and Allan Marquant,[72] Professor and Director of the Princeton University Art Museum, showed that Kingsley was now established as a specialist in medieval architecture. His expert opinion was constantly sought and highly valued.

On 24 October 1917, Kingsley wrote to Raymond Pitcairn, architect of Bryn Athyn Cathedral in Pennsylvania, to offer praise for his design:

> I had expected much of the Bryn Athyn church, but nothing like what I found. If it existed in Europe, in France or England, it would still be at once six centuries behind, and a hundred years ahead of its time. But on the soil of great architectural traditions, it would be in a measure comprehensible, and the presence in the neighbourhood of the great works of the past would in a way prepare the mind for this achievement of the present age. For your church, alone of modern buildings, in my judgement, is worthy of comparison with the best the Middle Ages produced.[73]

Kingsley was so appreciative of Pitcairn's work that he included an illustration of Bryn Athyn Cathedral as the frontispiece in his book, *Beyond Architecture* (1918).

The Porters also supported the war effort by attending several exhibitions and auctions that had been organized to raise funds. It was always important for Lucy to give her time to charitable organizations and over the years she served on many committees that funded artists, students and various minority groups. On 11 November 1917, Kingsley exhibited some of his art works at the exhibition of Italian paintings that was held at the Kleinberger Galleries in New York, the receipts for which went to the American war relief.[74] That same afternoon, Kingsley gave a lecture on medieval architecture at the Metropolitan Museum of Art.[75] On 19 December, Lucy attended the sale of Professor Elia Volpi's art treasures, at the American Art Gallery in New York. She purchased a seventeenth-century Italian velvet table cover, that was bordered with gold lace, for $320.[76]

During the early months of 1918, Kingsley continued to lecture at Yale while researching his latest book, *Beyond Architecture*. On 13 March he was invited to give a lecture on French Gothic architecture at Harvard's Fogg Art Museum.[77] Following on from the success of his lecture, Kingsley loaned two early Italian paintings to the museum.[78] One of the paintings was a rare fourteenth-century Gothic triptych by Simone da Bologna; the other painting was attributed to Jacob di Cione, brother of Orcagna, and was described as being very rich in colour. Thus began Kingsley's bittersweet relationship with Harvard.

During 1918, Kingsley's reputation reached new heights when he was awarded the prestigious Grande Médaille de Vermeil de Société Française d'Archéologie.[79] This great international honour was indeed a sweet salve after Mâle's relentless criticism.

In June 1918, Kingsley's fourth book, *Beyond Architecture* (based on a series of articles he had written), was published by the Boston publisher Marshall Jones Company. In the preface he wrote that this 'baby of peace' was born 'amid the shrapnel and groans of a great war'.[80] The main text discussed the components that must be present in any art – including architecture, painting, stained glass, sculpture, music and literature – to constitute a work of beauty and value.

Kingsley postulated that in all great art, the intention of the artist must be to bring forth a creation from the depths of the soul, from the sublime well of emotion: 'For the essence of all great art is joy: the joy of grandeur, the joy of poetry, the joy of gloom, the joy of tears perhaps, but always joy. The genius imbues the object with a spark of this divine joy, so that it may awaken in others the same or a kindred emotion.'[81]

While modern-day artists often focused on producing art for commercial purposes, Kingsley held that Gothic artists achieved 'absolute unity of composition . . . Each capital, each statue, each bit of tracery, each moulding, was a masterpiece.'[82] This wonderful spirit of creativity also applied to the work of medieval stained-glass artists, in which 'the flow of line, the rhythm, the composition, and above all, the colouring, are sources of unending delight'.[83]

This book, more than any other, shows Kingsley's absolute love of art. It is apparent that great art could stir his emotions and ignite his spirit – perhaps a great deal more than most people could ever excite or interest him. Art was more than a pastime, more than a career; it was an indelible need, bringing him close to the exhilaration he felt when wandering in the depths of nature. He strongly disagreed with the popular opinion that Greek monuments were 'self-restrained, metallic and icy, colourless as the moonlight on the snow'. For Kingsley, Greek art was highly erotic and charged with sexual imagery, culminating in the depiction of the male nude:

> Greek art was not anaemic, but red-blooded, not pale, but full of strong colours, not neurotic, but pulsating with life. Indeed, in this very vitality lies the secret of its illustrative power. It is full of sex. The emotion it conveys is the emotion of sex, the beauty it interprets is the beauty of sex! This fact has very largely been misunderstood or ignored because the type of sex which appealed with especial power to the Greeks is considered per-verse and repulsive by the modern age. Not being willing to grant that an art obviously of the highest type could have been inspired by ideals which seem to us depraved, we have willed not to understand. Yet delight in the nude, and especially in the nude male, is the key-note of Greek art. Where else has the vigour of youth, the play of muscles, the glory of manhood found a like expression? It is the ideal of masculine sex which the Greeks eternally glorified; this is the beauty they never wearied of interpreting... And the sculptures were the idealization of male sex, that and that only. Thus the entire Greek temple was made a glorious hymn in praise of sex.[84]

Kingsley's open appreciation of the male nude as created by the ancient Greeks was indeed courageous in the repressed New England society in which he lived. His description of the Greek temple as 'a glorious hymn in praise of sex' might have been construed as profane and indeed vulgar. Fortunately, his views on the sexiness of classical art passed without notice.

The early months of 1918 were busy for Lucy as she entertained friends and family for dinner and lunch engagements at their New York home.[85] Lucy's engagement diary for that year was full of social events and cultural outings, including evenings at the Boston Symphony, the opera, chamber music recitals and theatrical performances. Lucy was a full-time hostess, constantly arranging afternoon teas and dinners for the Wallace family, the Porters, the Merritts, and for their vast network of friends and acquaintances. On Thursday mornings Lucy volunteered for the Red Cross, where she learned the rudiments of nursing.

These were also busy months for Kingsley. Lucy marked set times in her diary for Kingsley to be alone, to write and study.[86] He was often asked to lecture at prestigious universities, including Princeton. He also made regular visits to Louis and his family in Stamford. It was mainly at weekends that Kingsley and Lucy could unwind and spend time together. No matter what events or lavish entertainment Lucy attended during the week, it was always these quiet times spent alone with Kingsley that were the most precious.

During the summer of 1918, the idyllic world of perfect form and shape in which Kingsley loved to dwell was far from the minds of millions of Europeans. War still raged in Europe, and unspeakable carnage and destruction littered the cities and countryside after a four-year onslaught by the Allies to defeat Germany. Kingsley was contacted by the Commission for Historical Monuments on behalf of the French government and invited to join the Works of Art Service in the Armed Forces Area of Paris. Kingsley was delighted with the honour as he was the only non-French expert invited to assist in the preservation of French monuments.[87]

Kingsley had recently established a career as a lecturer in Yale. He was now aged 35, while Lucy was 42. It is not known whether either of them wanted a family, though it was certainly unusual at the time for a couple who had been married for six years to be childless, unless there was some physical problem that prevented a pregnancy. Lucy would certainly have been within her rights to want a permanent home. The prospect of relocating to France in the midst of a world war would have been abhorrent to most women. However, Lucy appears to have embraced this momentous adventure with great fervour. In none of her diaries or correspondence does she portray the least trace of fear or apprehension about relocating to a war-ravaged zone.

Kingsley was subsequently appointed to a panel of experts to assess the damage that had been inflicted on medieval monuments in France.[88] The appointment suited him, as he was eager to begin research in Europe for his new book, *Romanesque Sculpture of the Pilgrimage Roads.* Yet it was a dangerous undertaking; although the war was moving into its final phase, atrocities were still being carried out on all sides.

During mid-July, the Porters visited family and friends in Stamford and Washington.[89] In her diary, Lucy failed to mention how their relatives greeted the announcement that they would be leaving the safety of their East Coast life for the chaotic shores of France, in the midst of a deadly war. In early August they met with Monsieur Hubert who was to arrange their passage to France.[90] The Allies had just begun their offensive against the Germans in northern France, centring on the town of Amiens, between 8 and 11 August. In Lucy's engagement diary, several dates were marked for their departure, but they finally left New York on Sunday 11 August.[91] Their destination was Paris,[92] and their official assignment was to assess the damage that had been wreaked on medieval monuments.[93] Kingsley's own mission was to save every sculpture, monument and Romanesque structure from ruin or oblivion.

Chapter five

War and Separation

As the First World War was nearing its final, desperate throes, the Porters left the safety of their privileged East Coast life to face the perils of an Atlantic voyage. They landed at Bordeaux without incident on 29 August 1918[1] and made their way to Paris, where they booked into the Hôtel de France to await further instructions.[2] They carried a letter of introduction to allow them to travel unhindered by officials. The letter was signed by Robert Lansing, the United States Secretary of State, on behalf of Kingsley's uncle, Schuyler Merritt, who was currently serving as a representative in Congress.[3]

Lucy arranged lunch and dinner engagements with American friends in Paris during September and the early weeks of October.[4] Travel within France was still hazardous as the Allies continued their offensive in northern France. On 12 September the Germans were forced to retreat to the Belgian border after the Battle of Havrincourt. From 18 September to 10 October, the Battle of the Hindenburg Line was fought until the Allies finally broke through German lines.

In late October, Kingsley was required to go to Italy to survey the damage inflicted on Roman monuments.[5] Lucy had trouble obtaining a visa to travel into Italy, so reluctantly she decided to remain in Paris until her papers were issued.[6] Kingsley was distraught at leaving Lucy behind. However, Monsieur Hubert promised that within a week Lucy would receive her papers.[7] In the meantime, Lucy had her maid, Natalina, for company.[8] On Friday 25 October, Kingsley travelled to Rome, alone.[9] Lucy recorded in her diary entry for that day: 'Our first separation.'[10]

15. Soldiers removing art works from Cathedral in Reims, c. 1918.

From *Rheims and the Battles for its Possession*, Illustrated Michelin Guides to the Battle-Fields (1914–1918) (Clermont-Ferrand: Michelin & Cie, 1919; published in eBook format by Project Gutenberg, 2011), p.23.

Before crossing into Italy, Kingsley met up with Monsieur Hubert and was given a busy workload, to visit churches and monuments in Dijon,[11] Bourg-en-Bresse[12] and other devastated regions of eastern France. He also tried to secure a pass for Lucy to allow her to travel within the war zone in Paris so that she could make an assessment of the damage inflicted on some of the churches and monuments.[13]

Kingsley and Lucy corresponded on a daily basis. Some days they wrote several letters to each other as well as sending telegrams and postcards. The separation was acutely painful to both. Their letters were passionate and romantic, written by two people who were very much in love and evidently distressed at being separated. Kingsley had just parted from Lucy when he wrote to her from Dijon, calling her 'My Bobbie', in a state of deep loneliness:

My Bobbie,

If you know how long and weary the moments of this our first (and may it be the last – until that final one comes) separation. I reached the station at eight o'clock and thought the half hour until the train left would never pass . . . I never so wished for time to pass before as I do now. To see you again!

. . . Even you will not guess how much love goes with it. To-night I know what homesickness is like – but it is not home, it's you.[14]

When he reached Bourg-en-Bresse, Kingsley was disappointed not to find a letter from Lucy waiting for him, but he surmised that she was sending the letters on to Rome.[15] He wrote to her instead, telling her of the places he had visited and of the boxes of damaged art objects that he had been assessing:

The Commission des Monuments Historiques has established a depot in the church and there are cases of stained glass and other objects piled in the chapels. To-day Hubert was going over the paintings from the Musée of Epinal – opening the cases, checking off the inventory and examining the pictures. There were several of considerable interest, most were second or third rate or worse – all were of the French, Flemish, or German schools, of the xvi, xvii, xviii centuries. No one seems to know anything about them. Almost all had been more or less injured by dampness, due to the fact that they had been packed in paper and left in an unheated building. It is a good point to know. If I had been in charge I should have supposed it to be more dangerous than its absence. So far I am not much impressed with the efficiency of the service. But I must not breathe anything of the sort even to you.

To-morrow I shall be in Italy... I need no photograph of you because you are always in my mind. I can see you now as distinctly as if you were present, and I know each gesture, each intonation of your voice – and I love it. How good it will be to see you again. Good night.[16]

On 28 October, Lucy replied to Kingsley with equal intensity and desire to be reunited: 'My baby, I am so lonely tonight, not let you know how much. You have been too good to me. I have leaned so heavily on you I can't walk alone. When you left me everything stopped in my life.'[17]

Kingsley travelled by a network of first-class trains from Bourg-en-Bresse to Turin, then on to Genoa, and finally arrived in Rome at noon on 30 October.[18] He booked into the Grand Hotel and was delighted to find two letters from Lucy waiting for him. Then he went for a walk around the city. He felt headachy and sick in the evening and took sleeping tablets to ensure a good night's rest. In the morning he visited several contacts, including Mr Keene who invited him to attend a 'Halloween Frolic' at the YMCA. Kingsley complained that the food in Rome was very poor. Fish was the only dish available and that was very expensive. He reported to Lucy that all the food that the Italians are famous for was unavailable, except for grapes and good wine. He immediately began the task of trying to obtain a visa for Lucy to cross the frontier, and of getting permission for their car to be released. Although it had been less than a week since they parted, Kingsley was bereft and wrote to Lucy that he could not enjoy the beauty of Rome without her.

During her time alone in Paris, Lucy took French lessons and also continued to meet friends for lunch and dinner.[19] In her engagement diary she marked down the dates when telegrams arrived from Kingsley. On Saturday 2 November she wrote: 'One telegram from K – at one. 3 more at 8.30. Sent answer.'[20]

Despite Kingsley's daily excursions to churches and monuments in Rome and the surrounding countryside, his feelings of loneliness and deep angst continued. While staying at the Grand Hotel he wrote to Lucy each evening, always longing for their reunion:

My Bobbie I love you

Without you the world is hollow and empty: there is unhappiness in it.

I see people and people and more people; and no one satisfies or satiates for an instant the yearning which is in the innermost parts of my being.

I shall not have one moment of happiness until I see you again. I want only you – nothing else counts – neither success, nor friends, nor even the incomparable loveliness of Italy.

I love you, my Bobbie. I love you with the most intense deep love. I love you because I know what you are.

I am homesick and lonely without you, my Bobbie. Come to me quickly!

> L'absence est le plus grand des maux.
>
> (Absence is the greatest evil)[21]

For Kingsley, the separation was made unbearable by the absence of Lucy's letters. Although she wrote to him daily there were times when the post was invariably delayed. On 5 November Kingsley wrote to her in a state of deep anxiety:

> No word from you to-day. I wonder where you are. There is no joy in life without you. I watch and watch the empty letter-box, and run to it a hundred times in the day. There is no life without you. Rome and peace! What a combination. But the sun only bores me, I see the beauty of the city with my intellect but not with my heart. Without you there is nothing which counts – If I only knew where you were.[22]

Kingsley's previous aloofness and lack of overt affection suddenly disintegrated under the strain of parting. There was a new depth of passion and intimacy that permeated his letters. It was as though no endearment could ever be enough to express his love to Lucy: 'I love you, little girl, and think of you every moment... Good night, and a thousand kisses.'[23] There was also a new sense of freedom and ease in the personal anecdotes he shared with Lucy: 'My pyjamas have gone to the wash, and I shall have to sleep naked for a night or two. It is so hot here the flannel ones are unthinkable.'[24]

Yet his love and devotion also began to take on a mystical dimension. He began using the language of a poet to describe the depth of love for his wife: 'I love you more than the seven worlds or the nine heavens. I only live because of you and when I am beside you. Every moment when I am separated from you is a moment of living lost from my life. I love you. Goodbye. Sleep well and how good it will be to come back to you!'[25]

Throughout his time in Rome, Kingsley continued the task of assessing damage to sculptures and monuments. He also made time to work on the drama he was writing, entitled *The Seven Who Slept*. On 2 November he wrote to Lucy, telling her that he was considering submitting the finished manuscript to Marshall Jones Company in Boston for publication: 'I worked this morning on *The Seven Who Slept*. I think I may send it to Jones. There are parts of it that seem to me to be rather good, but I am probably wrong. I don't think it will get very well launched with Jones.'[26]

Kingsley also worked tirelessly in his efforts to obtain a visa for Lucy. On 3 November he wrote to the ambassador, in an attempt to get Lucy's papers secured.[27] He also complained that his work to recover and assess important works of art was hampered by formalities. He reiterated that country churches in the devastated regions, as well as irreplaceable art objects, were being lost, damaged or stolen but that this trend could be reversed if he was allowed to carry out his task unhindered.

In early November, Kingsley was introduced to a Contessa in Rome who was quite influential.[28] He asked if she might find employment for Lucy in a hospital so that her visa would be granted. The Contessa said she was powerless to help, since Italian workers were returning from the front and there were no positions open for an American nurse in Rome. It appears that the Contessa developed a romantic interest in Kingsley and that she tried to seduce him in her boudoir.[29] In a letter to Lucy, dated 5 November, Kingsley turned the event into a farce and made light of the Contessa's amorous intentions: 'I went to see the Contessa this afternoon. She has an attractive studio and is no end kittenish – says she wishes every day she was divorced, lies on the sofa and kicks her legs in the air. All of which is interesting, as we were alone in a half dark studio.'

In the same letter, Kingsley praised Lucy's cleverness in persuading Hubert to give her a copy of important documents from the embassy.[30]

He also admitted that he was completely lost without her; he was gauche and awkward, whereas Lucy possessed great social skills. Lucy was left in no doubt that the amorous Contessa meant absolutely nothing to Kingsley and that his heart was devoted to her alone.

The following day he confided that he was discouraged after another fruitless day.[31] He still hadn't managed to secure Lucy's papers and he had discovered that there were great shortages of gasoline so that it was unlikely that their car would be released for quite a while. He also wondered if the Germans were going to fight it out until the bitter end.

On 7 November, Kingsley wrote to the American Embassy in Paris, stating that he needed Lucy to help him in Rome with the task entrusted to him by the Commission for Monuments.[32] The same day, however, Kingsley discovered that there were difficulties in crossing the Italian border and getting back into France, so he advised Lucy to stay in Paris.[33] His new plan was to obtain papers to enable him to cross back into France.

During his time in Rome, Kingsley dined with several acquaintances. He felt ill at ease in these social situations, where there was constant 'gossip about Roman society', and little talk of art or books.[34] He dearly missed Lucy's social grace and finesse to guide him during these tedious dinner engagements: 'without you I just spoil everything, and nobody cares for me without you. My Bobbie, how I need your sympathy and your tact.'

On Monday 11 November at 6 a.m., Germany signed the armistice of Compiègne. The First World War officially ended at 11 a.m. One could cross the French–Italian border without being issued with special papers, and on Wednesday 13 November, Lucy left Paris and travelled to Nice.[35] Kingsley wrote to Lucy just one last time from Rome.[36] He had lunched that morning with fellow American archaeologists and Harvard professors Edward Forbes, George Edgell and Chandler Post, and had afterwards gone to the Church of St Francesco Romano to view a signed painting of Gimbaldo Ibi. He had also visited the Contessa and her daughter, who were both seriously ill, and he had sent them a dozen roses. Later he met Pompelly who handed over the necessary papers to have his automobile released. He hoped to have secured all the visas, including one for their chauffeur, Anfossi, by Saturday.

16. Letter from Kingsley Porter in Rome to Lucy Porter in Paris, dated 13 November 1918.

Harvard University Archives, HUG 1706.114, Correspondence of Arthur Kingsley Porter and Lucy W. Porter 1911–25, 1918.

Kingsley finally left Rome and travelled north towards the border.[37] Lucy wrote to him from Hotel Alexandra in Nice: 'Love – my Kingsley, my baby, from your Bobbie. It does sound sentimental, forgive me this once.'[38]

On Tuesday 19 November, Lucy travelled to Monte Carlo and booked into the Hotel Westminster.[39] Kingsley finally reached Monte Carlo that evening and they were reunited. Lucy recorded the moment in her diary: 'We met at last! The joy of it!'

The following morning the couple awoke to beautiful sunshine.[40] They lunched in the village of La Turbie, perched high above Monte Carlo, where they could survey spectacular views along the Riviera.[41] Life had never seemed so glorious. They had survived the final months of the war; they were both infused with a burning zeal to continue their mission to save their cherished Romanesque monuments; and they had never been more in love.

Chapter six

Travels in France

The Porters could now begin their task of assessing the damage inflicted on monuments during the devastating war throughout France. Their motor was finally released and Anfossi purchased the parts needed to get them back on the road.[1] On Saturday 23 November 1918 they travelled to St Raphael. They stopped at the village of Esterel for lunch, set amid the pink rocks of the Esterel Hills and the pounding seas of the Côte d'Azur. At St Raphael they visited the exquisite Romanesque church.

During the final week of November they slowly made their way back to Paris, stopping at Lyons to visit the famous cathedral and admiring the sunlit scenery en route to Avalon in the region of Burgundy.[2] At Avalon they photographed a portal that Kingsley very much admired: 'Of all the Chartres-esque portals of France, this is the most archaic and the most crisp.'[3] The design of twin portals with tympana grouped under a larger tympanum was a typical feature of the region.[4] Kingsley noted that the tympanum, sadly, had been destroyed.

Back in Paris, they visited Monsieur Hubert to receive an update on their assignment.[5] On Christmas Day they attended the Catholic service at Notre Dame. Although both Lucy and Kingsley had been brought up in staunchly Protestant families, neither embraced religion or attended church regularly, yet both were entranced by the sacred, mystical power of a medieval cathedral and fascinated by the simple beauty of a small country church.

After the armistice, there were two million American servicemen left in Europe.[6] It was a logistical nightmare for the US government to begin shipping these men home. Also, since the armistice treaty was a ceasefire and not an end to war, it would have been premature to disband the entire US forces that remained in Europe. The US government therefore set about finding ways of occupying these men, including introducing athletics programmes and training courses. One school that was established for this purpose was the Art Training College, opened in Bellevue on 24 March 1919. As an expert on architecture, Kingsley was asked to give a series of lectures on aspects of French art at the new college.[7]

During the early months of 1919 the Porters continued to assess the damage to monuments in Paris and in nearby regions.[8] On 20 February, Kingsley wrote to Joseph Breck, Curator of Decorative Arts at the Metropolitan Museum of Art in New York, describing the work he was doing in Paris:

> Our trip in France has developed in a very wonderful way and incredible material has passed through my hands. I have been given the mission of compiling a list of the objets mobiliers which have disappeared in the devastated regions, and it is exciting work running things down. I have the strong impression that probably a majority of the missing things, from statues to stained glass and paintings have not been destroyed, but were really stolen by the Germans, or even in some cases I regret to say by allied troops. I imagine that when normal transportation is restored quantities of such things will turn up on the New York market.[9]

Kingsley had been asked by Breck to take up a position with the Metropolitan Museum.[10] He refused the kind offer and outlined his future plans: 'I have, however, come to the very definite decision that I want to write. As accurately as I can see this seems to be the line in which lies such strength as I have, and I am quite clear that I must keep my eye single on this one purpose alone.'

Kingsley also inquired if Breck might know of anyone who would like to rent their New York apartment, as both Lucy and he had fallen under the Parisian spell: 'Life here in Paris is exceedingly pleasant – so pleasant that for the moment, I confess our strongest desire is to avoid returning home.'[11]

During 1919, Lucy began to write a travelogue of her experiences in a series of diaries.[12] Although Lucy kept appointment diaries when living in the US, she only recorded personal feelings and anecdotes when travelling in Europe. Lucy wrote hurriedly, with letters tumbling over each other, barely stopping for breath in case she failed to capture a significant moment. Sometimes she drew tiny faces to illustrate her feelings of happiness or sadness. Sometimes she listed paintings and artists she had seen at a gallery that particularly interested her, or wrote detailed accounts of frescoes, sculptures or church interiors that she specially admired. The years that she spent travelling through France and Spain were her most prolific. In the mid-1920s her notes were less copious. Her scant descriptions of their visit to Egypt in the winter of 1928 were the last of her entries.

During March 1919 the Porters began to explore regions in eastern France that had suffered appalling devastation.[13] Working side by side with Kingsley, Lucy became his invaluable partner, photographing churches and monuments throughout France, and later in Italy and Spain. Lucy loved the luminous beauty of the landscapes they encountered during these trips: 'Went off through the goldened carpeted forests to photograph beautiful grey lichens, [not sure of this word] untouched by war. The fields dotted by slow majestic white oxen and by horses turning, harrowing and rolling the brown earth. We are happy in all this beauty and peacefulness.'

Yet the dreadful carnage of war was never far from her vision. The lasting effects of the atrocities were visible not only in ruined churches and crushed monuments, but also in the poverty encountered throughout the French countryside and in the rotting human and animal remains that lay strewn on the roadsides:

A bare footed filthy little boy of 8 yrs was singing at only the skylarks, singing in these devastated regions . . . We had luncheon

17. Cormicy Church (c. 1918).

From *Rheims and the Battles for its Possession*, Illustrated Michelin Guides to the
Battle-Fields (1914–1918) (Clermont-Ferrand: Michelin & Cie, 1919);
published in ebook format by Project Gutenberg, 2011, p.145.

at Chevigny. Baby shot to pieces, horses lay under their load of
trucks, helmets, blood, everything told of the hasty retreat of the
Germans in 1918. The French must have driven them from their
shelters after the French took Chemin Des Dames.[14]

The damage inflicted on churches and monuments was often
extreme. Sometimes all that was left of a church was a pile of rubble.[15]
The Porters also experienced the destruction of cemeteries that had
been badly shelled, where graves lay open and body parts were
exposed. Coupled with all this destruction, there was the ever-present
danger that unexploded shells still lay in the fields where they walked.
Lucy was particularly fearful that locals would be maimed or killed by
accidentally dislodging one of the deadly shells when farming the land.

During April they continued their tour and assessment of damaged
churches.[16] Some evenings they were exhausted after their day's work
and were happy just to eat a simple meal and get an early night. They

still managed to find time to keep up a regular correspondence with family and friends. Kingsley often took walks alone in the woods around Chantilly while they were staying in the medieval town of Senlis in northern France. This may have been Kingsley's way of unwinding and of gaining solitude. In a letter to her sister Ruth, Lucy mentioned Kingsley's penchant for spending time alone: 'Kingsley took pictures alone and a walk in the woods by himself.'[17]

There is no mention in Lucy's diaries of how either of them came to terms with the unspeakable horrors they witnessed on their travels. Both were sensitive, caring people who were used to dwelling amid every comfort that wealth and privilege provided. Yet by their own choosing they had entered a war-torn world that must have required great courage and strength to face on a daily basis. Ultimately they had each other. Kingsley was particularly fortunate to have a wife who looked after his every need, who nursed him when he was ill and soothed him when he had over-exerted himself.

Lucy was described by all who met her as Kingsley's perfect companion. She focused exclusively on her husband's needs, interests and passions and became fully immersed in his academic and literary world. An article in the Bulletin of the Fogg Art Museum described Lucy as:

> the beloved companion and helpmate of his travels, research and writing, fostering by her protection his never too robust health so as to preserve him for the hard tasks which he set himself, enthusiastically submerging herself in the many subjects that interested him, aiding him with suggestions and penetrating criticism, and even making herself a distinguished photographer in order to assist him in the illustrations of his books.[18]

From Lucy's diaries, however, it is clear that she was more than an assistant to Kingsley. Lucy had an innate love of art and had developed an impressive knowledge of architecture. She was involved in discussions with Kingsley as to the dating of monuments, and the style and importance of frescoes and art objects that they photographed during their travels. Lucy's photos would ultimately fill nine volumes of the ten-volume work, *Romanesque Sculpture of the Pilgrimage Roads*, that was published in 1923. Kingsley was remarkably fortunate to have a wife who shared his passion for art and architecture. Lucy was an accomplished photographer and also a gifted writer, though it was much later that her own writings were published. There is little doubt that Lucy's talents, enthusiasm and devotion contributed a great deal to Kingsley's success.

During May 1919, Lucy must have been deeply saddened to hear of the death of her elder sister, Elizabeth, wife of James B. Waller, in Chicago. Elizabeth had been a well-known patron of the arts, and her death was acknowledged in *A Magazine of Verse*: 'Elizabeth Wallace Waller, who died last May in Chicago, was always ardent in her support of the arts, as in all the other activities and sympathies of a spirit both strong and delicate.'[19] Lucy continued to correspond with her mother and younger sister, Ruth, though she must have felt very far from home, ensconced in the depths of the French countryside.

The summer of 1919 was a busy one for the Porters.[20] On 2 May they revisited the medieval town of Senlis. According to Lucy this was the 'most devastated region'. Still, Kingsley gleaned what he could from the ruined monuments. He later wrote that the tympanum of Senlis appeared to have been inspired by the apse of St Maria in Trastevere, Rome, inferring that French sculpture had been influenced by Roman mosaics.[21]

Two days later they travelled to Villers-Cotterêts.[22] Conditions were often uncomfortable and primitive in the small boarding houses they stayed in. That Sunday, Lucy wrote in her diary: 'Awake and go to sleep in the rain. Some faint sunshine too. The grandmother brought hot water at 7.30 and drunk delicious hot tea and toast and butter at 8. At 9.30 we were off.'

Although Kingsley delighted in their bohemian lifestyle, the sheer pace and breadth of their itinerary began to take its toll. On 6 May he became ill during the night and had a splitting headache.[23] Lucy finally managed to nurse him to sleep. Then she got dressed in the dark and crept downstairs for coffee, making sure not to wake him. Since Kingsley developed a fever they backtracked to Senlis and remained there for several days until Kingsley regained his strength.

When Kingsley recovered, they were driven by their chauffeur, Anfossi, to the town of Soissons, in Picardy.[24] Here they spent Sunday reading the papers and catching up with correspondence. They also took photos of the magnificent Gothic cathedral there, that had sustained serious damage to its nave during the war, using the new eight-by-ten plates they had bought. On Monday they visited the old Benedictine Abbey of St Medard and went for a five-mile walk down the Ossen River. Lucy added a little note in her diary: 'We enjoy our fresh boiled eggs for supper. We have lovely talks together and are so happy although we see no one.'

On Thursday 22 May they returned to Paris and spent several days catching up on various errands.[25] The following Tuesday they were back in Senlis: 'Cloudy but only sunshine poured upon us. We slept late and enjoyed hot bath and soft bed. Kingsley felt headachy but a beautiful walk, first through the walled passage-ways of the town and then through the adorable hamlets (the suburbs of Senlis) and at last into the forest cured him.'

For the next week they stayed in Senlis and began to fall under its spell.[26] On Monday 2 June, Lucy wrote: 'After supper a quick little turn. Senlis like most good things, can't be shown off, you have to live here to appreciate its beauty. More letters to be written this eve. These happy, restful days, quite little to record.'

The following week they encountered a series of problems when they motored to Chalons.[27] The hotel was jammed full of guests, there was no milk for Lucy's precious coffee, and Anfossi had to work on their motor all day to repair some trouble that had developed. There were days like this when Lucy must have yearned for her comfortable life in New York, where every luxury and convenience was within easy reach. Yet she was never one to complain and remained as resilient and resourceful as ever.

While researching in France during the summer of 1919, the Porters met fellow American Bernard Berenson and his wife, Mary. Although Berenson's field of expertise was Renaissance art, he was happy to accompany them on various trips to visit Romanesque churches.[28] Mary Berenson also had a lot in common with Lucy as she had become an art historian in her own right and accompanied her husband on many expeditions.[29] During one of these trips, Kingsley told Berenson that his work in France was coming to an end and that he was in a quandary over whether to return to Yale or to remain in Europe.[30]

Berenson accompanied the Porters on an excursion to Vézelay, located in north-central France and famous for its spectacular abbey.[31] This was the town where many medieval pilgrims set out to travel Chemin de St Jacques (the Way of St James) en route to Santiago de Compostela.[32] It is also the reputed burial place of Mary Magdalene. On the way back to Paris, Berenson fell asleep, allowing Lucy and Kingsley some space to dream about their future: perhaps, if prices and taxes kept rising at home, they conjectured, they might remain in Vézelay, and live in a little house beside the abbey.[33]

In many ways the past year in France had been perfect for Kingsley. It had provided him with an occupation, which was always important for his self-respect, while also allowing him the freedom to live a nomadic existence. There was something about Europe that really appealed to his artistic nature. It was certainly an enormous distance from Connecticut or New York and hence he was virtually anonymous. It was as though he had a new identity in France, where he did not have to conform to anyone's preconceived notions. Perhaps the scandal of his early years still dogged him and made him long for privacy and seclusion. Whatever the reason, from 1919 he was actively seeking a European retreat, a new home outside of the States.

Amid his medieval research and extensive travels, Kingsley somehow managed to complete his first play, *The Seven Who Slept*. It is based on the legend of the seven sleepers of Ephesus in Ancient Greece, now a famous archaeological site in Turkey.[34] It was published by Marshall Jones Company, Boston, in July 1919. The themes of truth, lies, illusion and the danger of facing the truth run through the play's entire preface.[35] The tone and content of the writing is undoubtedly gloomy and cynical, and is in strong contrast to Kingsley's wonderful, soaring ideals of great art and genius postulated in *Beyond Architecture*, published only the previous year.

The New York Times reviewed the play thus: 'All Society – all everything, is based on illusion, according to the author of this play. *The Seven Who Slept* is a fanciful play, in which the writer attempts to prove his pessimistic theory.'[36]

Kingsley had completed the preface on 1 April 1919.[37] The whole preface and the short allegorical drama reveal Kingsley's disillusionment with the human race. He states that religion, art, literature, initiative, achievement, scholarship, patriotism and love are all ideals built on illusion. It is remarkable that even the citadels of his own life, his marriage and his work as a scholar, are placed in the same category of lies, delusion and deceit. A study of *The Seven Who Slept* reveals a dispirited and sadly frustrated man who no longer believes in once cherished values.

It can only be imagined what Lucy thought of the following passages, written by the husband she adored, on the absurdity of the romantic tradition that marriage should be founded solely upon sex or love:

> Of all illusions, the most transparent, perhaps is love … So they live together more happily than ever, until one day there comes to knock at their door a gentle god, disguised as a stranger. So on the foundation of illusion is built the mansion of happiness. Possibly an indistinct and instinctive realization of this is the basis for the romantic tradition that marriage should be founded solely upon sex passion. Considered materialistically, nothing could be more insensate than to found an enduring relationship upon the most volatile and least abiding of human whims.[38]

Lucy's diary from this time reveals nothing of a personal trauma that could have precipitated Kingsley's general cynicism. The horrors of war that Kingsley had observed at close quarters may certainly have caused deep shock and disillusionment with the whole human race: the gruesomeness of trench warfare; the devastation caused by modern weaponry; the millions of young men who were killed and maimed; the destruction of so many irreplaceable monuments through greed, stupidity and madness. Always a thoughtful and sensitive man, the sheer futility of so much killing and carnage must have affected Kingsley deeply.

What is difficult to understand, however, is the extent of Kingsley's disillusionment. The presentiment that at any moment a stranger might call and lure away one of the marriage partners must have filled Lucy with at least a measure of anxiety. If a prospective lover did exist during their European travels then no details have ever surfaced. There is no doubt that Kingsley was an attractive, accomplished, cultured and wealthy man in the prime of his life. Yet, throughout their brief separation in October 1918, Kingsley was never more passionate than within the pages of his long, ardent letters to Lucy.

However, the cramped living conditions and countless hours spent travelling with Lucy may have begun to take their toll on Kingsley's innate need for solitude. All through their married life, Kingsley had been busy studying, teaching and writing, often at Yale, while Lucy spent time with friends and family, and attending various social events in New York. Lucy often referred to Kingsley's restlessness, his urge to explore another village, to investigate yet another church, to take a walk alone even when they had spent all day walking and working. In the context of later revelations, this may have been the time when Kingsley first became aware of an inner secret that lurked in the depths of his psyche, threatening to unhinge his orderly life. If this was indeed the case, then Lucy appears to have been oblivious to the source of Kingsley's distress.

Then there was Kingsley's chosen vocation as an author, teacher and scholar, that he had dedicated the previous fifteen years of his life to perfecting. The whole process of research and scholarship was also placed in the realm of fantasy: 'Scholarship, which seems so cumbersome, so bound hand and foot to fact, is in reality based on illusion.'[39] Kingsley revealed that the scholar collects facts to justify his initial theory. Hence all research and the ensuing results are tinged with deceit and falseness. Kingsley saw this as yet another illusion, where true inquiry and scholarship was erased.

Whatever the effect of the drama's publication on Kingsley and Lucy, they returned to Senlis in July to carry out more in-depth assessment of damage incurred to churches and monuments.[40] Lucy noted that many churches in the region had been almost destroyed but that the statues that had been hidden during the war for safekeeping had been put back in place. It was the town of Senlis that kept up their spirits. In the afternoon they often walked around the walled town, delighting in the exquisite design of St Pierre's Cathedral, with its Renaissance dome that sparkled in the misty sunlight. Lucy was entranced with the town; on 8 July she noted that 'the beauty of this place is extraordinary but is only realized after long acquaintance. We

18. Notre Dame, Pontorson, France, taken by A. Kingsley Porter.

Courtesy of Brooklyn Museum Archives, Goodyear Archival Collection, General correspondence (1.1.066): Porter (1910).

are happy here together even when not feeling well.'

During August the Porters completed their work in northern France by photographing monuments in Amiens, in the devastated Somme region.[41] In Dijon and Paris, Lucy continued to capture the fascinating symbols carved on Romanesque churches: gargoyles and angels; sinners condemned to hell, virtuous saints soaring towards heaven.

In August they took a day trip to Burgundy, accompanied by Berenson whom they collected from the Ritz in Paris.[42] Lucy and Kingsley were always anxious to get the tea basket ready and to leave early in the morning so they could visit as many churches as possible.[43] Kingsley always followed the advice given in 1909 by his friend and mentor William Goodyear, and religiously photographed every aspect of a monument so that the images could later be used for reference.[44] For lunch they stopped at a small inn.[45] To save time, Kingsley remained in a church taking notes and photographs and would only eat his lunch in the back seat of the car when they were driving to the next village. It may have been Kingsley's enthusiasm, coupled with the excitement of the chase to visit as many churches as possible in a day, that opened Berenson's eyes to the wonders of medieval art.[46]

In September the Porters travelled to Semur in Burgundy,[47] to photograph examples of pointed arches and tympanums that were reminiscent of those at Cluny.[48] They continued south to Arles in the Camargue, then onto Aix-en-Provence, where they photographed the cloisters of the Cathedral of the Holy Saviour.[49] Kingsley was also interested in the sculpture of 'the powerful lions of Aix-en-Provence' that displayed 'vigour and massiveness'.[50] They travelled further south to the magnificent Côte d'Azur where they visited St Raphael and Nice.[51] On 15 September they crossed into northern Italy and spent several weeks photographing monuments in Genoa, Florence and Padua.

In October 1919 the Porters decided to return to New York.[52] Lucy had been having pains in her lower abdomen for some time and Kingsley insisted that they travel home so that their doctor, Dr Horton, could examine her. Lucy felt it might be a hanging fibroid or uterus that was causing the pain, but Dr Horton diagnosed a cyst on the ovary.

He invited Dr Frank Matthews to give a second opinion, and Lucy noted the outcome in her diary: 'Anyway all addressed having detected lump remained. Dr Horton advised leaving Dr Frank Matthews do it and it was done on Dec. 19 at 5.'

Kingsley brought Lucy to hospital to have the lump removed.[53] That evening he stayed in the room next door while Lucy lay in recovery after the operation. From Lucy's account of the episode, Kingsley greatly feared that she would not survive the operation. He was incredibly relieved when she woke up after the procedure, in pain but glad to have got through it. But this was not the end of the matter: it appears that after the operation the doctor thought that Lucy might be pregnant. Lucy recalled the incident in her diary:

> We had the scare of my being pregnant (again K was so wonderful and kept assuring me he'd find a way out which wouldn't warrant injury to me). I fear he would mean killing the child (which would be there in embryo after all) as well as my bidding adieu to the sunlight... We read much of Shelley's and Keats', death – the end of full life seemed to fascinate us...

It is unclear from Lucy's diary entry if a pregnancy would have caused a threat to her life. If there was no such threat, then Kingsley's reaction to his wife's alleged pregnancy was indeed extreme. Perhaps he feared that a child would curtail their travels, or the thought of fatherhood may have brought back painful memories of his own father's deviant behaviour. Certainly, at the age of 43, Lucy was no longer a young woman; pregnancy and the birth of a child may have been difficult for her to endure. Whatever the cause of Kingsley's reluctance, he need not have worried as it was later confirmed that Lucy was not pregnant.[54] Relieved that there was no pregnancy and that Lucy would make a full recovery, the Porters made plans to book their passage to Italy.

Chapter seven

European Travels

While Kingsley Porter made plans to return to Europe in early 1920, he was unaware of the fact that one of the most illustrious universities in the world was carefully tracking his progress. During 1919, Edward Waldo Forbes, Harvard art historian and director of the Fogg Art Museum, began his pursuit of Kingsley.[1] Forbes's task was to persuade him to accept the position as Professor of Fine Arts at Harvard. Forbes believed that no one at Harvard had the range of attributes that Kingsley possessed: he had taken studio art classes at Yale as an undergraduate; his graduate work at Columbia had focused on visual qualities and materials; and he always advocated the combination of art practice with art history. Kingsley also stressed the importance of viewing art objects and walking through buildings before writing about them, hence his frequent travels to Europe. He also employed scientific methodology in the gathering of data and the presentation of his findings.

Harvard University, located in Cambridge, Massachusetts, was the oldest institution of learning in the United States and also one of the wealthiest and most influential in the world. It was exclusively male and was attended by students from America's most elite families. The appointment would have been highly prestigious, yet Kingsley was unsure whether or not to remain full-time in France. It took months for him to make up his mind. In a letter to Berenson he expressed some of his concerns, particularly his lack of confidence in his own abilities: 'As I grow older I seem to see quite clearly that my chief problem in life is time. Where you, for example, are brilliant and intuitive, I am dull and plodding (and how I dislike the characteristics!) If I am ever to have a peek at the farther shore even through a telescope I have no time to waste.'[2]

All through life, feelings of ineptitude and shyness caused Kingsley to hanker after a life of solitude, study and writing. Kingsley's literary and scholarly talents were considerable, yet his inability to interact well with strangers or mere acquaintances caused him great difficulties. But the true dilemma he was facing may have run much deeper: the freedom to be himself and to live according to his own dictates, versus the status of becoming a Harvard Professor, under the watchful eye of the entire faculty.

In January 1920, Kingsley finally accepted the Harvard appointment, but with the stipulation that he would not begin teaching until the autumn of 1921 and he would also be allowed several months leave each year to travel and to research.[3] He had chosen to accept one of the most prestigious academic posts in the world while building in a clause that would guarantee him several months of freedom each year. This would also give him sufficient time to complete *Romanesque Sculpture of the Pilgrimage Roads.*[4] On 9 January, Kingsley wrote to Berenson, outlining his reasons for accepting the Harvard post:

> As I see things, an official position, like a social background (or what passes for such), or a real reputation, is of value in that it does save time and energy which would otherwise be wasted in the effort to assert one's self. But this official label of a university position is bought only at the price of time and energy. How does the balance stand?[5]

Kingsley also corresponded with Louis during that spring, still weighing up the pros and cons of leaving Europe to live in Cambridge: 'The golden minutes are flying by too quickly and I have an idea that I do not do as good work when I am having so congenial a time. Perhaps afterall Cambridge with prohibition and American prices and poor food and the general absence of all things that make life sweet may prove to be very wholesome.'[6]

On 13 March, Kingsley and Lucy arrived in Naples.[7] Their plan was to photograph medieval churches and monuments in southern Italy, in Florence and Sienna. They spent several days touring the region of Campania in southern Italy by train. They visited the church of St Angelo in Formis, near Capua, to study the crossed-legged figures depicted in the frescos there.[8] From Capua they travelled to the spectacular town of Ravello, situated above the Amalfi Coast,[9] where they relished their visit to Ravello's cathedral, famous for its bronze doors[10]. The following day they travelled to the exquisite town of Sorrento that overlooks the Bay of Naples.[11]

On 17 March they took a train up north to Florence, where they stayed for several weeks.[12] On 26 March they visited their American friends, the Berensons, at their spectacular villa, I Tatti. Berenson had built up a private art collection that fascinated the Porters. Kingsley was still contemplating whether or not to buy a second residence in Europe.[13] Suddenly, both he and Lucy fell in love with Florence and, with the help of the Berensons, began looking at villas. Berenson genuinely liked the Porters but he quickly tired of escorting them all over Florence to view a list of villas that they subsequently found unsuitable. He described their quest as 'having wonderful moments ... but was on the whole futile and fatiguing'. Kingsley, in contrast, greatly enjoyed 'the moments of pure joy in Florence', yet he couldn't make up his mind whether or not to settle there.

On 10 April, the Porters visited the Tuscan town of Sienna, with its spectacular Romanesque-Gothic cathedral, its museums and art galleries.[14] Lucy recorded in her diary: 'The view from the sacristy window was what Bernardino must have seen when he climbed a tree and was so moved looking back on Sienna he could barely speak.'

Anfossi spent a great deal of time searching out parts for the old motor, changing tyres or tuning up the engine.[15] Lucy loved the luxury of travelling by motor since she could always include her tea basket. In her diary she commented: 'Had tea (how I love my tea-basket!) under pine trees near an ancient cross while Anfossi blew up another tire.'

Lucy also had Natalina to attend to her needs, including ironing her summer linens.[16] The Porters remained in Sienna for over two weeks. On 27 April they travelled to Florence where they spent one night, and next morning they crossed the French border en route to Marseille. Kingsley's plan was to visit as many towns as possible that were stopping points along the routes that pilgrims had travelled for centuries on their way to Santiago de Compostela. Travelling conditions and lodgings were not always ideal as they made their way through southern France, yet Lucy looked on this time as one of her happiest. She travelled, ate, slept and worked diligently beside Kingsley.

One evening during that Spring, the Porters took a walk by the River Lot.[17] Lucy remarked in her diary:'The willows grew in an exact Corot way – a boat with a touch of red in it, would have completed the Metropolitan Museum picture.'[18]

The following afternoon, Lucy lay in a meadow just outside the town of Espalion, in the Rouergue region.[19] The red sandstone church of St Foy de Perse was close by. An old château perched on a massive rock of basalt was facing her. Earlier that morning, Lucy had photographed the church while Kingsley had written notes on the various sculptures within. Now Lucy rested while Kingsley went to explore the surrounding area, and Anfossi slept in the motor that was parked at the side of the road.

From their early days of courtship, Lucy felt inexplicably fortunate that Kingsley had chosen her as his companion. Eight years after their marriage that same feeling of delight and pride in being Kingsley's wife was palpable in Lucy's next diary entry:'In about two hours I heard his whistle and saw him coming in the softness of the August afternoon, the castle, the pastures and ripe blackberries setting off exactly his dear, sensible face. So tall and fair and mine!'[20]

Lucy sat up in the meadow and continued to write of her deep contentment. She usually wore her hair in a bun, so that the grey streaks would be less noticeable. She was sensitive to the fact that she was seven years older than Kingsley and at times this caused her some concern. Kingsley was undoubtedly a handsome man in the prime of life, and Lucy must have sometimes secretly feared that some younger, prettier woman would catch his attention. As an afterthought, she picked up her pen and added a darker foreboding: 'Again, almost fearful because of our great happiness.'[21]

The past two years had been filled with intrigue, romance and adventure as the Porters had struggled heroically through war-torn France to save their beloved monuments and later to photograph many of the most glorious examples of Romanesque architecture in existence. Besides a brief separation during late October and early November 1918, Lucy and Kingsley had been inseparable, although Kingsley still managed to find space and solitude during his forest walks. Lucy had been more than content to fling herself headlong into Kingsley's world. Yet Kingsley's deep cynicism and disillusionment with all facets of life must have hit her deeply in July 1919, after the publication of *The Seven Who Slept*.

Perhaps it was this lurking scepticism that Lucy detected in Kingsley that made her fearful and wary of being too complacent. Outwardly they were the perfect couple, with every attribute and advantage that anyone could ever wish for. Although Lucy kept a diary throughout their travels, she never left any clues as to the state of their emotional or sexual life as a married couple. For a female reared in New England in the late 1800s it is no surprise that such intimacies would remain private. Yet on this afternoon, amid the beauty of the French countryside, Lucy does reveal a dramatic contradiction: feelings of great happiness, coupled with anxiety that something undefined may be lurking that could destroy all that she held dear.

The Porters also visited the twelfth-century abbey at Conques.[22] The Sainte-Foy abbey church was a popular stopping point for pilgrims on their way to Santiago de Compostela.[23] Kingsley ascribed the sculptures in Conques to the end of the eleventh century. He inferred that the sculptors who had executed them had previously worked at Santiago. Lucy photographed a section of the tympanum, depicting *The Last Judgement*.[24] On the left, angels lead the righteous to heaven while on the left, a procession of devils escort the condemned to hell, right into the mouth of a demon. In her diary Lucy wrote: 'Sculptures are very lovely. Tympanum with Christ and angels, cross placed off axis; column in centre, caryatid figures on three sides appealed to me the most.'

During their stay in Paris they happened upon Edward Forbes, who had hotly pursued Kingsley over many months to accept the Harvard post.[25] Forbes later described their meeting: 'I remember meeting him in Paris in 1920 on a bleak October day, and he and Mrs Porter invited me to go on an inspection tour with them through the desolated fields, forests and ruins.' Kingsley confided in Forbes that he was presently absorbed by the idea that the medieval French literary epic had developed along the pilgrimage roads. Perhaps, he suggested to Forbes, sculpture and architecture might have also developed in the same way.

On 8 May 1920 the Porters travelled to the medieval town of Montpellier in southern France,[26] which pilgrims returning from Santiago often visited.[27] Kingsley did some research at the university there and Lucy photographed reliefs that Kingsley believed were influenced by those at Santo Domingo de Silos.[28] Kingsley's plan was to continue southwards into Spain,[29] and he had invited fellow Americans Georgina Goddard King and Bernard Berenson to join Lucy and he on their Spanish travels.[30] King was an historian and professor at Bryn Mawr, Pennsylvania, specializing in the architecture of Spain. It was King who may have first whetted Kingsley's interest in the study of Spanish art when, in 1914, he attended a lecture given by her at Haverford College, on the importance of pilgrimage to the development of Spanish sculpture.

In his letter of invitation to Berenson, Kingsley wrote:

> It would be amusing to follow the route of the Lombard masters, as nearly as convenient, and see what we can see along the road ...There are a quantity of glorious things all through the region which I am on fire to see. Possibly you might even be tempted to recross the frontier into Spain. You have recently skimmed the cream, but that country is so little known it might not be an entire waste of time to browse around. I am hopeful

that Puig y Cadafalch of Barcelona may know some interesting and unknown things.[31]

Neither academic took Kingsley up on his offer. On 12 May 1920, Lucy and Kingsley, driven by Anfossi and accompanied by Natalina, crossed the French border and entered Spain, en route to Barcelona.[32] This was the Porters' first excursion into Spain. In Barcelona, Kingsley viewed several superb altar frontals in the museum.[33] They also photographed the tympanum at the church of San Pablo del Campo that had been consecrated in 1125.[34]

The Porters' main destination was Santiago de Compostela, and Kingsley's mission was to visit as many of the pilgrim sites as he could along the route. He possessed a copy of the guidebook for pilgrims that had been written in the twelfth century, where the four main routes that led to Compostela were clearly designated.[35]

The motor was a faster and more convenient mode of transport than the train and it allowed them to carry their essential camera equipment.[36] They also had greater flexibility to stop at any time to photograph the architectural monuments along the route. Much of this area had remained unspoilt and undeveloped for centuries. Kingsley's discoveries in Spain were the subject of seven chapters in *Romanesque Sculpture of the Pilgrimage Roads* (1923) and also inspired his later work, *Spanish Romanesque* (1928).[37]

For the next two months Lucy and Kingsley explored central and northern Spain.[38] They spent almost a week in Madrid, where Kingsley researched at the Royal Academy of History and the National Archaeological Museum. On 21 May they travelled north-west to El Escorial, before continuing their journey to Segovia.[39] Continuing in a north-westerly direction they visited the towns of Avila, Salamanca and Zamora to photograph medieval churches and monuments.

On 10 June they finally reached their destination: Santiago de Compostela.[40] They visited the famous cathedral that borders the main plaza where, according to legend, the remains of Saint James are buried. Lucy was smitten by the sculpture in the cathedral, in particular the

19. Photograph of Spanish monument, Santillana del Mar, Santander, Spain, taken by the Porters, n.d.

Courtesy of Brooklyn Museum Archives, Goodyear Archival Collection, Visual materials (6.1.012): miscellaneous photographs.

south passageway. In her diary she recorded her thoughts about the carvings on the altar, pleased that St James took centre stage: 'It seems right Christ should take second place here.' Lucy remarked that the nude figures were 'perhaps the loveliest of all', while the devils depicted were 'exquisite'.

Throughout their Spanish travels Kingsley had been honing his hypothesis that Spaniards had been creating architectural works of great beauty long before the rest of western Europe. Kingsley firmly believed that medieval artists had known no national borders but had shared their trade secrets as they travelled the pilgrim roads that led to Santiago de Compostela. On 14 June the Porters drove to Lugo, famous for its Roman walls, where they stayed for over a week.[41] Here, they photographed the restored Christ figure on the northern portal of Lugo Cathedral.[42] They then drove eastwards across northern Spain and spent several days exploring the towns of Laredo and Burgos.[43]

Kingsley delighted in visiting these medieval towns and photographing their unique monuments. He yearned for the medieval world, devoid of machines, mass production and industrialization.[44] He saw himself in the romantic role of knight, pilgrim and adventurer. He had been raised in Connecticut at a time when families were encouraged to settle out west on unclaimed land, although the American frontier had officially closed in 1890, when Kingsley was just 7 years old. Still, Kingsley had inherited much of the pioneering spirit that seemed to push him onwards, delving into a lost, medieval world, fuelled with romantic notions of discovery and exploration. This was also the time when art history was beginning to emerge as an academic discipline in the US and Kingsley was a leader in his field, the first American to discover the significance of various medieval churches and forms of ornamentation in Europe.[45]

On 1 July they arrived at Santo Domingo de Silos.[46] Kingsley was particularly impressed with the two-storey cloister of the Benedictine monastery, named after St Dominic of Silos.[47] He considered the monastery to be one of the finest examples of Romanesque architecture.[48] He also noted that one of the unique features of the cloister was the carving that had been executed by Muslim slaves.

For Kingsley, Spain was the perfect region for his explorations, as much of it remained unspoilt. He abhorred progress; he loved natural landscapes and original architecture that was untouched by poor attempts at restoration.[49] It was his quest to prove that the Spanish, who were considered backward by many Europeans, had in fact surpassed the whole of Europe with their technically brilliant and creatively exquisite designs. Kingsley's acute idealism may have been charming and inspirational to many but it also left him psychologically weakened whenever reality or practicality intervened. This over-optimism seems to have hidden a darker pessimism that had emerged with full force during the writing of *The Seven Who Slept* (1919).

The Porters drove to Pamplona on 6 July, in time for the festival of San Fermin, where a herd of bulls charges through the streets, pursued by screaming inhabitants.[50] They also visited the cathedral of Pamplona. In medieval times, the cathedrals of Pamplona, León and Burgos were also centres for teaching the art of sculpture.[51] Kingsley and Lucy continued east through Tarragona, where they photographed various features in the cathedral,[52] before arriving in Barcelona.[53] On 22 July they met their friend Bull Durham at the Spanish border.[54] Durham had driven their new Fiat motor from Italy, so Kingsley and Lucy, accompanied by Anfossi, Natalina and Durham, crossed the border and entered France in great style.[55]

20. Porters in car with chauffeur.
Harvard University Archives, HUG 1706.125, Box 1, folder 1.

The Porters had spent two months travelling and photographing throughout Spain and were exhausted when they reached France.[56] Their rigid schedule had taken its toll. Their photographic work demanded great patience and persistence. They often had to wait for hours until the sun was in the right place to photograph a church or a sculpture without shadows.[57] Then every evening they had to change the camera plates on which they had recorded their subjects. Using glass plates instead of adopting the recent invention of celluloid film was a tedious procedure[58] but Kingsley believed that the images created using this method were sharper. This task also required time and precision and had to be completed in the dark.[59]

Besides all the work, it had been a wonderful experience. There had been many carefree days when they sat outdoors and picnicked from Lucy's tea basket. Then in the evenings they found simple lodgings and ate marvellous meals made from the best produce in each of the regions they visited. Kingsley delighted in selecting and savouring the local wines. They both loved their afternoon siestas when the sun was at its height and the whole world around them turned silent. Then in the evenings they strolled arm in arm, along old village streets or in the midst of spectacular countryside.[60] Lucy wore a floppy hat to shield her from the sun and there was no one to comment on the simple, practical clothes she wore. The vagabond lifestyle seemed to suit them well with its lack of rigidity and formality.

Back in France, their first stop was to visit the famous abbey of St Michel de Cuxa. Lucy wrote in her diary: 'Once a famous Benedictine monastery, now served by a handful of Cistercian monks. Little left to its past grandeur.'[61] The cloister was missing in Cuxa. Berenson had previously bought the capitals to exhibit them in the Cloisters Museum in New York.[62] He had tried to obtain others but they had already been sold to a bathing establishment at Prades.[63] The French government intervened and seized the remaining capitals.

This was an era when little legislation existed to protect medieval monuments from being bought and exported to the US from France, Spain and other European countries.[64] Since the separation of Church and State in France in 1905, church lands became the property of the state, religious orders were dissolved and empty churches were left untended, becoming easy prey to being stripped bare by antique dealers and collectors. American art collectors, such as George Grey Bernard who amassed a vast collection of church artefacts that he later exhibited in the Cloisters in New York, had no scruples about displacing rare medieval monuments, once venerated by devout parishioners. It could be argued that art collectors such as Bernard Berenson and Kingsley Porter wished to save neglected monuments by preserving them in museums, since governments were disinterested in the preservation of their medieval treasures. The practice of buying and transporting rare artefacts continued until European nations began to enact legislation to prohibit the sale of culturally priceless art objects from the mid-1920s onwards.

While the Porters were in Carcassonne their precious camera somehow got damaged,[65] and Bull and Anfossi volunteered to travel to Paris to have it repaired. Natalina was already travelling by train, having arranged to meet the Porters at their next destination. Left alone, Kingsley and Lucy booked into the Hôtel de la Cité.[66] Without their camera they walked around the town, with plenty of time on their hands. They even stopped to watch a local wedding. Lucy recorded in her diary that the young bridegroom wore a horned cap. They also had time to catch up with their correspondence and Lucy at long last had the chance to finish her letter to Ruth.

That evening they walked arm in arm in the starlight, glad to be alone.[67] Lucy always loved to be alone with Kingsley. She revelled in social gatherings, meeting old friends for luncheon or entertaining family members, yet there was nothing as glorious as spending time alone with Kingsley, enjoying his full attention. The last eight years of marriage had been something of a roller coaster. Lucy had not married a conventional man who was content to live an ordinary life. Kingsley was infused with a burning zeal to analyse, to discover and to transmit his findings to the world. She had married a brilliant man, at times ethereal and elusive, but also fully determined and dynamic. Lucy had never met anyone like Kingsley; there was no one who could thrill or excite her like Kingsley. Being his companion in life was all she had ever dreamed of.

A few days later Anfossi returned with the camera that was now in working order again and they were back on the road.[68] During August and September 1920 they continued their tour of towns along the Chemin de St Jacques that medieval pilgrims had trodden.[69] They visited St James Church, in Villefranche-de-Conflent, in the Lanquedoc region. They also spent time exploring churches in Bordeaux, in the Dordogne region in south-west France. In mid-September they drove to the romantic seaport of La Rochelle that is associated with the Knights Templar and Eleanor of Aquitaine. They also visited Poitiers to photograph the celebrated Romanesque church, St Hilaire Le Grand.

On 23 October the Porters arrived in Limoges,[70] famous for its medieval enamels. The following week they travelled to Nice, where they remained until mid-November. It was a welcome bonus for Kingsley to spend time by the sea again; the fresh sea air always revived him, with its salty taste and pungent scent of seaweed. The sound of gulls and the sight of rowing boats wove a heady spell, pulling him down towards the shore. It was always a great release for him to break through the calm surface and plunge into the water's depths, where another world lay unexplored far below him.

On 15 November they arrived at I Tatti, on the outskirts of Florence.[71] Here, Bernard Berenson had amassed a magnificent library on Renaissance studies. The Porters agreed to spend five months looking after the Berensons' villa while they travelled abroad.

21. Bernard Berenson and I Tatti.
Courtesy of Wikipedia Commons.

Lucy was a little overwhelmed by the task of playing hostess at the Villa.[72] She wrote to Mary Berenson, admitting that she knew more about photography than she did about housekeeping. All through their married lives, Lucy had had many tasks to perform as Kingsley's wife, but managing the organization of a large house had not been one of them. Kingsley wrote to Louis, confiding that the Villa would be expensive to run. The main advantage, however, was the superb library where Kingsley began to write *Romanesque Sculptures of the Pilgrimage Roads*.

In December 1920, Denman Ross, Harvard professor and friend of Berenson, spent a week with the Porters at I Tatti, and Kingsley and Ross became good friends.[73] Another friend of the Berensons, Nicky Mariano, spent time with the Porters at the Villa that winter. In a letter to Mary Berenson, Mariano gave his impressions of the couple:

> You can imagine how nice and friendly the Kingsley Porters are to me and if this so often ill-used adjective 'good' can be applied in the nicest sense of the word to anybody I am sure it is Lucy Porter. He is a charming man, but not at all stimulating. He always seems lost in a dream and I do not want to disturb him.[74]

Kingsley's shyness continued to make him appear aloof to passing acquaintances. He may not have found any new friends in Florence, yet he loved the city, the countryside, the food and the wine. He felt a deep sense of freedom at I Tatti where he could write, go for walks and visit monuments whenever he chose. While Lucy's letters to Ruth are full of preparations to move back home, Kingsley was still grasping at straws, trying to find ways to remain in Europe.[75] In a letter to Berenson, Kingsley used Lucy's perceived fear of foreign countries for their decision to return to the US: 'Lucy although she will not admit it, I think secretly fears a little living in a foreign country. She thinks we should feel hostile towards the Italians and remit to American type. But I wonder whether this might not be rather a good thing. The promiscuous cordiality of New York seems to me much more dangerous.'[76]

Kingsley's reluctance to return to the US and to begin teaching at Harvard may have been due to his innate love of freedom and adventure, coupled with his shyness and lack of social skills among his peers. It may also have been caused by a strong desire to remain outside of regular social or work life, where his behaviour, opinions or motives were not being scrutinized. Even at this time of great freedom and tranquillity while residing at I Tatti, there was still some repressed inclination that drove Kingsley to seek seclusion. The above excerpt from his letter to Berenson shows Kingsley's propensity for self-deceit by covering up his true feelings. In this case Lucy was the scapegoat: it was Lucy's imagined fear of living in Italy that was used to cloak Kingsley's own anxiety. After living in Europe almost full-time since August 1918, including a period of great danger when war still raged in northern France, there was nothing unusual about Lucy's wish to return to the US and to set up a permanent home among her family and friends.

Kingsley's desire to remain in Europe may have been influenced by the conservatism he had experienced growing up in Connecticut. The 1920s in the US was a time of great social change and economic prosperity. Wealth was generated by a series of Republican governments that cut taxes and encouraged the creation of large businesses.[77] There was also growth in the construction sector as well as rapid expansion in the production of consumer goods, such as automobiles.[78] In many large cities, particularly in New York, Chicago and Philadelphia, music, architecture, fashion and all the arts flourished. Jazz, Art Deco, the development of all-talking feature films, shorter fashions for women and the popularizing of dance clubs signalled a new era of prosperity and freedom.[79] On 18 August 1920, American women were finally given the right to vote. Yet despite all of these changes there were still strict social and moral codes in operation in many States. The Prohibition of alcohol was enforced in 1920; laws to control the length of a woman's skirt were being considered for enactment in Virginia, Ohio and Utah. There was still great fear among the powerful, conservative elite that America would be overrun by communists, or that the fabric of society would be destroyed by decadence and promiscuity. For Kingsley, the freedom to choose a bohemian or unconventional lifestyle was of paramount importance, as he abhorred rules or dictums that interfered with his personal freedom.

Despite Kingsley's concerns, both he and Lucy began corresponding with friends and relatives at home, asking if they knew of a suitable house in the Cambridge area of Massachusetts, where they planned to settle.[80] Louis replied to Kingsley, describing the beautiful mansion called Elmwood that was on the market, located at 33 Elmwood Avenue in Cambridge.

Elmwood was a traditional New England four-square, white, wooden house with a handsome central hall and staircase.[81] It was listed as a colonial mansion that had been built in 1767,[82] and was the former home of the Vice-President of the United States, Elbridge Gerry, and also of the renowned poet, James Russell Lowell. The Lowell family occupied the house for over a century. Its location was perfect: just half a mile from Harvard's campus. The Porters asked Louis to go ahead and rent the house, but in the meantime they would continue their travels until the autumn of 1921.

On a beautiful day in March 1921 the Porters visited the elevated region of Monte Serrato in Campania.[83] Lucy noted in her diary that she had visited there with Kingsley in January 1913. In mid-April they left I Tatti and travelled southwards, arriving on 3 May at the coastal town of Taranto, in the Apulia region. They spent several weeks exploring southern Italy, including taking an excursion to visit the remains of the Temple of Tavole Palatine that dated back to 520 BC.

On Monday 23 May they arrived in Pisa, and during June they crossed the French border and travelled on to Paris.[84] Using Paris as their base they continued their research in central France. They left Paris on 9 July and travelled to Montoire, situated on the Loire, and on 16 July they visited Tours, famous for its association with St Martin of Tours whose shrine was visited by medieval pilgrims on the road to Santiago de Compostela.

On 29 July they travelled to Nice to enjoy the glorious Côte d'Azur.[85] The Mediterranean sparkled in the blinding summer light but the beaches were crowded with bathers. Kingsley preferred to seek out hidden nooks along the coast. Here he could swim and bathe in peace while Lucy sat and read in the shade.

During August they travelled to Vienne to visit the Romanesque cathedral of St Pierre.[86] It had been another remarkable sojourn in Europe but, as autumn approached, a whole new chapter was beckoning. In September 1921 they returned to the US in time for Kingsley to take up his position as Professor of Fine Arts at Harvard.

Chapter eight

Elmwood, Harvard and Further Travels

Kingsley began teaching at Harvard in September 1921. He was immediately in great demand to lecture on his travels and recent findings. Kingsley's Harvard colleagues Edward Forbes, Denman Ross and Paul J. Sachs were delighted to welcome such an illustrious scholar into their midst. Ross was also a friend of Berenson's and shared Kingsley's obsession with photography.[1]

During December, Kingsley gave a series of lectures at the Metropolitan Museum of Art in New York.[2] On 3 and 10 December he delivered a two-part lecture on medieval sculpture and Romanesque art. The lectures were later published by the Marshall Jones Company of Boston, with the title *The Sculpture of the West*. In many ways, *The Sculpture of the West* offered audiences a sneak preview of the elaborate theory Kingsley had devised as to the development of sculpture throughout Europe. The opening paragraphs of his lecture summarized his now deeply held convictions that he later expounded in *Romanesque Sculpture of the Pilgrimage Roads*: 'We should find that the road formed a river of sculpture, flowing through a region otherwise nearly desert in southern France and Spain. We should find that artistic ideas travelled back and forth along the road with the greatest facility, so that monuments separated by hundreds of miles of distance show the closest stylistic relationship.'[3]

On 4 December, Kingsley lectured on medieval sculpture and the pilgrimage to Compostela,[4] and on 11 December the topic of his lecture was Romanesque art in Apulia.[5] The lectures helped Kingsley to piece together the data he had gleaned from his time in Europe and to prepare the way for his monumental book, *Romanesque Sculpture of the Pilgrimage Roads.*[6]

22. Elmwood, Cambridge, MA.
Courtesy of Wikipedia Commons.

Lucy and Kingsley were delighted with their new home at Elmwood. It was the perfect home for a Harvard lecturer since there was ample room to turn part of the house into a study area for students. Their plan was to purchase Elmwood and to carry out important renovations, since the old mansion was in very poor repair. From the winter of 1921 to the summer of 1926, they carried out major alterations, including electrical work, roof and chimney repairs, carpentry, painting and decorating, grounds' work, plumbing, and repairs to the heating system. In total, the renovation costs amounted to $10,633.[7] This was an enormous expense to incur, yet the Porters took it in their stride. Their tax returns for 1922 showed that their interest and dividends alone amounted to $53,642.13, so the extent of their wealth was considerable.[8]

The Porters finally took up residence in Elmwood, when all the major work had been completed, in October 1922.[9] Their new home was an imposing twelve-roomed mansion, complete with formal dining room, library, wide lawns, guest house and carriage house.[10] The building was noted for its wonderful proportions and for its sense of illumination and light. Lucy had learned a great deal about managing a large house during her months in I Tatti and she now used this experience to turn Elmwood into a magnificent centre for dining and entertainment, and a luxurious showcase for medieval art.

When the Porters set up home at Elmwood, it became the treasured haunt of many of Kingsley's students.[11] They came to examine the Porters' collection of photographs and art works, to study in the library and to have fascinating discussions with Kingsley. As a lecturer there was something different about Kingsley, a passion coupled with an informality that made students flock to his classes. On Sunday afternoons Lucy played hostess to Kingsley's students, and Elmwood buzzed with lively discussions while afternoon tea was served. During these informal gatherings of like-minded scholars, Kingsley was very much at ease. He knew and liked each of these young protégés; he delighted in expounding his theories and drawing out their thoughts about architecture and art.

Although the Porters used the house mainly as a private residence, Kingsley also taught some of his advanced courses on the first floor.[12] Described by his friends and colleagues as shy and reserved, 'which involved an almost physical aversion to the limelight', Kingsley obviously felt more comfortable conducting classes at his own home than teaching within the hallowed walls of the Harvard campus.

Despite Kingsley's earlier reservations about his ability to teach, it was the opinion of students and professors alike that this was a vocation at which he excelled.[13] Frederick A. Sweet, art historian and museum director in Chicago, was a student of Kingsley's during the early 1930s and regularly attended classes at Elmwood on medieval Spanish painting and Irish High Crosses.[14] Sweet described Kingsley as 'a brilliant teacher and [he] made you feel that your ideas were just as important as his'. He also noted that Kingsley, unlike any other professor, only taught his classes for six months of the year, spending the rest of his time in Europe researching.

The Porters also regularly entertained their friends, relatives and a host of distinguished guests at Elmwood.[15] The house was filled with music, poetry and stimulating discussions at these luncheons, soirées and dinners. Both Kingsley and Lucy became good friends with several of the Harvard faculty, in particular Chandler Post and Edward Forbes. Morton Vose, a student of Forbes, described him as 'a loveable person, quite delightful'.[16]

Sweet also recalled that both Kingsley Porter of Elmwood and Paul Sachs of Shady Hill were the wealthiest professors in Harvard, each owning a private art collection.[17] However, according to Vose, Sachs had a reputation for being 'unpleasant and disagreeable' in manner and 'overbearing and top lofty'.[18] Among his faculty, Kingsley appears to have been on friendly terms with all his colleagues, including Sachs. As Associate Director of the Fogg Art Museum, Sachs enjoyed conversing with Kingsley on medieval Italian art.

In his student days, Sweet was a frequent visitor to Elmwood.[19] He sometimes did research in Kingsley's library where there were 'all sorts of rare books which I've never found anywhere else. He had a room at The Fogg Art Museum where portions of his library were brought down from the house and that we had access to.' Attending Kingsley's classes, where there were never more than twelve students, was always the highlight of the week:

> There was a great deal of discussion, constantly asking our opinions, and he always made us feel that our opinions were just as important as his and he gave you a great feeling of

self-confidence. Not self-importance but self-confidence. In other words, he respected his students' opinions. The idea was you wouldn't have been there in the first place if you weren't a serious student, and you were expected to do well. I think eventually everyone did. He was such a charming, delightful and at the same time brilliant person that you felt that you must do your very best. It would be an insult to the man to let him down in any way.

When it came to marking assignments, Sweet described Kingsley as a lenient marker: 'if you got an A on it you thought you'd done awfully well. Well, you soon realized an A wasn't that great in Kingsley Porter. It had to be an A-plus or, better still, "A-plus – Compliments." A straight with Kingsley Porter was more like a B with other professors.'[20] Kingsley had therefore escaped his father's perfectionist standards for academic achievement. Unlike Sachs, who was viewed by students as being 'demanding', Kingsley was noted for being a sensitive and understanding teacher.

Sweet never forgot the Sunday afternoon gatherings at Elmwood.[21] Lucy often invited some of the Boston debutantes, who thrilled the all-male Harvard fraternity. He remembered the house as being 'strange', an old American mansion that was decorated entirely with Italian furnishings and medieval paintings. Then there were the four full-time Italian servants whom the Porters employed to help with the running of the house: two butlers, a general servant and a cook called Angelo. Anfossi continued to be their chauffeur.[22] Sweet was greatly amused by the 'two Italian manservants in white jacket and white gloves who waited on table'.[23] Overall, Sweet described Elmwood as having 'a fascinating atmosphere'.

While Kingsley taught his students and worked on his book, Lucy developed a wide social network through joining women's clubs, attending lunch engagements and supporting various cultural events, such as concerts, ballet, opera and theatre performances.[24] Lucy's sisters were regular visitors to Elmwood, as were Kingsley's nieces, Beatrice,

Joyce and Louise. Lucy and Kingsley often visited Louis and his family at the weekends, sometimes staying overnight in Stamford.

Early in 1923, Kingsley's desire for further wandering suddenly resurfaced. It had been just sixteen months since Kingsley and Lucy had returned from Europe. They had recently moved into Elmwood, their magnificent home that had cost an enormous amount to renovate. Also, Kingsley's reputation as a skilful and much-loved teacher at Harvard had been established. None of this, apparently, was enough to satisfy Kingsley, and a deep restlessness for further travel began to emerge.

One would have to wonder what Lucy thought of this plan for another expedition. Certainly, Kingsley always had the alibi of research with which to defend his extensive travels. There was also his adventurous nature and his constant need for space and freedom. Yet Lucy would have been justified in feeling that there was something more profound and disturbing that drove his persistent desire to pursue these lengthy voyages across the Atlantic. There must have been times when Lucy questioned this wanderlust. Was there some mystifying dissatisfaction with his home, his career or his marriage that kept him constantly exploring faraway lands?

Now that *Romanesque Sculpture of the Pilgrimage Roads* had been completed, Kingsley accepted the position of exchange professor from Harvard to teach at the Sorbonne in Paris and at various provincial French universities.[25] He also took this opportunity for an extended European tour, taking in Greece, Italy and Switzerland. He planned to research Byzantine art in preparation for a course he was to give at Harvard later that year. In early 1923 the Porters let Elmwood,[26] and on 15 February 1923 they sailed from New York on the SS *Patria*, en route for Europe.

The SS *Patria* arrived at the island of San Miguel, in the Azores, on Thursday 22 February. Lucy recorded in her diary: 'After luncheon about 1.30 pm we walked about Ponta Delgada. In the Cathedral of San Miguel we were struck with the barocco wood altarpiece (not gilded) and by the blue and white tiles in sacristy. The priest said they were Italian. Looked about 18th century. It had wider borders. Scenes (large figures) represented a hunt et cetera.'[27]

On 10 March they arrived in Athens.[28] Kingsley had been here with Louis during their world tour in 1902. On this occasion he had great difficulty finding comfortable lodgings but finally secured a suitable double room in Hotel Grande Bretagne.[29] Lucy noted that the rooms were inexpensive.[30] After a rest she treated herself to some pampering: 'I had my head washed and my nails manicured for 25 cents. We had baths and a good dinner.'

The following day they walked to the Acropolis,[31] but they only had time to glimpse the celebrated Parthenon, dedicated to Athena, before it closed. They were disappointed, not only with the early closure but also with the new blocks of restoration that had been carried out. They also took a trip by car to the monastery of Daphni. Anfossi accompanied them and was very helpful in 'erecting scaffolding out of ladders, boards and tables upon which K could take mosaics'.

On 17 March their friends the Berensons arrived in Athens.[32] Due to a shortage of rooms, the Berensons were stuck with substandard lodgings, and Kingsley somehow persuaded Lucy to give up their pleasant room. Their new quarters were so cramped that there was barely room to develop their photographs. In the circumstances, Lucy was unusually sarcastic in her praise of Kingsley's heroic sacrifice: 'We fortunately decided at luncheon to give up our comfy rooms to the B.Bs. We took in exchange Number 75 on the first floor…K was so wonderful in helping me realize how good it was for us to adopt ourselves to taking more uncomfortable quarters.'

Over the course of the holiday, the friendship that had earlier blossomed between Kingsley and Bernard Berenson began to wane as they bickered about the importance of various eras to the development of art. Kingsley had little time for classical art.[33] At Olympia a row developed between the two scholars, as Berenson berated Kingsley for giving too much attention to Byzantine art.[34] If there was one event that could rouse Kingsley from his usual placid disposition it was a perceived attack on his current field of research. Berenson must have been shocked, indeed, to encounter a belligerent Kingsley, who ably defended the importance of the Byzantine era with regard to its monuments.

Despite the poor accommodation and the occasional heated debates, Lucy focused on all that was magical about Athens. She especially enjoyed exploring Byzantine churches with Kingsley, where they viewed fine Greek pottery and alabaster ornaments.[35] She loved their early morning walks to visit churches almost hidden in the mountains. Her exuberance that spring can still be felt between the faded lines in her diary: 'What weeks of pleasure at Athens!'

During April they travelled by train to Patras, west of Athens, with the Berensons, Professor Hammond and a German painter.[36] They had dinner together that evening, and the others remained drinking coffee while the Porters went to bed early, exhausted after their travels. They remained in Patras until 2 May. Lucy enjoyed taking train excursions around Greece; her great delight was to be served lunch on board the train while gazing out at the magnificent landscape and coastline. On one such trip she wrote: 'I was so impressed with the beauty of the sea I didn't notice much the mountains the other side of the train.'[37]

By 6 June they had travelled across the Ionian Sea by steamer and were staying at Brindisi, in the Apulian region of southern Italy.[38] They continued their excursions to churches in southern Italy with the Berensons and their friend Nicky Mariano. Lucy continued to record their itinerary in her diary: 'B.B. and Nicky came to hotel – to join us and we went to cathedral together. Saw four capitals placed on top of each other . . . Cathedral still being restored as it was last time we were there . . . We were tired and longed to be alone but Roger Loomis arrived for dinner.'[39]

Some snippets from Lucy's diary begin to give a glimpse of her growing annoyance. Roger Loomis was an authority on medieval literature and a lecturer at Columbia. Kingsley enjoyed long conversations with Loomis and even carried on a correspondence with him concerning Arthurian legends.[40] Lucy usually enjoyed meeting Kingsley's colleagues, but in Italy the strain of constant travelling and entertaining began to take its toll. She may have wished for greater privacy, but it is more likely that she had begun to yearn for the comforts and routine of home.

The following day, Lucy's friend Conassa invited her to visit a villa owned by an acquaintance.[41] Lucy, who was used to a high standard of living at Elmwood, greatly valued style and quality, particularly in home furnishings. In her diary entry she was unusually sharp in her comments about the decor of the room in which they were entertained and about the gaudiness of the utensils used: 'a modern reception room with uncomfortable cheaply made chairs of some unknown period. I sat and waited for coffee to be served in thin, shiny silver cups.' Lucy's renowned civility was beginning to wear thin, perhaps yet another symptom of their hectic pace and her growing need for stability.

In August 1923, while they were still travelling in Italy, *Romanesque Sculpture of the Pilgrimage Roads* was published.[42] Kingsley's reputation immediately climbed to new, loftier heights. The book had taken eight years of research and it contained 1,527 original photos, most of them taken by Lucy. Since nine volumes of the ten-volume work were devoted to photographs, Lucy deserved the status of co-author of the work. The book, however, was attributed solely to Kingsley. There is no indication that Lucy was in any way upset by this. The 1920s was still an era when most talented wives who were married to brilliant men were quite content with the role of helpmate and may never have dreamed of sharing the limelight. There was never a hint of jealousy or resentment towards Kingsley in any of Lucy's diaries or correspondence. Lucy was incredibly proud of her husband's achievements and always the first to rejoice when one of his books received a glowing review.

Romanesque Sculpture of the Pilgrimage Roads revolutionized the methods used to date medieval monuments.[43] Kingsley discovered that previous dating of monuments was erroneous. By using inscriptions, documents and comparative analysis he devised a new system of dating for Romanesque structures.[44] He argued that proponents of medieval architecture were often more interested in ascribing fabulous dates to their national monuments than arriving at unbiased and realistic chronology.

Until the publication of *Romanesque Sculpture*, archaeologists hypothesized that churches were constructed slowly, or had been demolished and reconstructed, so that dates set by documents were considered to be inconclusive.[45] Kingsley refuted these theories and included a list of 425 dated monuments in *Romanesque Sculpture* to illustrate his findings on the basis of the comparative analysis of various monuments that he studied along the pilgrim routes. He offered a new, exciting vision of the creative landscape of the medieval ages. Instead of bleak and blank years with little or no construction, there had been a constant flow of craftsmen of great genius, executing some of the most marvellous stone sculptures ever created in Europe.

Kingsley devoted a large section of his book to the Benedictine abbeys at Cluny in France, the cloisters of Santa Domingo de Silos in Spain and the throne of San Niccola of Bari in southern Italy. He carried out detailed comparisons between the iconography on important monastic sites and medieval book illuminations, and arrived at some startling findings:

> The mastery of line and delicacy of technique characteristic of Silos are paralleled in the frescos of the life of St Alexius in the lower church of S. Clemente at Rome. Even a closer analogy is to be found in the capitals of Cluny (1088–1095). The faces at Cluny though of different type are like those of Silos in being archaic and conventionalized.[46]

Romanesque Sculpture of the Pilgrimage Roads inspired wide debate and was frequently met with storms of protest in academic circles. The main thesis of Kingsley's book was that medieval architecture developed throughout France, Italy and Spain, through an exchange of artistic ideas and techniques along pilgrim roads. Kingsley also included several references to the influence that Irish manuscripts[47] and Irish miniatures[48] had had on European sculpture. Kingsley also hypothesized that stone sculptures were often made from designs found on much older ivory carvings.[49] This was particularly the case in Spain, where there was a strong Moorish influence, so that many famous craftsmen worked with ivory.[50]

Although Kingsley may have been a classic introvert in social situations, when it came to writing he spoke fearlessly with a powerful and passionate voice. His controversial theories were delivered with clarity and conviction. It is obvious that he had honed his craft for many decades and now revelled in speaking with great eloquence and authority through the medium of his pen.

The book was met with outrage from certain scholars, including Kingsley's principle opponent, Émile Mâle. Mâle once again postulated that France was the centre of medieval architecture, whereas Kingsley sought to establish a link between Roman architecture and French Gothic outside of national boundaries.[51] Despite criticism from some academics and archaeologists, the overall verdict was that Kingsley had produced another masterpiece. *The New York Times* arts reviewer was in raptures over the entire work: 'To read the text volume and study all the illustrations indicated in the other nine volumes, or rather atlases – for they are enclosed without stitching – is a liberal education in sculpture and iconography and logic... It is indeed a monument of erudition and of enthusiastic labor.'[52]

Towards the end of August the Porters arrived in Geneva.[53] Reluctantly, Lucy had to endure the inconvenience of a bathless room. On 1 September, while Kingsley studied, Lucy accompanied her new friend Madame Bertaux by motor to the town of Ferney-Voltaire in eastern France. They visited the home of the writer and philosopher Voltaire, but the old mansion was closed and they could only read the church inscription through the fence: 'Deo Erexit Voltaire' (Erected to God by Voltaire).

On 3 September, Lucy wrote in her diary that she had a digestive upset.[54] Since she did not have a fever, she felt her symptoms were not severe enough to warrant a postponement of their trip. She felt strangely compelled to keep up with Kingsley's frantic schedule. They continued their travels by motor to Lausanne, where Kingsley photographed the Cathedral of Porche des Apôtre, and then they drove to Vevey, located on the spectacular north shore of Lake Geneva. The following day they travelled to the Alpine village of St Moritz, where they photographed the treasures of various churches.

By mid-September they had crossed the Italian border and were staying in St Monty Chiavenna in northern Italy, enjoying the sunshine, the mountain air and the spectacular lakes.[55] Lucy delighted in revisiting the church of St Fidelis of Como that she had first visited on her honeymoon:

> The little Romanesque chapel where S. Fidelis was decapitated in the 3rd century AD as he hastened to escape into the mountains. In the 16th century a Bishop of Como found the body of martyr and church at Como was erected in his honour. His body still rests there in the church of St Fidelis. We are now 4.30 pm – in the midst of taking a picture of frescos in apse, without light. A Christ stands in the centre (high waist). His face is much re-done. The two angels, one on either side bow before him. We are taking one at his L [Left]. They wear a white tunic, and over shoulders and falling on the backs in circular folds they wear a yellow garment, a reddish serviette ... Kingsley and I were here in 1912.[56]

Kingsley began lecturing at the Sorbonne in Paris and at other French universities during the autumn of 1923.[57] The bohemian lifestyle that Europe seemed to engender in Kingsley was never easy to relinquish. Instead of travelling home in early 1924, he obtained a further six months' absence from Harvard to take up the position as visiting professor to Spain. Lecturing in Europe did not faze Kingsley, as he was an excellent linguist, having learned the usual classical and modern European languages, as well as Catalan, and various Scandinavian languages.[58]

Lucy made no reference in her diary as to how she felt about remaining in Europe. There is little doubt that it was Kingsley who prolonged their stay. Neither Elmwood, his recent appointment at

Harvard, his family or friends could draw him back to Massachusetts, to a life of stability and routine. It was as though Kingsley was blind to the many inconveniences of travel and immune to the usual physical tiredness caused by constant motion. There must have been a point when Lucy began to wonder if Kingsley would pursue his unfathomable quest indefinitely.

By June 1924, Kingsley had completed his lectures in Spain. At this stage they had been travelling continuously since February 1923. Instead of feeling relieved that they could finally return home, Kingsley decided to continue his research of Spanish monuments.[59] After sixteen months of living out of a suitcase, even the glories of Europe must have begun to lose their lustre for Lucy. The excitement of visiting new towns, of staying in luxurious hotels and of photographing medieval churches must eventually have become monotonous as weeks turned into months, in an endless stream of packing and unpacking, of booking tickets and waiting at stations.

Lucy continued to sleep in hotel beds and to frequent dining rooms that were sadly anonymous. It was only natural that she must sometimes long for home and the routine of meeting her sisters for luncheon, tending to her garden, playing with her cats, and having afternoon tea with cherished friends. Elmwood, the magnificent home that had become an icon of style, luxury and comfort, could not have been far from her thoughts.

Though she never overtly recorded her misgivings about Kingsley's restlessness and his abhorrence of living a normal family life, Lucy must surely have begun to question his motives. She was a highly intelligent and perceptive woman, who must have asked herself: what is Kingsley searching for? What is he escaping from?

Lucy would have had some notion as to what drove Kingsley to work so tirelessly and to travel so frequently. She would have known of his early attachment to his mother and the terrible loss he suffered by her sudden death. Freud's theories as to the importance of people's early experiences to their subsequent psychosexual development would have been widely circulating by the 1920s. His theory of the

Oedipus Complex, where a young male child must pass through a stage of being in love with his mother and a jealous rival to his father, would have also fitted Kingsley's later experience, of becoming attached to his pretty governess and then losing her to his lecherous father.[60] In adulthood, Kingsley had managed to shed much of the baggage of his exceptionally difficult childhood and to form a loving attachment to his wife. Still, there was some deep desire that lay unfulfilled and for which he yearned that kept him compulsively pushing forward.

But Lucy could go without anything except her beloved Kingsley. She never once thought of going back home, of leaving Kingsley alone to pursue his relentless adventures. For Lucy, home had no meaning, no definite shape or form unless she was beside Kingsley.

For Kingsley, the prospect of taking to the road again was one he greatly relished. This time his plan was to travel across north-eastern Spain in the Fiat and to wring every last drop of adventure from his sabbatical. As ever, Lucy threw herself with full gusto into this new experience. If Kingsley wanted to wander across Spain then she would make the best of the situation. And there were some lovely moments that they shared: stopping under shady trees to feast on the many delicacies that Lucy had packed in her precious tea basket; going for walks along country roads as the sun set and the landscape was set alight in a blaze of spectacular colour. Sometimes after lunch they would sit, read and nap under clear blue skies. Lucy wore her lightest linens, her sun hat and sensible shoes, while Kingsley walked around in shirt-sleeves, forever scribbling notes. Lucy followed his instructions and photographed all the important monuments. Sometimes she spotted a perfectly chiselled face of an angel or a deranged demon that intrigued her. It was then that she captured the image for her own delight, like any enchanted tourist.

Kingsley was most preoccupied with San Pedro de Jaca Cathedral, in Aragon.[61] He made a close study of the tympanum over the west door of the cathedral and concluded that the designers chose symbols that were deeply significant to the Mediterranean region, such as paired lions at the gateway.

23. Arthur Kingsley Porter in Spain, c. 1924.
Harvard University Archives, HUG 1706.125p (Folder 13), W272203_1.

The ornately carved sarcophagus of Doña Sancha, located in the Benedictine Convent in Jaca, also caught Kingsley's special attention.[62] The central sculpture on the front of the sarcophagus contained two angels carrying a naked figure. Three priests marched forward under an arch. To the right, a woman sat on a throne, with two servants beside her. The back of the sarcophagus contained two warriors in combat.[63] Kingsley located a document that dated Sancha's death as August 1097. From this he inferred that the building of the sarcophagus took place around 1096.[64] His findings were revealed in an article entitled 'The Tomb of Doña Sancha and the Romanesque Art of Aragon', published in *The Burlington Magazine* in October 1924.

The Porters finally left Naples on the SS *Duilio* on 5 September 1924 and arrived in New York on 20 September, just in time for Kingsley to begin teaching the autumn term at Harvard.[65] It had been eighteen months since they had set eyes on their majestic home. Despite the extent of their foreign travels, the Porters' income from interest on their investments continued to assure them of a very comfortable lifestyle. An article in *The New York Times* in October 1924 reported on the largest taxpayers in New York City. Kingsley Porter was listed amongst them, with a 1924 tax return of $17,366. Louis H. Porter was also named as one of the top earners, having paid a staggering $40,433 in tax.[66]

During the autumn of 1924 the Porters' social life at Elmwood resumed. Lucy took great delight in playing hostess and she organized a series of luncheons, dinners and elaborate parties for friends, Harvard colleagues and family members. After their long absence, it was almost like a homecoming. Lucy welcomed all their old friends and arranged a grand celebration to mark their return. They issued a special invitation to the President of Harvard, Abbott Lowell, and his wife to attend a musical evening on 9 November 1924.[67] Meanwhile, Kingsley resumed his Harvard duties and continued to teach students at Elmwood. Lucy confined the students' socializing to Sunday afternoon gatherings so that Kingsley could have space to write and study during the remainder of the week.[68]

A major family crisis that concerned Lucy's favourite niece, Ellen, erupted that autumn in Chicago. Ellen had married John Borden, explorer and financier, on 2 February 1907.[69] The couple were well known in Chicago's elite social circle. They had two daughters, Ellen, aged 16, and Mary Elizabeth, aged 14. During 1924, John Borden met Mrs Courtney Letts Stillwell. Mrs Stillwell had divorced her husband in Paris earlier that spring.[70] Then, in the autumn of 1924, Ellen filed for a divorce against her husband on grounds of cruelty. This caused quite a sensation in Chicago. The divorce was finalized on 14 December when a settlement was made and Ellen was awarded custody of the two children.[71] Three months later, the 40-year old John Borden married the former Mrs Stillwell, who was thirteen years his junior.[72] All through this crisis, Lucy supported her niece. After the divorce Lucy continued to be in close contact with Ellen, often inviting her to spend holidays at Elmwood.

During the early months of 1925, Kingsley continued his lectures at Harvard. In January he was appointed to the newly established William Dorr Boardman Memorial Professorship of Fine Arts.[73] Lucy continued to play hostess and patron to many cultural and artistic events that were taking place in Cambridge. On 14 January, Lucy was one of the organizers for a song recital in aid of the New England branch of the Women's Farm and Garden Association.[74] During March, Lucy played host to Kingsley's niece, Joyce, who was Louis's second daughter.[75] Joyce was a student at Low-Heywood School at Shippand Point in Connecticut and she spent her spring vacation at Elmwood. Throughout the spring of 1925 the Porters' world consisted of Kingsley's lectures, Lucy's women's groups, attendance at cultural events and their joint entertainment of family and friends at Elmwood.

As soon as Kingsley's classes were finished for the summer, the Porters made plans to return to Europe. In early June 1925 they sailed on the SS *Martha Washington* from Boston.[76] Kingsley had been invited to teach as Hyde lecturer at various universities.[77] He also planned to continue his research of Byzantine art in Greece. They invited the Berensons to join them on a cruise of the Aegean Islands. Mary

Berenson declined the offer, writing that it was 'awfully temping for you are the people we like to travel with', and added the excuse that they 'dreaded the heat of July and August on the blazing sea & the furnace rocks'.[78] It is more than likely that the Berensons were still smarting from the constant rowing that had ensued between Bernard and Kingsley the previous year in Greece, and that they did not relish the prospect of another acrimonious holiday.

That summer, Lucy and Kingsley chartered a Greek freight sloop and cruised around the Aegean Islands.[79] The turquoise blue of the Aegean Sea, the secluded beaches, the craggy coastlines and the exotic villages with their narrow streets and Byzantine churches must have delighted the Porters. Compared to their previous long treks through France and Spain, the cruise was much more relaxing and invigorating, with lots of time for rest, reading and gazing out to sea. On their return home through Europe, however, a catastrophe occurred when Kingsley's case was stolen. This contained many negatives of his photographs and a large part of his notes on Byzantine art. The theft resulted in Kingsley having to abandon the book he had planned to write on his research in Greece. He was greatly annoyed by this senseless act that had destroyed many years of painstaking work.

In the autumn of 1925, Kingsley returned to Harvard to take up the newly created William Dorr Boardman Professorship of Fine Arts, to which he had been appointed in January.[80] The Porters also completed their major renovations of Elmwood.[81] Kingsley continued to compile his findings on Spanish architecture. He wrote to Berenson on 11 November 1925, thanking him for his encouragement to do further research in Spain: 'You have done lots of nice things to me, but never anything for which I am more grateful than pushing me into the Spanish Romanesque field once more. I have seldom worked at anything with such breathless interest as this new book.'[82]

During 1926, Kingsley continued to teach his classes at Elmwood. He also contributed articles to several journals.[83] In June, however, the disillusionment he had previously disclosed in *The Seven Who Slept* (1919) began to resurface. Although he had spent several decades

24. Faculty members of Harvard's Fine Arts Department in the courtyard
of the new Fogg Art Museum, January 1927. Standing (left to right):
Meyric R. Rogers, Langdon Warner, George H. Edgell,
Arthur Kingsley Porter, Chandler R. Post, Martin Mower, Kenneth Conant;
seated (left to right): Paul J. Sachs, George H. Chase, Denman W. Ross,
Edward W. Forbes, Arthur Pope.
Harvard University Archives, HUG 1706.125, Box 1, folder 11.

postulating theories of the development of European architecture, he
now questioned the validity of his findings in a letter to Berenson:

> The insuperable difficulty with artistic scholarship I suspect is
> intellectual dishonesty – I don't mean wilful, but the more danger-
> ous subconscious kind which makes it almost impossible, even for
> the few who try, to look at things without bias, whether derived

from herd instinct, reaction, self-interest or what not, I don't suppose unemotional thinking along our lines is attainable and I am convinced that most people are warped by some complex or other. With a crooked outlook, the resources of scholarship merely become a tool for befogging the general opinion.[84]

The implications of Kingsley's claim to Berenson, that all scholarship is dishonest, are indeed chilling. Kingsley, who had spent his life researching, had arrived at the conclusion that scholarship was doomed, because every scholar coloured his results to suit his own agenda. He starkly referred to the deviousness of the subconscious and its propensity to fool the self into believing motives to be true when in fact they were completely false. For scholars such as Berenson, these ideas must have been blasphemous. Berenson must have wondered if this revelation was based on Kingsley's self-analysis. Had he discovered 'a crooked outlook', some kind of complex within his own psyche that had remained hidden from the world, but still warped and befogged his true intentions? While staying at I Tatti, Kingsley had previously written to Berenson, blaming Lucy's perceived fears of living in a foreign country for their anticipated return to the US.[85] His fear of being confined to a teaching position at Harvard, where he would have to give up much of his freedom, was never alluded to. Perhaps Kingsley was beginning to gain insights into his true motives and feelings and this was causing him to question his deepest values and most cherished beliefs.

It was also during 1926 that Kingsley made a presentation of a rare medieval monument to the Fogg Art Museum at Harvard.[86] This deed was later to evoke great international controversy.[87] Throughout 1924 and 1925, Kingsley had been researching Romanesque architecture in Spain, with particular concentration on Leónese monuments. He had begun to suspect that León was the artistic focus of Spain and beyond.[88] He became especially interested in the sarcophagus of Alfonso Ansúrez, the son of Count Pedro Ansúrez, an influential nobleman in the court of Alfonso VI.[89]

The sarcophagus was commissioned by Pedro for his young son, Alfonso, who died in 1093, and it was originally located in the monastery of St Beneto de Sahagún near León.[90] It contains the epitaph: 'On the sixth day of the Ides of December in the year of the Era 1131 [10 December 1093] died Alfonso, the dear son of Count Pedro Ansúrez and Countess Eylo.' The iconography on the sarcophagus denotes 'a mass of the dead performed in heaven'.[91] Alfonso is portrayed taking his last breath, a symbol of the body being resurrected on the Last Day of Judgement.[92]

25. Sarcophagus of Alfonso Ansúrez, son of Count Pedro Ansúrez.
From the monastery of San Benito, Sahagún, León, Spain.
Courtesy of Wikimedia Commons.

The lid of the sarcophagus was considered to be one of the finest examples of European sepulchral sculpture in existence from the Middle Ages.[93] The discovery of the burial slab gave Kingsley the proof he had been searching for that Romanesque sculpture was practised in Spain during the eleventh century.[94] The sculptured style of decoration on the coffin lid was a divergence from tomb construction of the time. It contained large figures representing souls that had passed into the other world, Evangelists and Archangels, all in human form.[95] The figures were depicted with large bulging eyes and the Archangel

Gabriel had long chiselled curls.[96] Therefore, as an art object it was invaluable to archaeologists to further their knowledge of eleventh-century Romanesque Spanish sculpture.

26. Lucy and Kingsley Porter at Elmwood, Cambridge, MA, photograph, c. 1920.
Harvard University Archives, HUG 1706.125p, Hollis No: olvwork272201; Photo no: W272201_1.

The details of the transaction are unknown but the stone slab somehow came into Kingsley's possession and was transported to Cambridge. The previous year, Kingsley had made a gift of a thirteenth-century stained-glass medallion to the Fogg Art Museum.[97] This latest artefact, however, differed substantially from any other medieval object that Kingsley had ever collected, for this had been the covering tombstone of a young boy who had been buried with all the ritual and honour bestowed on a nobleman's son at the court of Alfonso VI. For archaeologists in that era it was common practice to excavate tombs and to distribute and sell treasures that had adorned the dead. The haphazard excavations in Egypt during the early 1900s have been well documented,[98] when archaeologists were more interested in monetary gain than in preserving the Egyptian culture. Although Kingsley's zeal to obtain the precious slab was driven by academic research, he also chose to ignore society's innate taboo against removing burial or funerary objects. Nevertheless, the Fogg Art Museum was delighted with its latest acquisition and displayed it in a prominent position.[99]

As Kingsley struggled to untangle the enigmas in his inner world, Lucy surrounded herself with a rich and varied circle of friends. Her sisters Ruth and Eleanor were frequent visitors to Elmwood. Lucy was particularly fond of her nieces, Joyce and Beatrice, and held a party in their honour on 4 December 1926.[100] After five years of renovation and superb decoration, Elmwood simply sparkled as party revellers arrived at the colonial mansion that evening. Each guest was greeted by the tall, slim figure of Kingsley, dressed in a three-piece suit, and by his adoring wife, Lucy, attired in evening dress, chatting and smiling as she stood beside her celebrated husband.

Chapter nine

Accolades and New Horizons

The Porters spent a quiet Christmas at Elmwood. Although the first term of 1927 was to begin at Harvard in February, Kingsley yet again secured eight months' leave from teaching to pursue further travels. This time he had no pressing project to work on. He needed to return to Europe to stimulate his mind in the hope that some new venture would absorb him. On 29 January 1927, he and Lucy sailed aboard the SS *Roman* from New York, en route to Spain.[1] They arrived on the Portuguese Island of Madeira on 4 February. Lucy enjoyed their short time on the island: 'The walks up the pine-covered mountains (all of young growth) with the barren grey peaks beyond was beautiful but became chilly in the shadows.'

They sailed on to Gibraltar, where they met Anfossi, who drove them to their hotel.[2] They spotted the African Pillar of Hercules in the distance. The next day they drove along the Spanish coast to Malaga. Kingsley's plan was to explore southern and western Spain to expand his knowledge of Andalucian architectural styles, dominated by Moorish design. Ever since his valuable notes on Byzantine art had been stolen he had contemplated a suitable subject for his next book. He decided to return to Spain to continue his research of Romanesque monuments.

On Wednesday 9 February they drove to Ronda.[3] Lucy noted in her diary: 'Ronda was inaccessible natural fortress for west with arable land which it protects at the south; also a meeting place of 3 passes. Art objects are lacking.' They visited the stone church there before driving on to Jerey and Cadiz.

Throughout February they continued their travels of Andalucia, exploring churches and monuments in Seville, including Alcalá de Guadaíra, with its impressive towers and town walls, and the Roman town of Carmona.[4] During March they made their way north-east towards Catalonia. They stayed in the town of Tarragona, famous for its Roman ruins, and both fell in love with its quaint mixture of culture, landscape and cuisine. Lucy noted: 'Stayed 3 nights. What air and wine and monuments.'

27. Passport photograph of Arthur Kingsley and Lucy Porter.
Harvard University Archives, HUG 1706.125, Box 1, folder 4.

On 22 April they arrived in Barcelona,[5] and from here they toured the surrounding towns and countryside. Lucy made copious notes in her diary about the frescos and sculptures they photographed.[6] She was particularly taken with the small church in Campo, in Aragon:

> After luncheon went to Roman Temple. One stone of much interest to us. As are two reliefs in (little modern church in Campo) ... 3 disciples, one beardless ... two bearded. Bartholomew at end. Judas!!
>
> Opposite: 3 bearded ones with scrolls – prophets. Cloisters of X1 and X11 centuries.[7]

Later that summer they travelled on to Germany.[8] At Marburg University, Kingsley was awarded an honorary Doctorate of Letters to mark the 400th anniversary of the oldest protestant university in Europe. In August they met up with the Berensons and travelled to Minden.[9] The Berensons' friend, Nicky Mariano, accompanied them on various expeditions.[10] Mariano reported that Kingsley was like a 'hunting dog' when he was in pursuit of a photograph of some monument or sculpture to supplement a theory.

In September the Porters reluctantly left Europe to travel back to Cambridge for the autumn term,[11] and on 18 September they arrived in New York on the SS *Cedric*. Kingsley returned to teaching, while Lucy's social life gathered momentum.

Kingsley always dreaded returning to Harvard, not because of the teaching involved or the interaction with students, but due to the dull formality that was imposed by the whole educational system. Kingsley was different from other professors because he actually enjoyed discussing his evolving research with students. Fairfield Porter took Kingsley's course in pre-Romanesque art. It was the lack of formality that delighted students and developed in them a genuine interest in art and architecture: 'It wasn't a set course. He didn't know everything yet. It was as he was discovering things he gave them to us. We were sort of watching his research.'[12]

While Kingsley pursued informality in his teaching, Lucy embraced everything that was expected of the best Bostonian families when it came to socializing. Although neither Lucy nor Kingsley originated in Boston, their social position, great wealth and old family money assured their inclusion within Boston's elite circle. Austin Warren, literary critic and author, was a frequent visitor to Elmwood. Warren noted that dinner guests were always of the proper lineage and social position: 'Mrs Porter's dinners remain for me an archetype of the traditional formal style of entertaining, such as I knew from the novels of James. The seating of the guests was carefully planned; each man seated between two women, with each of whom in turn he conversed.'[13]

Warren described the ladies who attended these dinners as 'stuffy, stiff little persons'.[14] The whole affair was extremely formal, and traditional Bostonian etiquette was always adhered to:

> I was content to talk, first to the lady on my right, and then to the lady on my left. The whole art of social conversation engaged me. Not to be shy or gauche, not to be diffuse of words or specialized; to give and take; not to be too heavy or too light; too personal or too impersonal; not to be too brilliant or too witty: such are the desiderata... After dinner parties, the men were left to their cognac and cigars or cigarettes, while the women withdrew to the drawing room.

It was the food rather than the calibre of guest that delighted Warren: 'The food at Elmwood was delectable partly because it was European, and Italian, yet not the lower class Neapolitan food I associated with Italian cookery, the kind I had had at American-Italian restaurants. The pasta was delicate and various. The sweet was likely to be some confection with chestnut paste as its foundation.'[15]

Within the first week of their arrival home, Lucy organized two intimate dinners.[16] The first was for Lucy's mother and Kingsley's colleague Chandler Post. The second included Kingsley's uncle, Schuyler Merritt, and Lucy's niece, Ellen. There was also an evening spent at the theatre, a day trip to New York and a weekend visit to the Porters and the Merritts in Stamford.

From her appointment pad it is clear that Lucy needed to keep herself busy.[17] Occasionally there were evenings when there were no dinner engagements and Kingsley had a faculty meeting to attend. Then Lucy would write the ominous word 'Alone' in her pad. There is little doubt that Lucy disliked being alone. It was something of a priority to fill her mornings, her afternoons and her evenings with social engagements.

The remainder of 1927 was packed with entertainment.[18] The servants at Elmwood were kept busy preparing lunches, afternoon teas and dinners for intimate family engagements. A large dinner party was organized for Louis on 29 October. Joyce and Beatrice were among the dinner guests on 20 November. Then there were outside events to attend, such as symphonies, afternoon lectures at the Fogg Art Museum, the Harvard Christmas play, and a rendition of Handel's *Messiah* in Boston.

28. Kingsley sitting on the steps at Elmwood, Cambridge, MA.
Harvard University Archives.

Lucy's 1928 diary began with a rare biblical quote from the Epistle of St Paul to the Galatians: 'For do I now persuade men, or God? Or do I seek to please men? For if I yet pleased men, I should not be the servant of Christ.'[19]

During 1928 the lectures that Kingsley had given at the Sorbonne were published in two volumes as *Spanish Romanesque Sculpture*.[20] This was another major achievement for Kingsley as it contained the fruits of eight years of research into Spanish architecture. In this work, Kingsley set out to prove that Spanish Romanesque sculpture had a distinct development that was not a mere reflection of French sculpture.[21]

In the foreword, Kingsley reminded readers that within a five to ten year period the book's content would seem 'quaint', as research in architecture was ever changing and transitory.[22] He was again preoccupied with his failure to capture the truth, no matter how hard he tried: 'Archaeology is an ephemeral product of an ephemeral age. It runs the same race with truth that a parallel line runs with its fellow; it constantly tends to approach, but in this world coincidence will never be realized.'[23]

At the end of the second volume of *Spanish Romanesque Sculpture*, Kingsley finally acknowledged in writing the enormous contribution of his talented wife: 'The foregoing book is published under the name of A. Kingsley Porter, but anything in it which may be of value could not have been without Lucy Porter.'[24]

Once Kingsley's Spanish studies had been completed he immediately pressed on to discover further architectural wonders in foreign lands. On 3 June, the Porters sailed from Boston on the SS *Cedric*, making their first excursion to Ireland.[25] Their friends Joe Breck, Curator of Decorative Arts at the Metropolitan Museum of Art, and Peter Teigen, artist and Professor of Drawing at Princeton,[26] travelled with them. Lucy described her first glimpse of the Irish coast:

> What grey seas, until the last, when for two days the waves came out of the VE to roll mighty under us without giving us any perceptible motion.

Clouds livid over Ireland as we neared the South West and ran
along its shore. At midnight dropped anchor off Queenstown.
Rock! . . .

Ad old moon setting in the west.[27]

Ever since Kingsley's case had been stolen, that contained his collection of negatives and notes on Byzantine art, he had been eager to find
a new venture to whet his appetite for further research. Kingsley's interest in Ireland's High Crosses and portal tombs began in November 1926
when he corresponded with a Dublin photographer, Thomas Mason,
asking where he might obtain photographs of Irish medieval antiquities.[28] In *Spanish Romanesque Sculpture* he referred to the importance of
Irish carvings in the context of the development of sculpture in
Europe.[29] He discovered that High Crosses had preceded European
Romanesque sculpture[30] and he became fascinated with Ireland's role in
the development of medieval art, particularly in Spain and Egypt.[31]

On Sunday 10 June they arrived in Cobh.[32] There was bedlam on
the dock as luggage was sorted and Anfossi loaded the car. They stayed
that evening in Cobh. They had arranged to rent Bective House in
County Meath for the summer, a nineteenth-century manor located in
an estate of 180 acres.[33] Kingsley had previously written to its owner,
Charles S. Bird Junior, asking for the presence of six servants, a car and
driver and two riding horses.[34] On their first morning they drove
through Co. Tipperary and stopped for lunch in Cashel.[35] They visited
the Rock of Cashel before travelling on to Bective. Lucy's sister, Ruth,
and her niece, Ellen, had already arrived, intending to stay for the
month of June. Their friend Peter Teigen also visited for over a month.

The quiet Irish countryside suited the Porters, allowing them to
unwind, to take long walks and to write.[36] Lucy eloquently described
the sounds emanating from the Meath landscape at nightfall:

At dusk − 9.30 or later, quivering black clouds with croaking
sounds descending from them, began to settle in the trees. The
rooks became part of the landscape–as much so as the golden

asters in the fields, the stinking flax in the impoverished ponds and the grazing sheep and bullocks and many turkeys. These two weeks were strangely happy to me.

During their first week in Ireland they made two trips to Dublin.[37] On Wednesday they lunched at the Shelbourne Hotel before visiting the collection of prehistoric gold work at the National Museum. They also visited the National Gallery, where Lucy made two pages of detailed notes on paintings from the Dutch school, including Ruysdael, de Hooch, Rembrandt, Maes and Cuyp.[38] Lucy wrote critically and authoritatively about the paintings: 'Dublin Gallery. #131 Jacob Gerritzy Cuyp 1594–1651 Dutch School. A young girl with dog. Poor thing. Child convincing, dog suggests wood. Purchased in 1889. Father to renowned one: Aelbert Cuyp 1620–1691.'[39]

On Saturday they visited the Book of Kells at Trinity College.[40] They also took day trips to photograph several important Celtic High Crosses at Kells, Co. Meath, and the magnificent round tower at Glendalough, Co. Wicklow.[41] Glendalough was the location of a monastic settlement that was established by the sixth-century St Kevin,[42] a hermit priest who lived in a small cell in the mountains, overlooking two lakes.

On 24 June, Anfossi became ill and Lucy called a local doctor to treat him.[43] There was no improvement and the Porters became alarmed at Anfossi's condition so they drove him to Dublin to see Dr Lane. In early July he was admitted to hospital where he slowly improved. Meanwhile, the Porters were invited to attend various lectures in Dublin and they also received several lunch invitations from American acquaintances. On 3 July they visited Mrs Childers, formerly Molly Osgood from Boston, at Bushy Park in Terenure, for afternoon tea. Molly was the daughter of the Porters' Boston friends, Dr and Mrs Osgood.[44] Her husband, Erskine Childers, had been executed by the Irish Free State for gun-running in 1922. Her son, Erskine Hamilton Childers, later became the fourth President of Ireland, in 1973. The Porters celebrated Independence Day, 4 July, at the American Ambassador's residence at the Phoenix Park.[45]

Two days later they visited Co. Kildare to photograph the well-preserved High Crosses at Moone and Castledermot.[46] On 10 July they travelled to Tara Hill in Co. Meath, reputed to have been the home of the High Kings until the sixth century. At Tara they visited a selection of ancient monuments of great archaeological significance, including a famous standing stone known as the Lia Fáil, and a Neolithic passage tomb called the Mound of the Hostages. During July they also visited Monasterboice, Duleek and Clonmacnoise to photograph superb examples of High Crosses. At Clonmacnoise, Lucy wrote in her diary: 'Beautiful day. K took swim in Shannon, largest river in British Isles.'

On Monday 23 July the Porters returned to Dublin to visit the impressive library at Trinity College.[47] While there, they continued their research of the Book of Kells and the Book of Durrow. Two days later they returned to Glendalough. In early August they made an excursion to Durrow Abbey and also revisited Clonmacnoise.

No matter where the Porters travelled, they always made contact with American friends who would then introduce them to writers, collectors and academics whom they wished to meet. On Friday 3 August they were invited to lunch with Irish poet, mystic and member of the Senate, William Butler Yeats.[48] In 1923, Yeats had been awarded the Nobel Prize for Literature. Both Kingsley and Lucy enjoyed reading poetry, especially Keats and Shelley, so their interest may have extended to Yeats's poetry.

The following week was spent at the Dublin Horse Show, held at the Royal Dublin Society (RDS) in Ballsbridge.[49] On 15 August they left Bective, and Lucy drew an illustration in her diary of a sad face with tears streaming down. It had been a happy and satisfying holiday for both Lucy and Kingsley. From Bective they made their way to Donaghmore House in Castlefinn, located in the eastern region of Co. Donegal. The large nineteenth-century house was set on an estate that contained a Victorian cast iron greenhouse and an eighteenth-century walled garden. Lucy wrote in her diary: '2 happy weeks.'

This was the Porters' first excursion to Donegal. Kingsley quickly became fascinated by stories of the local saint, Columcille, who was

29. High Crosses at Clonmacnoise, Co. Offaly.
Michael Cullen.

reputed to have been born in Gartan near Glenveagh in the sixth century and to have established a monastery of great learning on the island of Iona;[50] a series of legendary High Crosses sculpted at Iona were destroyed by the Vikings. On 27 August the Porters travelled to Iona, off the western coast of Scotland.[51]

On 1 September they returned to Donaghmore House to pack up their belongings and to close up the house.[52] The following day they travelled to Larne, and after a short stay there they boarded a steamer for Scotland. Lucy recorded the event in her diary:

> I was on the way to Larne to photograph tower where sculpture is. Hotel at Larne, Olderfleet, by the quay delightful. We walked along the shore in late PM in rain and thought we saw Scotland in the mist. A smooth crossing. King's Arms Hotel at Stranraer, very English and comfortable. Boarded the steamer to Stranraer and spent a few days travelling around Scotland.

After spending several days in Carlisle they drove back to Glasgow.[53] Anfossi had resumed his duties once again as chauffeur. Lucy was particularly intrigued by Shelley's original manuscript of 'When the Lamp is Shattered', that was on display in the University of Glasgow. In her diary, she quoted the entire poem, that ended with the verse:

> When hearts have once mingled,
> Love first leaves the well-built nest;
> The weak one is singled
> To endure what it once possessed.
> O Love! who bewailest
> The frailty of all things here,
> Why choose you the frailest
> For your cradle, your home, and your bier?

After a brief stay in Oxford they travelled on to London. Kingsley spent time at the British Museum where he studied illuminated manuscripts,[54] and Lucy also visited the museum and enjoyed studying the various exhibitions on display there. In London, however, Lucy became tired and out of sorts. After four months of constant travelling, her usual calm and positive veneer began to wear thin. Her diary records this rare attack of ill humour on an excursion from London to Kent: 'Left London more dead than alive. Sat. Oct. 13. Gradually my state of mind (a horrid feeling towards Anfossi and other human beings) passed from me. At Rochester still hurrying and a little insane but Canterbury (and a good lunch) was like the hand of a big, fine friend (like K's) smoothing out the furrow of your brow.'

They had especially travelled to Canterbury to photograph St Augustine's Abbey but it proved to be a disappointment for Lucy as it was merely 'a rather mixed up mess of ruins'.[55] They continued driving to Portsmouth Harbour in Hampshire to photograph Portchester Castle with its Roman-Saxon shore fort and a restored Norman church within its walls. In late October 1928, the Porters sailed from Portsmouth to the Continent, stopping at Bruges and Venice. As November dawned – their sixth consecutive month of travel – they still had no plans to return home. Their sights were firmly set on travelling farther east, to explore the ancient tombs of Egypt.

Chapter ten

Depression and Confession

In November 1928 the Porters continued their journey to Africa. Kingsley's responsibilities lay many thousands of miles west, in Harvard. No matter how glamorous his home may have seemed, or how prestigious his Harvard position appeared, to the romantic adventurer it was still mediocre and he could only take so much mediocrity. For Kingsley, real living was crossing oceans, traversing continents, delving into exotic cultures and wallowing in the allure of great, sweeping landscapes. There had already been several times when Kingsley had fled the mundane. In times of crisis this need was even greater, such as when Louis was ill and his nerves were shattered after years of family litigation. The 19-year old Kingsley had conjured up a world tour to revive his brother's ailing health. When his own plans to develop a Faculty of Art History in Yale had been rejected, he accepted the French government's offer of relocating to France during the final, perilous months of a world war. His yearly flights from Harvard were his latest attempts to flee the constraints imposed by a conformist institution at the heart of an ultra-conservative society.

At the age of 45, Kingsley Porter possessed every asset that most mortals can only dream of. Within his chosen field of Romanesque architecture his ingenious theories, his original research methods and his brilliant publications were highly respected. Besides the mammoth books he had authored, he had also written countless articles that had been printed in leading periodicals and collective works in Europe and the US.[1] He was a lecturer who was truly loved by his students, celebrated by his peers and championed by one of the most influential universities in the world. Financially, Kingsley Porter possessed a fortune; romantically, he was adored by his intelligent, charming wife. Together with Lucy he travelled the world for months at a time, seeking out landscapes of exquisite natural beauty; visiting monuments, cathedrals and castles of rich cultural significance; meeting artists, writers and politicians: all doors were fully opened to satisfy his every desire.

Despite all of these worldly advantages, Kingsley Porter was growing more restless and despondent. At the very height of his success, Kingsley began to experience serious bouts of depression. An inner secret that had remained bottled up and hidden his whole life was about to erupt and shatter his private world forever.

The Porters arrived in Alexandria in early November.[2] Kingsley was pleased to get the chance to visit the new excavations and to do some research in the museum.[3] Mr Breccia, the Director of the Greco-Roman Museum, put his art collection and his library at Kingsley's disposal.[4] Yet even the glories of these incredible excavations could not raise Kingsley's spirits. Lucy mentions nothing in her diary about his darkening moods; it is only in his correspondence with Louis that Kingsley's true state of mind is revealed.

That same month, Kingsley confided to Louis for the first time that he was suffering from depression. Louis wrote back, amazed at the revelation: 'I am distressed to hear that you have been having fits of depression. I always think of you and Lucy as typical Buddhas. You seem to have reached the goal of Nervanah and I find it difficult to imagine depression in connection with either of you.'[5]

Louis was clearly shocked to hear of Kingsley's feelings of depression. Although the brothers had always been close, it appears to have been highly unusual for Kingsley to share his feelings with anyone except Lucy. The following week the Porters travelled to Cairo and stayed in a hotel under the shadow of the pyramids.[6] Kingsley was particularly pleased to receive another letter from Louis as it had taken a month to arrive. Kingsley replied immediately, updating Louis on his Egyptian travels. He told him that the loot from archaeological expeditions was in the hands of a few who showed it only to their special friends. He also outlined many changes that had taken place in Egypt since 1902, when Louis and he had visited Egypt on their world tour. He also informed Louis that Lucy and he would be back in Boston in late January, in time for his February lectures. He mentioned their plans for the following Tuesday, to visit the Coptic monastery of Wadi Natrun located in the eastern desert. There was no further mention of any feelings of depression.

The Porters' cruise on the Nile began on 3 December 1928.[7] Their first afternoon was spent with Captain Connell in Cairo. On Thursday 6 December they boarded the launch SS *Beatrice* at the Anglo-American pier at Gezira, a region of east-central Sudan, between the Blue Nile and the White Nile. Kingsley shopped while Lucy unpacked; she was more than happy with their comfortable quarters.

The following day they had an early start. Breakfast was at 6.45 a.m. and by 8 a.m. they were out on the east bank of El Massara.[8] Lucy wrote in her diary: 'we walked over ploughed fields to automobile road to village in a date orchard. Church clean and interesting enough for a photograph. Coptic priest sitting cross-legged on high seat overlooking the Mokattam Hills.'

Lucy lamented that they hadn't spent enough time enjoying the pyramids of Giza.[9] Further down the Nile they stopped at the pyramids of Dahshur as evening approached. Lucy was entranced by the magnificence of the scene that unfolded before her: 'Looking at those of Dahshur, light, medium, with a big red sun in back of it was stunning. It looked like a mosque with something wrong with its dome.'

Lucy was fascinated by the dark, exotic Arabs they met on their travels. In her diary, she described the young Egyptian girls who wore 'silver amulets and one gold nose ring with 3 dangles on it'.[10] The cruise was relaxing for Kingsley, who had time to work on a new drama entitled *The Virgin and the Clerk*. Lucy enjoyed reading books about Egypt in English and French.

There was, however, one incident that blighted their enjoyment. During a camel ride through the desert Lucy had a fall and injured her back.[11] Apparently Lucy didn't realize how serious it was and failed to record it in her diary; it was only later that it caused her great discomfort.

On 26 January 1929 the Porters disembarked from the White Star Liner, the SS *Cedric*, in Boston.[12] Lucy's engagement diary was very empty for the first few weeks after their arrival home. From 19 February, however, their social life became hectic again as Lucy's sisters visited and her luncheon club resumed its Thursday meetings.[13] Meanwhile, Kingsley began lecturing again at Harvard. Lucy slotted his classes in her diary for Monday and Wednesday afternoons.

March and April were very full months with various social engagements, including lunches, dinners and a visit from their niece, Beatrice.[14] On 3 April, Kingsley wrote to Louis at his New York office:

> With us there is no particular news. Everything has been going along as usual. I have been very much oppressed by various odds and ends of back work that I have not been able to get cleared up, and which have given me a feeling of being harassed and dissatisfied. Some day perhaps I shall learn that I at least probably will never be able to keep things in order, and let it worry me a little less. I still have on my table, uncorrected, important proofs that have been waiting there for nearly a month.[15]

On this occasion, Kingsley blamed his feelings of dissatisfaction on his heavy workload.[16] He also told Louis that Lucy and he were returning to Ireland for the summer, to Marble Hill in Co. Donegal:

> It is situated in the most wild and lonely part of the north coast, in what I imagine is one of the most desolate but also beautiful landscapes of Europe. The climate is said to be much more bracing than West Meath where we were last year...I am hoping it may give me a chance to gain a certain peace of mind which I feel I have rather lost lately in the archaeological scramble.

Towards the end of April, Kingsley's troubled mind appears to have taken its toll on Lucy. On 29 April, she underlined the word 'Alone' in her engagement diary.[17] The following Thursday, 2 May, Dr Osgood was called. Nothing was recorded as to the malady or the patient, yet it may have been Lucy's back that was causing her discomfort. Despite the ailment, May was again packed full with appointments. The Porters travelled to Stamford on 9 May to visit Louis before stopping off at Yale in New Haven for a lunch engagement. Lucy's sisters stayed at Elmwood on 29 May and an entire week of entertaining ensued.

Suddenly, in June, Lucy was ordered by her doctor to spend thirteen hours a day in bed and to avoid getting tired.[18] Kingsley wrote to Louis on 7 June: 'I have done a lot of worrying about taking Lucy to Ireland, and have had two talks with Dr Osgood on the subject.'[19] Kingsley confided to Louis that Lucy's back trouble began after the fall in Egypt, and he feared she would not be able to travel as much in the future.[20] Kingsley also reassured Louis that Lucy was determined to attend Joyce's wedding on 22 June before sailing to Ireland the following day.

Throughout June, doctors Osgood and Ross made several calls to Elmwood.[21] Kingsley wrote again to Louis on 23 June, saying he was perturbed that Lucy might not be able to travel with him to undertake research in Europe.[22] He was faced with a major decision: whether to carry on his work alone or to change the direction of his work to remain near Lucy.

Throughout 1929, Kingsley was battling with enormous personal conflicts that had been repressed for his entire life. Kingsley's torment may have also exacerbated Lucy's physical ailments. Since the mid-1920s, Kingsley had been reading books on psychoanalysis, desperately struggling to find the roots of the depression that had assailed him.[23] These books included *Studies in Psychoanalysis* (1922) and *Psychoanalysis and Aesthetics* (1924) by Charles Baudouin.

Even before the First World War, the ideas of psychoanalysts such as Sigmund Freud, Havelock Ellis and Ellen Key were being discussed by intellectual circles in Europe and the US.[24] The central theories of psychoanalysis – that sexual repression was harmful to the emotional

30. Signature of Arthur Kingsley Porter on the frontispiece of *Psychoanalysis and Aesthetics* (1924) by Charles Baudouin in Glenveagh Castle Library.
Michael Cullen.

and physical well-being of both men and women – were becoming widespread. The link between self-destructive tendencies and repressed sexuality was filtering into mainstream thought.

The literature that Kingsley was reading fitted into this category. *Studies in Psychoanalysis* contains twenty-seven case studies based on the analysis of the author's clients.[25] It is an in-depth account of the various symptoms that may be exhibited when trauma in childhood has been repressed. The patient may only be aware of suffering from a variety of symptoms, such as neurosis, but may have no actual memory of the event that caused the problem because it has become unconscious.[26] In particular, Freud's view of the sexual instinct is discussed, as this is considered to be the most potent instinct and the one most often repressed due to society's laws and expectations. A number of secondary tendencies are also discussed, that may occur when the sexual instinct is thwarted or repressed, including homosexuality, sadomasochism and exhibitionism. Baudouin states that patients may be cured from their 'perversion' by undergoing psychoanalysis and releasing repressed, painful memories.

Baudouin also refers to positive traits that may develop when a childhood trauma has been repressed.[27] These may include 'a moral, intellectual, aesthetic, or religious direction. This is what Freud speaks of as sublimation – a successful and beneficent derivation.' The author goes on to discuss the positive effects that may be derived from a lack of sexual expression and a redirection of the sexual drive:

Energy that was primarily sexual is thus looked upon as taking the form of a stream which divides into a number of branches, subsequently perhaps coalescing and separating once more. If one branch is dammed, the obstructed portion of the stream flows into lateral channels, and may there give rise to new derivatives which are sometimes of great moral and social value.[28]

Kingsley's interest in psychoanalysis stemmed from a growing feeling of despondency. As he continued his studies of Baudouin's books, he must have gained great insight into the causes of his depression. For instance, he learned that the sexual instinct can be thwarted or repressed; that sexual shame can occur in young children or those who are going through puberty; that the relationship with one's parents is of major significance in later life.[29] Although Kingsley's early years had been happy ones, it was after his mother's death that his family life disintegrated. This reached its zenith when Kingsley was approaching puberty, with the onset of his father's bizarre love life and the subsequent public scandal that blazed throughout the East Coast. But this was not the only revelation to emerge.

The truth finally dawned on Kingsley as he suddenly awakened from a lifetime of sexual repression. He somehow summoned the courage to confide in Lucy that, although he still loved her, he realized that he was homosexual. The exact date when this confession was made is unknown, as Lucy never recorded this or any other mention of her husband's sexual tendencies in her diaries. The effect, however, of this confession on Lucy can only be imagined. The man she completely adored, the absolute love of her life, was telling her that the sexual part of their married life had been a sham; that, in fact, Kingsley's true sexual feelings were not aroused by her at all. For Kingsley's sexual satisfaction could only be achieved with a male partner.

Whether Lucy had any suspicions of Kingsley's homosexual tendencies is pure conjecture. Although artistic and sensitive in nature, Kingsley had all the appearance of a happily married heterosexual male, handsome, athletic and passionate about the outdoors.[30] Perhaps if a reader of *Beyond Architecture* had been of a suspicious disposition, he or she would have pondered why Kingsley was so appreciative of the male nude in Greek art, yet he was an archaeologist and his admiration for an exquisite piece of sculpture would not have seemed atypical.[31]

Kingsley must have feared that his marriage was almost in tatters and his professorship at Harvard was hanging by a thread. He may have worried that Lucy would divorce him: her niece, Ellen, had divorced her husband in December 1924, and since the end of the First World War the divorce rate in the US had been rising,[32] so that divorce no longer carried the same social stigma as in bygone times. Whatever agonies Kingsley endured before he confessed the truth of his sexual orientation, he need not have feared for his marriage, as Lucy's devotion never wavered. Lucy was noted for her resilience and she certainly displayed this trait in abundance. Somehow she dealt with this catastrophic blow, managing to hold everything together. She turned a smiling face to family and friends without betraying the deep hurt and confusion she must have been secretly feeling. Like Kingsley, Lucy would have abhorred a scandal. In Cambridge, her lifestyle was formal, orderly and above reproach. Yet it was not out of any sense of duty that she remained in her marriage. For Lucy, the rare fact remained that, after seventeen years of marriage she was still totally in love with her husband.

All through their married life, Lucy had pandered to Kingsley's desires. She had lived a nomad's life without a permanent home for ten years before Kingsley agreed to settle at Elmwood. She had turned a blind eye to her husband's hobby of hunting, even though her sensitivities sided with the plight of the dying or maimed animal. Lucy's belief in her husband's goodness simply knew no bounds.

Kingsley's position at Harvard was less certain. The 1920s decade in the US was a time when conservative values and republican politics were at an all-time high. Prohibition had been introduced in 1920 and there was a major upswing in right-wing values promoting decency and morality. The President of Harvard, Abbott Lawrence Lowell, was known to abhor homosexuals.[33] Although Lowell had an excellent reputation as a liberal educator who wished to integrate students from different social classes and also staunchly supported academic freedom, there were deep fanatical tendencies in his nature that surfaced during his presidency. There were three groups in particular that he abhorred. He set out to limit Jewish enrolment at Harvard to 15 per cent; he tried to ban African American students from living in the Freshman Hall at the university; he completely outlawed homosexuality and carried on a campaign to have students and teachers who were suspected of being homosexual expelled. Much of his activity was covert, including a secret court that was held in Harvard in May 1920 to weed out homosexuals.

The secret court was held when a Harvard student, Cyril Wilcox, committed suicide and his brother brought evidence of homosexual activity to the university authorities.[34] Under the direction of Lowell, more than thirty interviews were conducted behind closed doors. The inquiry revealed that a number of men were involved in homosexual parties where, according to one witness, 'the most disgusting and disgraceful and revolting acts of degeneracy and depravity took place openly in plain view of all present'. After the inquiry, eight students were expelled, an assistant professor dismissed and a recent graduate disowned by the university. One of the students expelled, Eugene R. Cummings, committed suicide just days after the court's verdict was relayed to him.

During the 1920s and 1930s in the US, the authorities began to enact discriminatory measures to combat homosexuality and the act of sodomy was open to criminal prosecution in all fifty states.[34] Kingsley had always courted privacy. Since childhood and the appalling scandal that had raged for years over his father's sexual transgressions, Kingsley had greatly dreaded adverse publicity. The fear of becoming embroiled in a public scandal or criminal prosecution if the true nature of his sexual leanings became known must have been intense. Lucy must also have worried deeply, for fear that Kingsley's professional reputation would be tarnished. It was therefore of paramount importance that Kingsley's sexual orientation remain a closely guarded secret.

All through this time, Kingsley continued to lecture and to write. His lecture *An Egyptian Legend in Ireland* (1929) was published by the Philipp University of Marburg. Kingsley was becoming increasingly fascinated by Irish High Crosses. He postulated that this iconography derived from legends that were formulated in Egypt and were later carried by Egyptian hermits, who had embraced Christianity, to centres in France and Ireland.[35]

The main family event to take place during 1929 was the marriage of Joyce Porter to James Rae Arneill, a surgeon from Denver, Colorado. Joyce had graduated as a nurse from the Yale School of Nursing.[36] The marriage took place at Blachley Lodge on 22 June, and Joyce's sister Beatrice was maid of honour. Louis's only son, Louis Junior, was one of the ushers.

On 23 June the Porters sailed from Boston on the SS *Cedric*. Lucy wrote in her diary: 'A reasonable crossing. The days as uneventful as the sea. But we enjoyed them.'[37] They arrived at Queenstown on 1 July and travelled on to Liverpool.[38] Lucy's sisters arrived at Marble Hill on 2 July and stayed until 9 August. The Porters arrived in Donegal on 8 July and planned to remain at Marble Hill for two months. Ruth took over the housekeeping duties to spare Lucy, whose back was still giving trouble. A host of other guests arrived to stay with the Porters during July and August, including Mrs Osgood, Miss Nourse, Miss Williamson, Eric Nobbs and Russell Hitchcock. Hitchcock had studied at Harvard in the 1920s, taking several of Kingsley's classes.[39] The two men had developed a friendship and Hitchcock was a frequent visitor to Elmwood. Lunches and dinners were arranged and invitations received, including one from Canon Mitchell on 13 August.[40]

Despite the holiday atmosphere, Kingsley had other matters on his mind. He greatly feared public scandal and social alienation if rumours ever circulated at Harvard about his homosexual tendencies. Although Harvard's position on homosexuality was extreme, Kingsley was known by all to be a happily married man and there was no discernible reason to suspect him of any sexual indiscretion. However, on 29 August 1929 he drafted a letter to Edward Forbes and Paul Sachs, stating that he was thinking of resigning his Harvard post, citing his misgivings about his suitability as a modern researcher: 'With the great development of archaeology in the last few years the complexion of things has changed. It is no longer a field for a pioneer, but for co-operative production. The peculiar advantages I once possessed no longer count.'[41]

Kingsley's resignation was not accepted.[42] At least for the moment he was safe in his haven at Marble Hill. There was also the great consolation of meeting George Russell, known as Æ, who was their neighbour at Marble Hill, and they frequently invited him to dinner.[43] On the first evening they dined together, Kingsley and Æ immediately launched into an all-night conversation that delighted and inspired them both.

For thirty summers Æ had visited Donegal.[44] He stayed in a cottage in Ballymore. He was an Irish poet, painter, economist and philosopher,[45] and had known all the leading literary, artistic and political Irish figures, including William Butler Yeats, George Bernard Shaw, Lady Gregory, Harry Clarke, Padraic Pearse and Thomas MacDonagh. Publicity pamphlets printed for his second American lecture tour described him thus: 'Æ truly belongs to another age – an age when men had time to sit and talk and think and live. Contact with him is contact with peace and beauty.'

The Porters took many trips around County Donegal. Soon Kingsley discovered Lough Veagh and it was not long before he arrived at Glenveagh Castle.[46] Glenveagh derives from the Irish, *Gleann Bheatha* (the Glen of the Birch), and is located in the heart of the Derryveagh Mountains, in the remote north-west county of Donegal. The nineteenth-century castle is set within the hauntingly beautiful wilderness of rugged mountains and sparkling lakes. The raw beauty of the lakes and mountains must have reminded Kingsley of his carefree visits to the Adirondacks in New York State as a youth. This had always been his favourite holiday destination in the US, where he had swum, walked, hunted and fished with his brothers, and he had honeymooned there with Lucy in 1912.

When Kingsley first saw Glenveagh Castle it had been neglected since 1916. Its former owner, Cornelia Wadsworth Ritchie Adair, wife

31. Glenveagh Castle, set amid the spectacular lakes
and Derryveagh Mountains in Donegal; Glenveagh Castle exterior.
Both Michael Cullen.

32. View of Lake George, Adirondacks Region, New York, 1912.
Harvard University Archives, HUG 1706.125 (3).

of the notorious John George Adair, decided to remain in England, no longer returning to spend her summers in Donegal.[47] When Mrs Adair died childless in 1921 the castle remained unoccupied, until the anti-Treaty forces used the castle and grounds as their centre of operation during the Irish Civil War. When the Free State Army began to approach in 1922, General Joseph Sweeney of the anti-Treaty forces gave the command to Peadar O'Donnell to burn the castle to the ground.[48] Luckily for Donegal and for Kingsley Porter, O'Donnell disobeyed the order and the castle was left intact.

For Kingsley, the Victorian castellated mansion with an estate of over 30,000 acres of spectacular landscape[49] provided him with the opportunity to indulge his quixotic fantasies by becoming Lord of the Manor. It was also the perfect location to display his rare books and valuable collection of medieval art. He had also discovered a magnificent refuge, a world far removed from Harvard and from New England's puritanical social mores.

The beauty and rawness of the Donegal landscape had instantly ensnared Kingsley. Since 1919 he had set his mind on buying a home outside of the United States. He could have chosen any idyllic location but a mixture of fate, adventure and personal upheaval had brought him to the most north-westerly county of Ireland. Although Kingsley's romantic spirit viewed Ireland as a temple of glorious learning, artistic excellence and unrivalled heritage, its political and social structures were anything but enlightened.

The new Irish Free State had recently emerged after 800 years of British repression. Elections were conducted and a government was formed but the real power and influence lay in the hands of the Catholic Church. The State was governed by a 'chauvinistic and isolationist mentality... [that] restricted freedom of expression, and of intellectual and imaginative growth'.[50] Although Ireland possessed a great literary and artistic heritage, some of its most brilliant writers, such as James Joyce and George Bernard Shaw, chose to leave Ireland to pursue their creative expression in a freer and more liberal environment.

As the Porters arrived in Donegal that summer, the government had just passed the Censorship of Publications Act on 11 July 1929.[51] This Act banned works that were considered of dubious moral character. Harry Clarke, renowned stained-glass artist and friend of Æ, was about to have his masterpiece, *The Geneva Window*, rejected by that same government. The window had been commissioned by the government to represent Ireland at the International Labour Court in Geneva. It depicted scenes from works by Irish writers and included several sexually suggestive images and nude figures that offended the Catholic Church. For those seeking a haven far removed from fundamentalism in 1929, Ireland was not a wonderful choice.

From his first glimpse of Glenveagh, Kingsley was determined to secure the property. The castle and estate were on the market and Kingsley immediately set about completing the transaction. On 4 September he invited the estate agents for Glenveagh to dine at Marble Hill.[52] Lucy had pencilled in her diary that they would return to the US on 7 September, but the discovery of Glenveagh had changed everything. On Sunday 8 September, another invitation was issued to the Glenveagh agents who represented the executors of Mrs Adair's estate. The Porters had finally located their second home and they subsequently purchased the castle and entire estate for £5,000.[53]

Kingsley and Lucy had only recently completed the renovation of Elmwood but now they faced the prospect of salvaging a castle that had been badly neglected for well over a decade. During the Irish Civil War, much of the panelling had been burnt as firewood and very little of the original furniture was left.[54] Over the coming months Lucy helped Kingsley to redesign the decor, to keep the sense of antiquity while also building in modern conveniences. Plans were made to have a conical roof added to the round tower and then to paint and redecorate all of the rooms. The Porters managed to buy some of Mrs Adair's original furniture that was being sold at auction. They also paid ninety pounds for marble fireplaces from Ards House that had previously been owned by the Stewarts but was purchased by the Capuchin Friary. The fireplaces were installed on the ground floor of the Castle.[55]

On 17 September the Porters finally left Marble Hill.[56] They travelled to Liverpool and then on to Paris, and on 22 September they boarded a train to Barcelona. Lucy wrote in her diary on Monday 23 September: 'College opens.' Unlike their other adventures in Europe, this trip was hurried, essentially a way for Kingsley to borrow a little more time before returning to Harvard. On 5 October, the Porters finally sailed for America on the SS *Laconia*.

Throughout October the Porters' life at Elmwood resumed its usual pattern. Whatever catastrophe Kingsley feared would come to pass on returning to Harvard never materialized and he quietly resumed his lectures.[57] Lucy continued to entertain family and friends, attended dinner engagements, symphony concerts and college teas.[58] Monday 21 October was the Golden Wedding anniversary of Aunt Fanny and Uncle Schuyler, and on Thursday 24 October the Porters entertained their niece, Louise, before travelling to spend the weekend with the Merritts. That Thursday, however, was to take on monumental significance, as it was the day when the stock market at Wall Street collapsed and vast fortunes were wiped out within hours. This event signalled the Great Depression, that lasted for twelve years. The Porters were fortunate that most of their wealth remained intact.

In the midst of this personal and national torment, Kingsley's second play, *The Virgin and the Clerk*, was published. Set in the eleventh century, it is the story of a monk who sells his soul to the devil for the sake of art and friendship, but is finally rescued by the miracle of the Virgin.[59] There is one central question that is posed by the leading character, Theophilus: 'A man has the right to sacrifice himself, but has he the right to sacrifice others?'[60] In the coming years, this was a leading question that Kingsley would have to grapple with.

Chapter eleven

Glenveagh Castle and Inishbofin

Throughout the winter of 1929 and the spring of 1930, the Porters continued entertaining at Elmwood. On Monday 11 November, Lucy organized an intimate dinner party that included Kingsley's fellow professor at Harvard, Chandler Post, Lucy's close friend Rose Dexter, and Lucy's sister Ruth.[1] In December it appears that their niece Beatrice had a health scare. Kingsley wrote to Louis, advocating that Beatrice and her mother, Marion, should travel to Elmwood and see Dr Osgood.[2]

The remaining weeks of 1929 were packed with social engagements, culminating in an archaeological conference from 26 December that Kingsley attended.[3] Lucy marked on her engagement pad that she was alone during Christmas and the following two weeks. Besides attendance at the three-day conference, there was no mention of where Kingsley had spent his vacation. Lucy travelled to Washington and stayed there for several days before returning to Elmwood. Perhaps she needed time alone to reflect on the enormity of her bizarre marital situation. Whatever the circumstances of their apparent separation that Christmas, Lucy continued to be the personification of the ever-loving wife.

On the morning of 3 February 1930, Dr Osgood was called to Elmwood.[4] Whether Kingsley's depression had reoccurred or Lucy's back was giving trouble, the reason for the visit was not recorded. Lucy spent the remainder of that day alone. Dr Osgood also arrived the following afternoon, and two days later a doctor was again summoned.

Lucy's engagement pad shows a sudden lack of appointments and there is an increase in her evenings spent alone. Lucy's niece Ellen arrived on 16 February and they went to a symphony together.

By the spring of 1930, Kingsley was making plans to return to Glenveagh Castle for the summer; his need for space and distance from Harvard had become acute. When Kingsley broke the news to Berenson, however, he was appalled. On 16 February 1930, Berenson conveyed his dismay to their mutual friend, Paul Sachs:

> I am not happy about Kingsley. I regard his settling in Ireland with alarm, I wonder on how many blarney stones he will sit, & Lucy with him. He, like myself, may not be made for teaching and administration, but he is made to be a student. I cannot understand this shrinking from everything classical and his longing for the backwashiest puddles and stagnant pools of civilization. I suppose he too is a tree that the gods will not allow to pierce the sky.[5]

Berenson's opinion that Ireland was a backward, impoverished nation was not unfounded. The Great Depression that had hit the States in 1929 also wreaked havoc in Europe, causing widespread unemployment and economic hardship.[6] Since Ireland had been a colonized country for eight centuries and had only recently gained a degree of independence, its economic position was poor even before the Depression. The view of Ireland as a backward country, populated by poverty-stricken peasants, with substandard housing and hygiene, and a railway system where trains never ran on time, was widespread.[7] None of this affected Kingsley, however, as he loved the idea of living in a quaint, rural setting, isolated from progress, reminiscent of a medieval hamlet, as though the Industrial Revolution had never occurred.[8] Safe in a world of great economic and social privilege, he could well afford to indulge his romantic notions of a simpler, bygone age.

In February and March 1930, Kingsley gave a series of lectures at the Metropolitan Museum of Art in New York, entitled 'The Crosses and

Culture of Ireland'.[9] In his first lecture, entitled 'St Patrick and the Pagans', Kingsley stated:

> The Irish are thus perhaps the oldest of all European races. While the rest of the West has been melted down in the pot of invasion and recast in a different mould, the Irish are racially still what they have been since the La Tène period. No other existing culture of the Occident can boast over two millenniums of uninterrupted development.[10]

Kingsley put forward the premise that it was St Patrick and the coming of Christianity that brought foreign artistic influences to Ireland, including Egyptian symbolism that was incorporated into the decoration of High Crosses by Irish craftsmen: 'the first Christian art of Ireland had a strong Coptic tinge... It is thus that came about a curious phenomenon: an art that originated on the shores of the Nile passed to the extreme western island of Europe, and then returned to the centres of the Continent.'[11]

In early March, Kingsley dined with the Forbes'.[12] Lucy spent more evenings alone at Elmwood before travelling to spend three days in New York. Kingsley gave his first lecture at the Fogg Art Museum on 13 March: once again he spoke about his latest burning passion: 'The Crosses and Culture of Ireland'. The following week, on 18 March, he gave the second part of his lecture, entitled 'Colmcille'.[13]

From mid-March the Porters began entertaining again.[14] It was as though their forthcoming journey to their new home in Glenveagh Castle had given the couple a renewed optimism. The pending crisis had passed and their usual social life could be resumed. On 25 March, Kingsley gave his final lecture in the Irish series at the Fogg Art Museum. Early April witnessed Kingsley's dream being realized when his play *The Virgin and the Clerk* was performed by the Carnegie Institute. The Porters stayed in Pittsburgh from Sunday 30 March to Friday 4 April, to be present during rehearsals and to witness the main performance of the play that was held on the evening of Wednesday 2 April.

The remainder of April and the whole month of May were busy socially for the Porters, though Lucy still recorded that many evenings were spent alone.[15] On Sunday 11 May at 4 p.m. they set sail for Ireland. The following Sunday they arrived in Cobh and headed straight for Marble Hill; their plan was to remain at Marble Hill for a few weeks until some basic renovations on Glenveagh Castle had been completed. On 14 June, Kingsley and Lucy left Marble Hill, travelling to Liverpool and then on to London to begin a two-week holiday in Europe. They arrived in Paris on 17 June, and two days later they travelled by train to Florence. By late June they had returned to Ireland and were in the process of closing up Marble Hill and moving to Glenveagh Castle.

It is not known if the Porters were aware of the curse that had been put on the owners of Glenveagh. The first owner, John George Adair, known as Black Jack, became infamous for evicting defenceless tenants during the famine.[16] A woman whose family was evicted is reputed to have cursed Adair and all the future owners of the castle, swearing that they would remain childless and would die suddenly.[17] Adair had indeed suffered this fate.

The Porters moved into Glenveagh Castle on 16 July. Lucy marked in her appointment pad: 'Glenveagh – us.'[18] Ever since first setting eyes on Glenveagh, Kingsley had fallen under its spell. Always a strong swimmer and walker, he spent hours outdoors in the lakes and hills around Glenveagh.[19] The granite castle was also the perfect home for a man who loved all things medieval, where he could at last work, relax and dine in the most exquisite surroundings. The estate held another gem that entranced Kingsley: St Columcille, also known as Columba, was reputed to have been born at Gartan.[20] A monument on the estate is inscribed: 'Birthplace of St Columba 521–597. Son of Felim and Eithne of the Royal House at Aileach and Leinster. Grandson of Conal Culban. Founder of Columba Works in Ireland and Scotland.'[21]

Lucy later described Kingsley's growing attraction to Ireland: 'His thought was constantly returning to Ireland. The more he knew of its art, its ancient language, and its literature, the more the land possessed him… Another outcome of the spell of that land was the purchase of Glenveagh Castle. Alone in the wilds of Donegal, it stands on a mountain-girthed lake.'[22]

As an archaeologist, Kingsley must have felt the same sense of excitement as when he first discovered medieval monuments in Spain. Ireland was a land whose people had been brought to their knees by colonialism, poverty and constant revolutions, but Ireland also had a glorious past, once peopled by saints and scholars who had brought Christianity to Europe in the Early and Middle Ages. These artists and teachers had also shared their mastery of arts, crafts and manuscript illumination with the rest of Europe.

The Porters now enjoyed a period of deep solitude. Lucy described Glenveagh as 'a little kingdom of high mountains, wild moorlands, lakes and streams, and the nearest post office, seven miles away, was Mínanlábáin'.[23] On Monday 28 July they enjoyed a walk to the Poison Gap, a spectacular gorge surrounded by purple mountains and oozing with ancient legends.[24] The following day they picnicked in the castle grounds. Suddenly, life was slow and peaceful and there was no great need to drive anywhere. Both Lucy and Kingsley were content to spend that week alone, soaking up the mesmerizing beauty of the lakes, mountains and ever-changing light.

Lucy loved the castle gardens, the pleasure grounds and kitchen garden that occupied several acres.[25] She took an active interest in the planting of new shrubs and flowers, particularly rhododendrons. She also asked the gardener, Matt Armour, to sow dahlia seeds that later began to thrive and blossom. Lucy also enjoyed going hillwalking with Kingsley, safe in their own realm where all was beauty and tranquillity: 'When Kingsley and I walked inland over the high boglands we sometimes kicked up a dust of golden bees from the purple heather. This always meant bright sunshine so that even with a casual glance we could plainly distinguish four dots on the open Atlantic – the Tory archipelago.'[26]

On Wednesday 6 August they drove to Rosapenna and Londonderry.[27] The following Saturday their friend Russell Hitchcock arrived from the US to stay at Glenveagh. They also kept in close contact with their good friend, Æ. A correspondence developed between the Porters and Æ, and the letters were sent and collected from the post office at Mínanlábáin.[28]

The quiet beauty of Glenveagh was a perfect vantage point for Kingsley to continue his study of Irish High Crosses. He began to learn Irish and to conduct an in-depth study of the folklore and legends of Ireland by consulting many literary sources on the lives of Irish saints.[29] He also studied the iconography of various illuminated manuscripts and continued his study of the symbols carved on High Crosses located throughout Ireland.

It was during his years in Ireland that Kingsley wrote three plays that remained unpublished until 1952.[30] The first play, *Pope Joan*, is based on a medieval continental legend and clearly shows Kingsley's love affair with islands and the sea:

> We who live inland know nothing of islands. We never know what the sea is like with its spaces, its storms, its sadness, its exultation. We have never felt the wild wind sweeping unbroken from the rim of the world. We know nothing of islands. Why, the sea is full of islands, thousands of them, of all sizes – some with mountains rising high out of the water, others with low rocks and green fields and beaches with sea-birds. It is in islands that there is magic. It is in islands one breathes the fresh, salt air. Heavy-footed dwellers on the mainland never know joy. It is the island-dweller whose heart leaps and sings.

The other two plays were entitled *Conchobar's House* and *Columcille Goes*. Both plays deal with Irish heroes: legendary King Conchobar of Ulster and Kingsley's favourite saint, Columcille. St Columcille appealed deeply to his imagination, for Kingsley secretly yearned for a solitary life where he could live in a stone hut, spending his days studying and writing, surrounded by natural beauty and the ever-changing seasons.[31] Then there would be no responsibilities, no one to please and no pretence. The simplicity of a hermit's life might even bring him peace and stillness.

On Saturday 13 September the Porters sailed for New York in time for Kingsley to teach the autumn term at Harvard.[32] During the remainder of September and October, engagements were slack and there were a lot of 'Alone' times for Lucy. During November and December their social calendar was filled once again with concerts, lunches and dinners. Yet Glenveagh and Ireland were still very much on Kingsley's mind. Now aged 47, he had already explored many countries, spending months at a time in several European cities, but there was something different about his interest in Donegal. The ancient culture, the spectacular untainted landscape, the deep seclusion in a granite castle at the edge of a glorious lake – all this appealed deeply to Kingsley's imaginative nature.

To Kingsley, the entire estate of Glenveagh was idyllic, except there was no sea. The archipelago of islands off the Donegal coast included two inhabited islands, Tory and Inishbofin. The nearest island, Inishbofin is a landmass of just 300 acres. It lies almost 4.3 kilometres (just over two-and-a-half miles) off the shore from Magheraroarty on the Donegal coast. In 1931 just thirty people lived on the island.[33] They made their meagre living from fishing and farming. In spring and summer they fished for lobster, crab and Atlantic salmon, and gathered shellfish and edible seaweeds such as *cairrigin* (carrageen) and *creathnach* (dulse) from the rocks.[34] Their village, An Clachan, was little more than a scattering of houses. At night-time the island was pitch black, lit only by moonbeams and starlight.[35] The islanders were native Irish speakers. As a visitor to the island reported, 'the islanders were different; they kept to themselves, but if they took you in, you couldn't find finer people'.

Even while Kingsley was immersed in his other life of Harvard and Elmwood, he was making plans to build a fisherman's hut on Inishbofin. For the moment, this was the closest he could get to building his own hermitage. Lucy made no remarks in her diary as to what she thought of Kingsley's latest plan to establish a summer residence on a tiny island in the Atlantic. Kingsley thought up these unusual schemes and then expected Lucy to support them. Walter Muir Whitehill, a student of Kingsley's and a visitor to Glenveagh, unwittingly summed up their relationship in his description of the couple walking out together: 'That her short quick steps kept pace with his strides happened because she intensely willed it so.'[36]

On 21 November 1930, Kingsley received a reply to his enquiry from his contact in Donegal, Joseph McCarthy, about renting the beach from the islanders during the summer months so he could have total privacy:

Dear Sir,

. . . I had some difficulty in getting in touch with the Inishboffin people owing to stormy weather but I was speaking to a few of the principal people on the island about the exclusive right to bathing on the beach. They are willing to facilitate you as much as possible, but they point out that they will be using the beach for drying and burning seaweed during the months of May, June and possibly a part of July, (the season for burning seaweed does not always extend beyond the end of June). After that period they are willing to let you use the beach. In fact, they would have no objection to you using the beach at any time, but as they point out, the beach would be littered with seaweed (which when burning has a rather obnoxious odour) during the period already mentioned. They informed me that the exact number of landholders who have a claim on the beach is 30, they are also of opinion that the sum of £60.00 would be sufficient to compensate them for any privilege you would require. That sum does not include the site for the bathing box on Coll's property which would be £21.00. I am of opinion that if you did purchase the site, the Coll people should not be paid anything extra, that would mean that you would have only 27 to deal with which at £2 per head would be only £54.00. The ground that I thought would be most suitable is situated about 50 yards on the High Water bank on the beach on the North East side of the Island. Hoping that this will meet with your approval.

Yours truly,
Joseph McCarthy

The Size of the plot I mentioned to Colls was 30x20 feet but I gave them to understand that that was only approximate.[37]

Æ spent the winter of 1930 in the US, lecturing on economics, literature and poetry.[38] During the Boston leg of his visit he stayed with the Porters at Elmwood. Kingsley and Æ immediately launched into their usual deep discussions, oblivious to all that was going on around them. On the afternoon of Wednesday 7 January 1931, the Porters hosted a special lunch in honour of Æ.[39] Lucy gathered together a group of friends to meet Æ, including Dr Ross, Harry Davis and Mr Smith, and they were all enraptured by his remarkable eloquence.

The following Friday, 9 January, Lucy arranged a special dinner for the President of Harvard, Abbott Lowell, and a number of other academics, including Dr Lewis Perry, Principal of Exeter Academy in New Hampshire.[40] To ensure the success of the evening, Lucy left nothing to chance, even drawing out the seating arrangements in her engagement diary. The following week was again filled with social events: Lucy attended productions of *Hamlet* and *As You Like It*, while Kingsley spent time in New York. Then on Saturday 17 January a large dinner party for fifty people was held at Elmwood, again in honour of Æ. He stayed with the Porters for several days and lectured in various venues, including the community church and the City Club in Boston.

During the remaining weeks of January and the entire month of February the Porters were involved in a constant stream of engagements.[41] Lucy attended weekly meetings of the Tuesday Club and the Mayflower Club, and also went to French lectures every Tuesday morning. On 21 January, Kingsley gave a lecture at the Old Valance Club, and he also held lectures for his students every

Wednesday afternoon at Elmwood. During the last week of January the Porters took a mini-break and visited Stamford, Washington, Baltimore and New York before returning to Cambridge. The couple also regularly attended theatre and concert performances.

It was during the early months of 1931 that the controversy over Kingsley's transportation of the Sahagún sarcophagus slab to Cambridge erupted.[42] The Duke of Alba discovered that the sacred burial slab had been removed from León and shipped to Harvard. He immediately set about trying to have the coffin lid restored to its rightful place in Spain. The Spanish government also got involved in the negotiations with the Fogg Art Museum. Before any deal was reached, however, the Spanish King Alfonso XIII was overthrown by a revolution. For the time being, the sarcophagus slab remained on display at Harvard.

On Friday 13 March the Porters left Elmwood and travelled to New York, and at midnight they set sail for Ireland, now their second home.[43] Their local housekeepers, Mrs Molloy and Mrs Holmes, arrived the following Wednesday to begin work at the castle. Kingsley and Lucy enjoyed a week of tranquillity before their American friend Mrs Bird came to stay on 30 March. During April they took day trips to Derry and Dublin. On Saturday 18 April they travelled to Dublin to attend the wedding of their friends, George T. Rice of Westwood, Massachusetts, and Shelia Cornwallis Maude from Clondalkin.[44]

Lucy suffered with stomach pains for several weeks in late April and early May.[45] She rested for several days and the upset eventually cleared. Meanwhile, they began to explore Northern Ireland. They travelled to Armagh on 28 April, then on to Warrenport before making their way south to Dublin, where they stayed at the Shelbourne Hotel.

In May, Kingsley set about erecting a deer fence on the estate.[46] To satisfy his neighbours, he signed an agreement with each of them, allowing every family to graze their cattle between the existing line of the deer fence and the Calabber river. This agreement was favourably received by all concerned.

Kingsley had also purchased a rowing boat that he had christened *The Swan*,[47] but islanders considered the name to be a bad omen.

Despite the choppiness of the sea, Lucy often accompanied Kingsley as he rowed the little boat to the island. Owen McGee lived on the mainland and took care of Kingsley's rowing boat. On Thursday 7 May, Kingsley persuaded Lucy to row with him to the island.[48] Lucy recorded in her diary: 'Rowed from Magheraroarty to Inishbofin. Tea with Mrs Ferry while K walked to our "property". He was entranced with it.'

33. Repairs to ruined cottage on Inishbofin, photograph, c. 1929.
Harvard University Archives, HUG 1706.125 (10).

Kingsley was busy finding a local builder to erect his fisherman's hut on Inishbofin. On 13 May he received a reply from Edward Dixon, of Meenlaragh in Gortahork.[49] Dixon estimated that the cost of building the hut would be £325. Kingsley proceeded with the erection of the small stone hut that was to be located on the deserted eastern side of the island. None of the islanders would have lived there as they considered it too wild and lonely and too close to the treacherous cliffs.[50] Lucy described the cliffs as being 'like fingers narrowly opened, [that] stretch into the wide Atlantic'.[51]

Pat Coll was a fisherman who lived on the island.[52] He had lived through a gruesome tragedy when his boat capsized and he had to watch helplessly as his uncle and two cousins let go of the wreckage and drowned. Only he had been rescued. He was employed by the Porters to look after the hut.

Lucy and Kingsley began to build up a wide circle of friends in Donegal. On 14 May, they invited the local Catholic clergy to lunch: Fr Gallagher, Fr Cunningham and Fr McDwyer.[53] To keep the peace with all denominations, on 16 May the local Dean was asked to lunch. The Porters spent three days in Dublin in early June consulting Dr Lane, but Lucy gave no indication in her diary as to the reason for the appointment. They left Dublin on 11 June and drove to Athlone; the following day they stayed in Galway and then drove on to visit Tuam.

On 18 June they stayed at Fort Royal, a magnificent country house on the edge of Lough Swilly, in Rathmullan, north Donegal.[54] They also visited Castle Stewart in Co. Tyrone and called in to have tea with Lady Stewart. July proved to be a busy month for entertaining. Lucy's niece Ellen arrived, and also Lucy's good friend Mrs Crankshaw. When Æ came to stay at Glenveagh, Kingsley immediately rowed him to Inishbofin to survey his beloved island retreat. According to Lucy, 'He did not greatly enjoy it, nor was he interested in the individual islanders. He was too used to dwell on "things invisible to mortal sight" to differentiate people who had no intimate connection with his own life nor with his inner thought.'[55]

In the evenings, after dinner, Kingsley and Lucy would bring their guests to their favourite room located in the tower. Lucy described their evening ritual of relaxing in the spectacular library that overlooked the lake: 'The evenings at Glenveagh would find everyone gathered about Æ before the open turf fire in the library. This room, high in the tower, was swung over the lake into the sunset which lingered into the night, tinging to gold the orange of Biddie O'Donnell's home-spun curtains.'[56]

On Thursday 23 July Lucy went to Dublin with Ellen, while Kingsley and Æ brought Fr Gallagher to visit Dr Lane.[57] From Dublin they drove to Kells and Monasterboice, where they stopped off to study the wonderful High Crosses. On 25 July, Lucy brought Ellen to Adare

34. Library in Glenveagh Castle.
Michael Cullen.

for lunch and afterwards they visited Earl Dunraven's estate, before continuing their drive as far as Muckross House in Killarney.

The Porters rowed to Inishbofin on Wednesday 5 August, and on the Friday they brought Fr Gallagher to the island.[58] They visited Derry on 18 August and called into the Deanery there; on 22 August, Lucy organized a garden party and flower day as part of the open day at Glenveagh Castle.[59]

While Æ was staying at Glenveagh, Kingsley commissioned him to paint four canvasses.[60] Æ wrote to Kingsley on 7 August, telling him that the delay in sending the completed pictures was due to the framing. The paintings had arrived safely by 20 August, when Æ wrote again, hoping that 'the pictures will not prove too tiresome possessions'.[61]

The Porters were delighted with the paintings and hung them in the library, where they still remain to this day. Each of the paintings is a celebration of nature, creating a play of shadow and light, in rich tones of blue, green and ochre. The atmosphere created in all the works is one of mirth and lightness, as children play in the depths of the forest; nymphs fly beside cotton-wool clouds in a turquoise sky; a woman and

35. Æ (George Russell). Courtesy of Wikipedia Commons.
Paintings by Æ in Glenveagh Castle library.
Michael Cullen.

child sit peering at the magnificence of the emerald fields and purple hills; and children skip and dance in a shady meadow beside a lake.

During September 1931 the Porters played host to a number of guests. Mrs Appleton stayed for two weeks, while Lucy's sisters and a friend, Henrietta, remained until mid-October.[62] Lucy recorded in her engagement diary that the Garthorne-Hardys visited from 19 September.[63] Geoffrey Garthorne-Hardy was an author, adventurer and specialist of Norse history, who had lost a finger in the Boer war and a foot in the First World War. Geoffrey and his wife signed the guest book at Glenveagh Castle. Many years later, Lucy published a book entitled *Glenveagh Castle: Visitors' Book: 1931–1937*, in which she quoted from the comments inscribed by her guests, including the Garthorne-Hardys, along with two illustrations by Æ.[64]

Kingsley was also warmly welcomed into the circle of Irish academics, including the Royal Society of Antiquaries. On the evening of Tuesday 29 September, he read a paper at the Society's headquarters in Merrion Square, Dublin, on the relic of Labhraidh Loingseach that was housed in the sacristy of Armagh Cathedral.[65] The relic depicted the Irish chieftain as having ears like a horse. According to the legend, the chieftain used to have every barber who cut his hair killed, in case they might speak about his blemish.

The Crosses and Culture of Ireland was published by Yale University Press in 1931. In this controversial work, Kingsley interpreted the scenes carved on High Crosses in terms of Irish mythology and the lives of saints, instead of the usual scriptural interpretations.[66] Kingsley asserted that Irish High Crosses had developed as an art form during the Viking invasions when manuscript illumination was in decline.[67] He theorized that 'the constant pillaging of monasteries by the Danes may have forced the Celts into a form of artistic expression not so easily destroyed by a raiding party. A stone cross is not conveniently either burned or stolen.'

He again proffered the theory that Egyptian artistic influences had somehow filtered into Ireland during the early years of Christianity.[68] Irish monks and scholars then carried the wealth of its artistic tradition to the rest of Europe during the sixth to the ninth centuries. The work was a daring and highly original interpretation of the development of Irish symbolism.[69] Kingsley's portrayal of Ireland as an isolated haven for artists and writers with little connection to the rest of Europe, with devotion to a Church that was rooted in Irish mysticism rather than being influenced by Rome, was based on his own fantastical view of Ireland, rather than being derived from historical fact. Kingsley had taken his cue from the decades of the Celtic Revival, when everything Irish was lauded and given prominence, in order to instil a sense of national pride and positive Gaelic identity.

On the whole, the book was very well received as a major contribution to the study of High Crosses, though some of Kingsley's
contemporaries were sceptical of his novel interpretations.[70] The wealth
of detailed photographs of High Crosses throughout the book did,
however, receive unanimous praise.

Æ wrote to Kingsley on 13 October to thank him for his copy of
the book and to offer his congratulations: 'What an immensity of
labour and research went to the making of your book ... What a feeling
for beautiful design is in many of these crosses and the carvings on
them. You have certainly made a fine contribution to the culture of
your adopted country.'[71]

Lucy often surrounded herself with guests while Kingsley went
hillwalking or studied at his desk in the library.[72] A visitor to Glenveagh
recorded her impressions of the Castle and its mistress:

> We drove several miles after the castle came into sight at the
> edge of the lake, a turreted stone building, very romantic.
> Whitesides, a very, very proper butler let us in; the epitome of
> proper butlers, pale, mask-like face, adequate and imperturbable,
> slightly hunchbacked. Lucy Porter is small, vivacious, keen,
> kindly, busy. We went into the garden where guests were playing
> croquet. Father Gallagher there, very republican RC, Lucy
> Porter's two sisters, the Misses Wallace, and Mr Clapham, an
> English high-up official in Preservation of Ancient Monuments
> Bureau.[73]

Lucy enjoyed showing guests around the castle. The castle entrance
was through a small hallway that Lucy had decorated with shell
designs.[74] Then throughout the castle there were narrow corridors that
added a sense of mystery and romance. The main rooms on the ground
floor were the drawing room, where guests were entertained, and the
study. The dining room contained an enormous mahogany dinner
table, decorated with a pale-blue cloth and napkins. This was where
guests would sit down to dinner, to dine on the finest of fare. In

summer, delicious desserts were served, in vivid blue bowls, of wild fruits and currants from the hot houses. Guests would also be treated to various fine wines, liqueurs and coffees, served in the drawing room.

Then there was the magnificent library, situated on the first floor of the tower, where Kingsley liked to sit at his desk, with the medieval statue of St Jerome facing him, and survey the glittering lake below.[75] Here he was surrounded by his collection of books housed in an enormous dark mahogany bookcase. Lucy was particularly proud of the master bedroom with an enormous mahogany bed and canopy that she had had transported to Glenveagh. The remaining rooms were decorated with exquisite carpets and wall hangings that had been specially chosen by Kingsley to fit in with the medieval sculptures, paintings and antiques. Lucy often added an extra touch to the guest rooms when her favourite flowers were in bloom: a vase of red dahlias.

36. Master bedroom in Glenveagh Castle.
Michael Cullen.

Lucy also loved going for walks with her guests, along Kingsley's favourite path that was edged thickly on either side with huge rhododendrons.[76] Then there were the exotic peacocks, one pure white, which sat along the battlements over the courtyard, occasionally going over to the window to get crumbs from the dinner guests.[77]

Kingsley now possessed three homes, each appealing to a different aspect of his psyche. Elmwood, his colonial mansion, was part of his academic world, where he spent a great deal of time writing, teaching and entertaining colleagues. Glenveagh was his magical kingdom, his boyhood dream of climbing mountains and swimming in lakes, of hunting deer in the forests and roaming through miles of open fields. Glenveagh Castle was an abode fit for a medieval prince, perfect as a showcase for his Italian paintings and his vast collection of rare books. The hut on Inishbofin was his pilgrim's sanctuary, an austere stone refuge that was worthy of his hero, Columcille, with a view of the sea from his open door. In Donegal, so many facets of Kingsley's psyche began to be fulfilled. Yet, there was one space remaining that nothing so far had managed to fill.

Chapter twelve

Ellis and the Ménage à Trois

Despite the tranquillity of Glenveagh, Kingsley continued to have bouts of depression. He did not return to Harvard that September to begin the autumn term. On Sunday 4 October 1931, Lucy wrote in her diary: 'K to bed with headache.'[1] Then suddenly the next morning the Porters left for London. Lucy's plans to spend time with her sisters that week were crossed out in her diary: the trip to London must have been hastily undertaken. Kingsley finally made the decision to seek professional help, in the hope of finding a cure for his depression. The doctor he travelled to consult at his London premises was Havelock Ellis, British physician, psychologist and renowned sexologist. Kingsley would have known Dr Ellis's work from his studies of psychoanalysis. The book that Ellis had co-authored, *Sexual Inversion* (1896), was the first medical textbook in English that dealt with homosexuality.

Lucy was very sympathetic to her husband's situation and wished to help him in whatever way she could. Kingsley's subsequent appointments with Dr Ellis, their correspondence and the treatment that Ellis advised Kingsley to pursue remained a closely guarded secret, until Phyllis Grosskurth, Ellis's biographer, discovered the Porters' letters in 1980.[2]

During that first visit, Kingsley revealed to Ellis that he was a homosexual but had only realized this in mid-life. The 'cure' that Ellis recommended for Kingsley to alleviate his depression was an incredible one: an involvement with a 21-year-old American homosexual and aspiring novelist, Alan Campbell.[3] Campbell's birth name was George

37. Havelock Ellis, from Stefano Bolognini, *Havelock Ellis: Philosopher of Love* (Cambridge: Riverside Press, 1928), photograph by Houston Peterson.

W. Campbell. He had grown up in San Francisco before moving to London and becoming a patient of Ellis's.[4]

All through her married life, Lucy appears to have put her husband's desires above all else. Kingsley was her beloved companion. Her respect and admiration for him appears to have had no bounds. When faced with this extraordinary situation, Lucy agreed to Ellis's remarkable prescription and allowed Kingsley to take a young male lover. This must have stung Lucy to the very core, yet she appears to have supported Kingsley in every possible way. Perhaps the fact that a physician had sanctioned this singular arrangement made it easier for husband and wife to justify it. Ellis had also confided in the Porters that his own wife, Edith, was lesbian and that he had allowed her to take lovers.[5]

Lucy's appointment pad remains silent as to how this bizarre experiment affected her own state of mind. Lucy had been reared in a wealthy conservative New England home. It is probable that she had no lover until she met Kingsley so that her experience of sexuality and relationships was very proper, taking place within the sanctity of marriage. When faced with the most humiliating situation that any wife could encounter, Lucy somehow found justification for her husband's desire to take a male lover, suppressed her emotions and gave her consent. Always so careful to file their correspondence, the Porters removed every trace of their relationship with Ellis. Lucy's main objective from that moment was to keep the whole sordid affair secret. There was no one Lucy trusted enough to confide in. Even her diary was censored, though reading between the lines there are moments of heartache and loneliness that periodically filter through.

The Porters travelled to Oxford with a friend, E. McMillan, before returning to Ireland on Sunday 18 October.[6] The following Sunday, Lucy recorded in her engagement pad that they attended church. Perhaps the Porters had suddenly turned to religion as a panacea for Kingsley's depression, or maybe it was a way of mingling with the community. On Sunday 1 November, Kingsley was well enough to meet Mr Connor at 9 a.m. to discuss the erection of the deer fence on the estate. It was during that Sunday that Kingsley first wrote to Dr

Ellis, addressing him as 'Dear Mr Havelock Ellis': 'I should enjoy reading Campbell's manuscript if you care to send it to me. I shall be here until January 23rd... After that, my address is "Elmwood, Cambridge, Massachusetts".'[7]

Kingsley reported that he had read Ellis's *The Dance of Life*.[8] He was buoyant because he wholeheartedly agreed with Ellis's ideas: 'I remember Yeats telling how Spengler's philosophy had been revealed to him, a year or so before the publication of Spengler's book, by spirits who appeared to Mr Yeats. Perhaps similar spirits brought me knowledge of your thoughts!'

Ellis had apparently enclosed a letter that had been written by Alan Campbell to himself, so that Kingsley could get an idea of the type of person he was. Kingsley seemed to have formed a favourable impression of the young man: 'I was much interested in Campbell's letter which I return. He is lucky to have found his friend, and so early too. He is perhaps a bit Nietzschien in his treatment of his family. Yet, I know it is better and more right to be apparently cold-blooded than to be stiffed (sic).'[9]

On the following Sunday Kingsley was still unwell. Lucy recorded that 'K feared a headache, didn't go to church.'[10] In December, Kingsley again wrote to Ellis. By now, Kingsley viewed Ellis as a gifted mentor, almost as a wise father who could somehow lead him out of the mental torment he felt trapped in. Ellis had asked Campbell to send Kingsley a copy of his novel, *Starborn*, that he was trying to get published.[11] Kingsley reported to Ellis:

I have read 'Starborn' with emotion. Still you are right with your criticism and in judging it on the whole unsaleable. Still there are passages like the last page profound and moving, which it is quite extraordinary should have been written by so young a man.

I am returning the manuscript to Campbell and also sending him a letter expressing appreciation of his work and suggesting he stop over to see me in Ireland if he should decide to go to Calcutta via Europe instead of via Australia. As I think I mentioned to you, we shall be here only until January 23rd when we return to Cambridge.

Kingsley also discussed various books that Ellis had mentioned in his last letter.[12] At that time Ellis was reading *Soul of Spain*, and Kingsley had much to write about his own travels in Spain.

Despite the upheavals in the Porters' world, their guests continued to arrive. Milton Waldman came to stay on 25 November;[13] he was an American who worked in London as an editor. On 23 December, Mrs Crankshaw returned to spend Christmas at Glenveagh.

The Porters continued their correspondence with Æ, who was back in Dublin. His wife, Violet, had been ill and Lucy sent her a shawl.[14] Æ wrote to thank her, saying he had brought the shawl to the Adelaide Hospital where his wife was being treated: 'My wife desires me to thank you for a present which was beautiful to her eyes ... She cannot talk much but I think she likes me to be in her room. Yesterday she was able to read a little.'

Æ wrote again on 5 January 1932, saying he would have loved to visit them that winter but his wife's illness prevented it.[15] Nevertheless, he reminisced about the beauty of Donegal: 'You should be in the divine world of Donegal, and I think it is more wildly lovely in winter than at other times. I spent a good part of a winter on the west in Mayo and Donegal once and know what it is like, how unearthly the earth is.'

In early January, the Porters' friend Molly Childers visited Glenveagh.[16] When she left on 11 January, Kingsley and Lucy were left alone to walk the hills. This was the special time that Lucy enjoyed, when they would sit together in the library beside the open fire, while the pale winter sun dipped low behind the mountains, casting a wonderful glow on the glittering lake below. On 12 January, Lucy wrote in her diary: 'Only 12 days alone to departure.' Then she made a drawing of a little sad face.

The Porters returned to Cambridge on 23 January in time for Kingsley to teach the spring term.[17] While at Elmwood, Lucy recorded nothing in her engagement pad. It was as though she and Kingsley were merely going through the chore of living their American life, waiting expectantly for the following summer when they would once again return to Glenveagh.

Æ wrote to Kingsley on 17 February to tell him that his wife had died on 3 February.[18] He also told Kingsley that he hoped the economy would pick up in the US. Kingsley corresponded with Dr Ellis on 22 April.[19] He told Ellis that he was suffering from 'an over-loaded desk', and imagined that Ellis must be crushed by the amount of correspondence he had to deal with. He also wrote of his worry that he was taking up too much of the doctor's kindness and his time. He went on to describe the benefits that their therapeutic relationship was having on his state of mind: 'Hearing from you and writing to you have, in some way I do not fully understand, helped me more than I can hope ever to tell you: if patches of blue sky are now beginning to appear I know that it is fundamentally your doing.'

Kingsley told Ellis of his plan to return to Glenveagh in the summer and to finally meet Alan Campbell:

> Our plans for the summer are taking form. I am kept here rather late, as they are giving me a degree at Williams, but we sail on June 26th and go directly to Glenveagh. I should like to invite Campbell to visit us there for a week beginning July 5, but hesitate, never having seen him. May I leave the invitation in your good hands to pass on to him unless, when you see him, it should seem to you inadvisable?[20]

Kingsley also told Ellis about the circumstances of the death of a student at Harvard who had shot himself in a hotel room on 18 January.[21] The boy's father claimed the suicide was due to a nervous breakdown brought on by too much study, but the rumours circulating around Harvard claimed he was homosexual:

> The suicide I referred to was P.K. Stockton, a sophomore. I had met him at house parties and he had been to our house for

dinner once or twice. Of the details I know nothing beyond rumours of the usual indefinite type. The same sort of stories are circulating about one of the professors (or rather assistant professors) of philosophy who also committed suicide only a few days ago. And I see around me so many ruined lives. Yet any effort to help (the fundamental causes, of course, I mean) seems fraught with the anger of making a tragic situation more tragic still.[22]

It must indeed have been worrying for Kingsley and Lucy to be surrounded by stories of Harvard students and professors who were committing suicide because of their sexual tendencies. The need to escape to Glenveagh was becoming ever more urgent.

All through that spring and early summer, Æ kept Kingsley well informed of events in Ireland, such as Éamon de Valera's election as President of the Executive Council in March, and the Eucharistic Congress that was held in Dublin that June,[23] 'with its half million of imported, pious folk and its ugly decoration'. Æ was all too aware of the power that the Catholic Church wielded within Ireland's new Fianna Fáil. The country was led by a potent concoction of nationalism, religious fervour and conservative politics, all of which Æ abhorred.

However, in June 1932 the state of Ireland's political affairs was not uppermost in Kingsley's mind. On 15 June he again wrote to Dr Ellis: 'I received a letter from Campbell, written in Paris, saying he was about to leave for London. I am writing him, care of Cook's, London, asking him to come to Glenveagh for a few days on July 5th.'[24] Ellis apparently replied, stating his impressions of Campbell. Whatever Lucy felt about the strange arrangement, she allowed Kingsley to issue the invitation to Campbell before they left Elmwood. Kingsley was too caught up in his own feelings of anticipation to seriously consider the toll that the situation was taking on Lucy. He was wound up with excitement, focused fully on his own needs, while Lucy was left to deal with the aftershocks. He had made his decision. He would sacrifice a great deal to entertain Ellis's young protégé at Glenveagh.

Kingsley was awarded an honorary Doctorate of Humane Letters by William's University in Williamstown, Massachusetts, on 20 June.[25] Later that week, the Porters set sail for Ireland,[26] and their Donegal maids arrived on 27 June to open up Glenveagh Castle. On Sunday 3 July the Porters arrived at Glenveagh. The previous day, Kingsley wrote to Ellis,[27] saying he hadn't heard from Campbell and didn't know whether or not he would travel to Glenveagh. He concluded: 'Should he not, I shall be disappointed.'

Lucy recorded in her engagement diary on 3 July that Kingsley was annoyed because the Irish Free State wished to open Glenveagh to the public.[28] There were, of course, other more pressing concerns for Kingsley, who anxiously awaited news of his prospective young lover. He need not have worried: Alan Campbell arrived at Glenveagh on 5 July and stayed almost a week.[29] During that time, Kingsley and Alan became lovers. It was the beginning of a strange ménage à trois at Glenveagh and later at Elmwood.

Lucy recorded nothing of her first impressions of Alan in her diary. One can only imagine the sense of hurt and loneliness she must have felt when she heard the bedroom door close down the hallway, knowing that her husband was about to be sexually involved with a young man he barely knew. Lucy had always managed to keep her emotions in check: it was so rare for her to be annoyed, let alone to be angry or to be overtaken by jealousy.

There is no way of knowing whether arguments occurred or whether Lucy became cool and withdrawn by way of self-protection. What is known, however, is that rumours began to circulate between servants employed at various country houses that all was not well between the Porters. Annie McIntyre worked as a cook at Castle Grove Country House, near Letterkenny, during the 1930s.[30] Annie recalls that Kingsley had a room there, as the guest of Lady Grove, and he used to go fishing and sailing. Annie used to cook for him and even remembers the 'tweed Jacket belonging to him and his britches and leggings in the room'. She also recalls that there was talk among the servants that there was trouble between Kingsley and his wife over an affair. Perhaps the servants at Glenveagh Castle overheard arguments between husband and wife and passed on the story to friends who worked in other houses. It also seems more likely that an affair between Kingsley and a lady friend, rather than a male lover, was suspected locally.

As soon as Alan left, Kingsley immediately wrote to Ellis:

> Alan Campbell arrived Tuesday and left Friday. We both like him. Lucy feels that through fine-grained intuition he often appears at a rightness that usually is attained only through intellectual striving...her judgement reinforcing my own (which I am quite aware is liable to be unbalanced) means a great deal to me. Our gratitude to you for having put us in touch with Alan is very great. It is agreed that he is to return in September or October. He said he would see you in London, when he will no doubt tell you of our talks. I feel optimistic and more buoyant than for years. I realize of course that that very fact is likely to blind my eyes to some essential flaw in our foundations.[31]

Lucy must have hidden her feelings very well or otherwise Kingsley must have been seriously blinded by further layers of self-deceit, to believe that Lucy could take this bizarre love-triangle in her stride. Lucy was obviously in need of a friend and so she turned to Æ, inviting him to Glenveagh on 15 July.[32] Æ wrote back on 8 July, saying he had bought some canvasses, paints and stretchers and planned to paint during his stay.[33]

Despite the fact that her husband had just taken a male lover, Lucy wrote in her engagement diary on 14 July, seemingly jubilant that she finally had Kingsley all to herself again: 'Most beautiful night of Ireland. Rowed Curragh to Island... Went to Innisboffin for the night.'[34]

The following morning, Pat Coll called at the hut and Lucy made breakfast while Kingsley went for a swim.[35] They collected Æ from the station later that day. However, Kingsley's buoyancy was short-lived. Lucy recorded on 21 July that he was worried, but they still went to

Letterkenny. The following day, Lucy wrote: 'Kingsley most worried – write to England.' Apparently Kingsley contacted Dr Ellis. He had begun to yearn for Alan, hoping he could persuade him to return to Glenveagh very soon.

Alan did return on 25 July and stayed for several days. Lucy wrote in her engagement diary: 'Alan Arrives (I read in Bed).'[36] After twenty years of marriage, in which there had been a great deal of mutual affection and companionship, Lucy found herself sleeping alone, while her husband was again sexually involved with their young guest. Lucy somehow accepted the situation, dug deep within her own psyche and developed a rare form of unconditional love that was heroic. Louis had previously referred to Lucy and Kingsley as having the temperament of Buddhas.[37] Throughout the summer of 1932, Lucy's level of enlightenment was sorely tested. Somehow she emerged stronger and more protective than ever of Kingsley. As well as being Kingsley's nurse when he had bouts of sickness, Lucy now became his healer, in tandem with Dr Ellis. There was little she would not have done to help her brilliant but wounded husband to heal and flourish once again.

It is not clear how long Æ actually stayed at Glenveagh, or whether his own visit overlapped with that of Alan Campbell. It is highly unlikely, however, that Æ was ever privy to the singular arrangement that the Porters had entered into with Campbell and Dr Ellis.

On 31 July Kingsley wrote again to Ellis, expressing gratitude for having put him in touch with Alan:

> Alan Campbell came over for several days visit last week, and is to return again in about a month after his trip to Salzburg. Our impression of him continues to be in every way favourable. On the whole the experiment seems to me to be working exceedingly well – better than I should have dared to hope. I feel a deep sense of gratitude to you, deeper than I know how to express, for having put me in touch with Alan.
>
> Today the therapeutic side seems far away from me. Yet I imagine that from a scientific standpoint you may be interested

to hear of it. The extreme nervousness of a year ago has entirely disappeared after having been on the mend for sometime. To my triumphant delight, I found myself coming over on the steamer able to sleep quite undisturbed through noises which kept my wife awake. Spells of depression have continued quite persistently. But this week I have had none, and I have an inner conviction that they are things of the past, though of course it will require more time to prove this. On the other hand lassitude and disinclination (ever in ability) to settle down in my old habits of hard work continues. I am still hoping for the energy of past years to return, but its passing may be due to the obvious explanation of age.

What the future may hold we foresee only dimly and uncertainly. But we look forward to it with confidence that the foundations laid are right and solid. And those foundations we owe to you.[38]

For almost the whole of August, Lucy's engagement diary is blank. Then on Friday 26 August, Lucy wrote: 'Inisboffin . . . for us tonight.'[39] The following day she reported: 'Returned to meet Alan.'

With Alan's return, 'the experiment' continued. Then, on Sunday 28 August, in a rare moment of emotional honesty, Lucy wrote: 'Again the feeling solitude brings – perhaps for the 5th or 6th time in my life. Things connected back to childhood and girlhood.'[40]

The loneliness of their strange entangled arrangement finally hit Lucy with full force. She had experienced being left out as a child and as a young girl, but now she was being left out of her marriage. The husband who had written such long passionate letters, filled with deep love and yearning during their brief wartime separation, was now all but oblivious to her feelings of sadness and isolation.

On 30 August, Lucy and Kingsley travelled to Dublin while Alan remained alone at Glenveagh.[41] The following day Kingsley had a bad headache but it seemed to clear up within twenty-four hours. Alan remained living at Glenveagh throughout September, meeting the

Porters' friends, including the Bishop of Raphoe who called to tea.

On 20 September, Kingsley wrote to Ellis, sounding in great spirits after spending several weeks with Alan:

> Alan Campbell has been with us now nearly a month, which has been one of intense happiness for me, and what is more marvellous and important, I do not think Lucy has been entirely unhappy. Alan's character is one of extraordinary beauty – sweet, unselfish, straight from the shoulders, unclouded by dark moods. I believe in his genius and should be not in the least surprised if he turned out to be your spiritual successor. We both of us (Lucy and I) envy the parents who have such a boy.
>
> The future is still obscure for me. I feel I can never be again what I have been. Yet I am deterred from burning bridges by a doubt whether I shall be able to justify my existence by any other means than those by which I have been attempting to do so in the past. I feel that no solution postulated on idleness can be right or really satisfying. That is something I must fight my own way through, and it would not be difficult if only I could recover my old hunger. Perhaps I may yet.
>
> Alan is leaving in a few days for a trip to Mallorca, but promises to return in November. We are planning in a general way to be here until January, when I am returning to Harvard for I have promised to teach again the second term this year any way.[42]

Kingsley also remarked to Ellis that 'Donegal is very beautiful – for me one of the loveliest landscapes I have seen.'[43] He invited Dr Ellis to visit Glenveagh so he might enjoy its peace and beauty. It is obvious from the above letter that Kingsley had once again deluded himself that Lucy, who was deeply in love with him and would do virtually anything to alleviate his depression, was 'not entirely unhappy' with the fact that he was involved with a male lover. Kingsley took a gigantic further step by placing Alan in the role of a son, as though Lucy and he should be proud to be 'parents who have such a boy'.

The most incredible twist of all was that Lucy did become fond of Alan. Perhaps she saw Alan as a lost soul, needing affection and guidance that he had never received from his own parents. Alan finally left Glenveagh on Monday 26 September.[44] Two days later Lucy wrote in her diary: 'Kingsley and I talked.'

Kingsley received a letter from Ellis, reporting that Campbell had visited him and had discussed his stay at Glenveagh.[45] On 2 October, Kingsley replied to Ellis:

> You have made over my life. You know it. I do not need to tell you. And I know that that knowledge, combined with infinite similar knowledge, makes your happiness.
>
> I hope it is not entirely egotism which makes me desire that you should have about you some physical reminder of what you have done for me. I have thought and thought what might please you. Perhaps a drawing? I was about to go to London to see if I could discover some object you might like.

Kingsley then addressed the fact that Alan was a young man who was probably in need of friends of his own age: 'It seems to us obvious at his age, companionship with other young people is very necessary and should prove extremely developing. Just how to manage that for him when he is with us is a problem which may however perhaps little by little solve itself. My wife joins in warmest regards and deep gratitude.'[46]

Kingsley sent another letter to Ellis on 12 October.[47] This time he was more subdued because he had just read an article about two American men, Rudolph Stoddard and Herbert Brown, who had been shot in a suicide pact.[48] The article described them as 'inseparable companions', and rumour was rife that the men were lovers.[49] Kingsley told Ellis that if he hadn't replied to his last letter he would have travelled over to London to talk to him. He appeared to be grappling with the notion of resigning from Harvard, as he was afraid that 'if one doesn't burn one's boats, some one else may, which is worse'.

In the above letter to Ellis, Kingsley displayed a more realistic fore-boding of the type of scandal that would descend on Lucy and he if the truth of their situation became widely known.[50] Kingsley, with the help of Ellis, had attributed his depression solely to his lack of sexual fulfilment. In the autumn of 1932, Kingsley's growing desire for Alan Campbell threatened to destroy the fabric of his social and academic world, much in the same way that his father's desire for pretty young women had led to the unleashing of a public scandal and the disinte-gration of his family.

The remaining months of 1932 were very quiet for the Porters. Kingsley got a nine-pointer dog and they enjoyed walking him across the fields.[51] Æ continued to correspond with Kingsley about books, politics and economics. On 10 November he wrote to Kingsley, telling him that he was writing *The Avatars*, but he was finding it a very slow process.[52] He also teased Kingsley about his 'yearning for a simpler age without mechanics', and admonished him thus:

> You really ought to thank Heaven that you being born in a comfortable age can investigate uncomfortable ages without their dirt, smells, bad cooking, lack of sanitation etc. I wonder would you in the world of Abelard or Columcille have felt much different from Mark Twain's Yankee at the Court of King Arthur. The age we are born in fits us really like a glove.

Æ had also penned a poem that had been inspired by his summer visit to Glenveagh:

> The pool glowed to a magic cauldron
> O'er which I bent alone.
> The sun burned fiercely on the waters,
> The setting sun,
> A madness of fire: around it
> A dark glory of stone.[53]

On 24 November, the Porters spent Thanksgiving alone.[54] Lucy remarked that they did 'nothing festive'. Lucy recorded in her engagement diary on 9 December that they went out walking but that Kingsley was not feeling well. Christmas was dark, cold and quiet. After an emotionally turbulent 1932, the year drifted away amid morning walks across the freezing fields and evening talks alone beside the library fire.

Sunday, the first day of January 1933, began sunny but cold.[55] Both Kingsley and Lucy went to church in the afternoon. Lucy had invited Æ to visit them in the New Year, and Æ wrote back, saying he would arrive in Letterkenny on Tuesday 3 January.[56] Æ arrived as arranged amid a glorious storm.[57] The Porters' other guest, May Lucas, left that same day. Wednesday 4 January was a spectacular day: Lucy described it as 'A jewel of blue and gold in cold sunshine.' Lucy held a lunch for

her lady friends, Lady Grove, Mrs Moore and Mrs Crankshaw. Kingsley made time that day to write to Ellis, saying he was delighted that he had selected a drawing of the Shannon as a present.[58] He also reported that Alan had written a few days previously from California: 'I think all seems to be going well for him. His book is finished, and he is hoping you will consent to read the revision. Also he has had an article accepted and paid for by Asia.'

38. Porter holding pages of a newspaper or photographs.
Harvard University Archives,
HUG 1706.125, Box 1.

Alan's father had been taken ill and was staying at a sanatorium.[59] Alan had set his mind on becoming a nurse. Kingsley admitted to Ellis that he was despondent that Alan couldn't visit him until the spring and that 'depression has been gaining again since Alan went to California'.

Friday 6 January was cold and rainy but Lucy, Kingsley and Æ went for a long walk and had a good talk.[60] On Saturday, Lucy wrote, 'Æ left in as wild a storm as he came in.'

For Kingsley, the thought of returning to Harvard and his old life was a distasteful prospect. He wrote to Ellis on 12 January to give vent to his melancholic feelings:

> I fear I am hardly turning out to be the prize exhibit of the results of your kindness and sympathy, as I had so confidently hoped. The fault for this, I see or think I see, is not in your treatment which was the very best possible to the point of miracle, but to its having been undertaken too late. Comical, isn't it, that I who was so proud of my perspicacity, failed to discover the one fact I should know, although it was written in letters of fire across the sky. As late as 1928 I read Si le grain ne meurt [If the grain dies, from John 12:24]... wondering what the title could possibly mean!
>
> In this condition it is out of the question to give my course at Harvard. Perhaps the good New England virtue which I have may help to pull me together. If not, I should find some excuse for getting away.
>
> As for Alan's nursing, I am on the whole inclined to agree with you. I feel of course selfish regret, for it means the unsolving of my own life, but it is really his choice that is of course the end of it.
>
> ... We are still sailing on Saturday. Unless the vapours pass we may be coming back almost by return steamer.[61]

The Porters' guests had all left and the maids were closing up the castle until summertime.[62] Kingsley and Lucy reluctantly packed their cases in preparation for their return to the US on Saturday 14 January. Kingsley was unsure whether or not he could summon enough strength to teach at Harvard. But even if 'the good New England virtue'[63] of hard work and duty failed to revive him, there was always a way out: for a multimillionaire of considerable talent, there were many escape routes and always 'some excuse for getting away'.

Chapter thirteen

Harvard Witch-Hunt

The seven-day journey across the Atlantic was a weary one for the Porters. Their fairytale life in Cambridge had lost much of its sparkle as they valiantly struggled to keep the world from discovering their explosive secret. On Monday morning, 23 January 1933, they arrived in New York and met Lucy's sisters for lunch.[1] There was great excitement in the Wallace family as Lucy's favourite niece, Ellen, was to be married the following Monday, at Elmwood. Lucy was delighted to focus on this happy event, surrounded by her closest family and friends.

Ellen and her husband-to-be, John Alden Carpenter, stayed midweek at Elmwood to prepare for the wedding. Carpenter was a prosperous Chicago merchant and composer.[2] Lucy spent Friday at the beauty parlour with her friends, Agnes Mills and Alice James.[3] Ellen's daughters from her first marriage, Mrs Adlai Stevenson and Mrs Robert S. Pirie from Chicago, were present at the wedding.[4] Lucy was delighted that Ellen, who had divorced her first husband in 1924 amidst great scandal,[5] and Carpenter, whose first wife had died two years previously,[6] had at last found happiness.

On Tuesday 31 January the Porters dined with their friend, Chandler Post.[7] On Thursday evening, 2 February, they entertained another friend, Harry Davis. Lucy reported that it was a 'brilliant evening'. What was so brilliant for Lucy was that she was once again encircled by warm, trusted friends and life almost felt normal.

Æ continued his correspondence with both Kingsley and Lucy. During his New Year visit, Æ appears to have become closer to Lucy. He no longer addressed her as 'Dear Mrs Porter', but as 'Dear Lucy'.[8]

In a letter dated 4 February 1933, Æ wrote to Lucy from his Rathgar home in Dublin, discussing Irish and American politics, and mentioning Kingsley's gloominess that he interpreted as being caused by economic factors:

> Our election is over and nobody knows what use De Valera is going to make of his majority. If he bribes labour enough he can keep in for a long time... But what reason is there to meditate on the state of Ireland when you have America in as bad a way on a more gigantic scale. You have two countries in a bad way tied round your neck! Whereas I have only one. I won't write about Ireland any more or depress Kingsley who staggers gloomily under the weight of USA and Cole's Guide, which is I think a very good guide to economic reality.[9]

Saturday 4 February was also the day that Alan arrived at Elmwood.[10] The following Monday, Kingsley resumed teaching. The peculiar ménage à trois had now been established in Cambridge, in the very heart of homophobic Harvard. Lucy continued to entertain and to attend social events with friends.

Now that Alan was part of his life, Kingsley's spirits soared and he even reported a new zest for teaching at Harvard. He immediately set about helping Alan to fulfil one of his dreams to become a nurse. On Monday 13 February, Alan was introduced to Dr Wood and began working in the hospital in Cambridge the following morning.[11] In her engagement diary, Lucy disclosed nothing of her feelings about this new extended family arrangement. Lucy visited the hairdressers, had lunch with Mrs Gray and attended a musical event while Alan spent his first day at the hospital. That evening she wrote: 'A.C. came back very happy.'

The following day, however, both Lucy and Kingsley went up to the hospital and found a very distressed Alan.[12] It seems that Alan wasn't cut out for nursing after all. The following day, Lucy recorded: 'Alan appeared at front door bag and baggage.'

The Porters' social life continued in mid-February with visits to the Fogg Art Museum, lunch engagements and attendance at a lecture given by T.S. Eliot at the New Lecture Hall.[13] The week beginning Monday 20 February, however, was different. Lucy marked in her engagement diary: 'Monday (evening): Alone'; 'Tuesday (evening): Alone'; 'Thursday: All day alone.'

While at Elmwood, Alan began corresponding with Dr Ellis. On 22 February he wrote a fifteen-page letter in which he discussed his friends, the books he was reading and his life with the Porters: 'Last week I gave Kingsley your "Psychology of Sex" and of course we both jumped immediately to your chapter on homosexuality. From a single reading it seems to me the most sympathetic and balanced account of that subject, of its brief length, that I know.'[14]

Alan told Ellis that the Porters had arranged for him to work in a hospital but that he had only lasted three days.[15] He thanked Ellis for his praise of the first chapter of *Starborn* and was still hopeful that the book would be published. He hoped that he could make enough money from writing so that he could go away, settle down, live on his own money and write. He also mentioned that his parents were delighted that he had found paid employment as a secretary with the Porters: 'My parents are overawed with the idea of a Harvard professor and his wife – and I left home without any money from father, and Mr Porter sent me my fare – and I work three hours a day for Lucy and Kingsley, and they give me 30 dollars a month, so that I am independent financially.'

Alan also confided in Ellis that he was broken-hearted to find, on his return to California, that his boyfriend, Moray, was living with someone else.[16] He wrote, with obvious pain: 'I feel I have lost part of myself.'

Yet, Alan still planned to return with Lucy and Kingsley to Ireland on 18 July.[17] He told Ellis that he was fond of the Porters but that it wasn't an ideal situation. He admitted he didn't feel the same about Kingsley as the professor felt about him, particularly during the sexual act:

> It is my own fault that I am not really happy here. Lucy and Kingsley tried to find me work, and I quit. We have very

enjoyable times together. There is no discord – their friends and acquaintances treat me cordially. Only I long to be alone – as I was at Stratford.

It is consoling to know my presence here is of such value to Kingsley. Only I know it is an unequal exchange since I physically give him what he seems unable to do without, and he physically is only a sympathetic release to me – so far a cry from the harmonious sensations I had with Moray.

The following Friday the Porters travelled to Stamford to visit Louis.[18] Then suddenly, on Monday 26 February, Kingsley was summoned to Lowell House, the home of the President of Harvard. The following day, Lucy refused to attend three prior engagements and spent the day alone. Whatever transpired at Lowell House, Kingsley continued to attend his own engagements that week, including a meeting at the Faculty Club and a lecture on sociology. The Porters visited Louis again in Stamford on 5 March and the following day Lucy and Alan had tea with Rose Dexter.

On 7 March Alan again wrote to Ellis:

> These last few days I feel a truly extraordinary harmony between the three of us in this delightful old house – I guess it will be many years before I realize the value of this friendship. Kingsley would enjoy thinking it is perfect. Perhaps it is in ways ... there is no pain – no jealousy – nothing has been lost – their friends have accepted me – I am almost beginning to believe, for myself! The only imperfection is in myself – I want to be alone ... because I have lost Moray.[19]

While writing to Ellis, Alan reported that Kingsley had just walked in, after having received a letter from Ellis, dated 24 February.[20] Alan continued his letter: 'He looks awfully well, but all this financial havoc must be upsetting him considerably. Mrs Porter is, of course, marvellous about it. No matter what happens, she will be so interested to see how it works out, and how people react under a new set of conditions, that I think she will retain her marvellous buoyancy.'

From Lucy's appointment pad that March, it appears that she had completely accepted Alan's presence, as he was included in many of her luncheon and dinner parties.[21] On 18 March, she invited Roger Loomis to dinner, along with her own friend, Mrs Bowles. Alan was part of a dinner engagement on 22 March that included another of Lucy's friends, Mrs Robinson, and on 25 March he had dinner with the Porters' niece, Beatrice. If Lucy had any fears that the true relationship between Kingsley and Alan would be detected, she certainly put them out of her mind and got on with the situation as best she could.

Æ continued to correspond with Kingsley.[22] He wrote on 16 March in a jovial mood, imagining all the great miracles that the newly elected President Roosevelt could perform for America, calling him 'the Douglas Fairbanks of politics'. He had just completed *The Avatars* and was in high spirits.

During the spring of 1933, negotiations resumed between the Spanish government and the Fogg Art Museum to secure the transportation of the Sahagún burial slab back to León.[23] Spanish officials had sent several letters to Harvard since 1931, but due to the political unrest in Spain the Fogg Art Museum had refused to enter into further dialogue. Since Kingsley had given the sarcophagus lid to the Fogg Art Museum as a gift, they needed to obtain his consent to return it to Spain. In the circumstances, Kingsley must have had a change of heart and agreed to its return.[24] The Spanish government offered the Fogg Art Museum a number of artefacts in exchange for the venerated slab, including a marble column from the Benedictine Monastery of San Pelayo, Santiago, dating from the first half of the twelfth century; a double capital of the thirteenth century from the Monastery of Santa Maria de Aguilar de Campoo in Palencia; and a collection of Iberian pottery and figurines.[25] The exact date for the transfer of objects had not yet been arranged but it was hoped that the matter would be put to rest before the autumn.

In the first week of April, Kingsley continued to give lectures and to attend faculty meetings.[26] On 6 April he wrote to Ellis:

> Your good letter has lain unanswered for some weeks, not because I wasn't full of eagerness to write, but that I am aware what a burden your correspondence must be. Also Alan has kept you informed of our news in which I know you are interested.
>
> We have all been reading your psychology which Alan gave me. You tell some truths that are bitter to me, but I am the better for knowing them.[27]

Kingsley then told Ellis that he hoped that someday he would write about the 'withering and rasping effects of abstinence, as they appear evident to me among Catholic priests, elderly spinsters and Anglican Catholic bachelors of my acquaintance'.[28]

He also advised Ellis to write about 'the intertwined relationship of art and sex. But I note that you hesitate to put down the aesthetic impulse as primarily sexual.'[29]

Kingsley then went on to discuss Alan:

> Alan seems on the whole well and happy. He is gay, full of interest in what is going on, always amusing. At times he talks of wanting to be alone, half teasingly, for he knows I want him to stay, as does Lucy too, but I hope he doesn't mean it seriously. At any rate, he has given up a plan to go to Florence in April.[30]

It would appear a gross exaggeration to imply that Lucy wanted Alan to remain at Elmwood, but there is little doubt that Kingsley desired his presence. Kingsley still had Lucy's devotion and had also found a young male lover of whom he had grown very fond. He told Ellis that Alan was working as his part-time secretary, but he thought that Alan needed something more fulfilling, perhaps to become a writer or to start a bookshop.[31] Then Kingsley turned his attention to Lucy:

Lucy is wonderful. She has always been selfless – now has come a sort of heroic quality that gives her a new power and dignity. She appears to have grown and developed in every way under the experience of the last months. She seems too very happy, perhaps happier than ever; and I am sure that in that she couldn't deceive me. As far as the three of us are concerned, the situation is as perfect as anything in this world is likely to be.

Kingsley finished his letter to Ellis with a report on his own progress but also mentioned some dark clouds that were gathering over Alan's presence:

I too have been very well. Since returning from Europe until a few days ago there was unqualified happiness. I have never done such good teaching, and people have seemed to like me as they never have done before. All traces of depression disappeared, and my face altered completely. The shadow which has arisen is that it has been reported to me people are talking about Alan – not for any thing he has done, but the boy of course always wears his nature on his sleeve, which indeed is one of the most valuable things about him. I have foreseen he must arouse comment, and rather intended that he should. Yet now the situation is here, I find myself assailed by anxiety. But Lucy is so splendid; nothing matters. However faltering my courage may be, hers never flinches.[32]

However strong and heroic Lucy seemed to be, the moment she must have feared for several months was rapidly coming to pass. On Monday 10 April, Dr Osgood was called to visit.[33] That evening Kingsley was summoned once again to Lowell House. The following day Alan wrote to Ellis, oblivious to any anxiety that the Porters were feeling.[34] He told Ellis that he wanted to be alone and to write. He had asked Kingsley if he could remain behind at Elmwood while Lucy and Kingsley travelled to Ireland, and Kingsley had told him it would be unwise to remain there, but wouldn't tell him why. Alan was becoming restless, no matter what the Porters did to keep him happy. He admitted as much to Ellis: 'Lucy and Kingsley do practically everything possible to give me time to myself. But I cannot write, because inside of myself I do not feel alone, living in the same house as them . . . I want to get the Atlantic Ocean between us again, when I settle down to writing.'

Then he informed Ellis about Kingsley's latest outrageous plan to keep him satisfied:

> Kingsley, poor innocent darling, thinks if he could find for me a young lover, my problem would be solved . . . but I think you can understand, I would not want to enter upon a serious relation with another boy and at the same time be living in Kingsley's house – because if Kingsley and I continued our relation this other boy would be bound to guess it, and if we changed our relation it would be a false position, because Kingsley's desire would certainly still be there . . . and besides all that, I have not seen anyone to whom I am really attracted. Kingsley of course, can stand anything, except my having a relation with an older man – he draws that line at thirty five.[35]

Alan finally made it clear to Dr Ellis that, although he was fond of Kingsley, he was not in love with him:

> It is difficult, isn't it, to be as fond of anyone as I am of Kingsley, and at the same time, not to feel for that person what they feel towards you? Every time we are together, Kingsley is so much refreshed and I am so afraid my presence is becoming a habit to him. I am once in a while nervous that if the opportunity offers itself for me to be alone and to write, Kingsley will not be cured.[36]

The Porters continued entertaining at Elmwood during the remainder of April.[37] They attended a concert with Alan on 12 April and had lunch the following day with Dr Park. The following week, however, Lucy's engagement diary is full of refusals and evenings spent alone. On 24 April, Kingsley was again summoned to Lowell House. What actually went on at these meetings is pure conjecture but it is clear from Lucy's diary that they began to keep a low profile, refusing lunch and dinner engagements with some of their oldest friends.

The beginning of May did not bring any respite, as Kingsley was once again called to Lowell House.[38] The following evening a large musical dinner that had been planned for weeks was held at Elmwood. The next two days must have been anxious for Lucy as morning,

39. Lowell House at night, Harvard, Cambridge, MA.
Michael Cullen.

afternoon and evening appointment spaces were filled with the word 'ALONE' in large, heavy dark print.

It would appear that the President of Harvard was not letting Kingsley off the hook. The following Monday, 8 May, Kingsley's students took their oral exams; that evening he was summoned again to Lowell House.[39] That Wednesday was open day at Elmwood, in aid of the Women's Division of the Architects' Emergency Relief Committee.[40] Lucy wrote in her diary that Kingsley slept soundly that night while she lay awake.[41] On Saturday they visited the countryside; Alan went for a walk by the lake while Lucy and Kingsley walked together, frequently stopping to sit and talk, presumably trying to find a solution to their dilemma.

On Monday 15 May, Kingsley had more students for exams.[42] That evening, Lucy noted in her engagement pad: 'K not go to Lowell House.' Perhaps Kingsley had finally had enough of the ongoing witch-hunt. He spent the remainder of that week helping students to get through their annual exams. The strain of the last few months was beginning to take its toll. To add to the chaos, there were tradesmen working at Elmwood, papering, cleaning and redecorating some of the rooms. Lucy recorded on Tuesday 23 May that Dr Winslow was called to deal with a bad toothache, and Kingsley, Alan and Lucy were each examined by the dentist.

The Porters suddenly decided to pack their bags and return early to Glenveagh.[43] They cancelled all their outstanding plans and booked their passage to Ireland. On Thursday 25 May, Kingsley, Lucy and Alan travelled to New York, and the following day they lunched at the Union League and later met Lucy's sisters for supper. At noon on Saturday 27 May, the threesome boarded the SS *Cameronia*, en route to Ireland.

Chapter fourteen

Rendezvous on Inishbofin

The Porters arrived in Derry on Sunday 4 June in a glow of afternoon sunshine.[1] Alan had parted company with Kingsley and Lucy and had made his way to Stratford-on-Avon. It must have been a great relief for the Porters to leave the mounting problems behind in Cambridge and to feel safe once again in Ireland. There is no doubt that Kingsley realized he was on the brink of a scandal in Harvard. Those evening meetings with President Lowell led to a fraternity meeting to discuss Kingsley's future. The fraternity appears to have been divided, with some professors demanding that Kingsley be expelled while others spoke in his favour. Kingsley was told that the final decision would be reached during the summer.[2] Added to this, Kingsley had become deeply troubled by a fall in his investments.[3] With two great weights suspended above him, it was imperative that Kingsley could speak with Dr Ellis.

The Porters set off for London on Tuesday 6 June and arrived at the Connaught Hotel on the following day.[4] Lucy recorded an appointment for 3.30 p.m. at Herne Hill, but there was no mention that this was, in fact, the premises of Dr Ellis, and that Kingsley had arranged an urgent appointment.[5] The content of their conversation is unknown but there is no doubt that Kingsley needed to meet with his psychoanalyst, to get everything about Harvard and Alan off his chest. That evening Kingsley and Lucy dined at Rules.[6] On Thursday they took the 2.30 p.m. train to Liverpool, and by Friday they were back in Dublin. Lucy noted: 'K very tired.' Kingsley immediately wrote a short note to Ellis from the Shelbourne Hotel: 'Thank you very much for seeing us on Wednesday and for all your kindness and help.'[7]

That afternoon they took the 3 p.m. train to Letterkenny, finally arriving at Glenveagh at 9.30 p.m.[8] The next day Lucy wrote in her engagement diary: 'Mail delivery began; slowly a pull uphill in sunshine.' To help divert their minds away from Harvard, both Lucy and Kingsley began working in the Glenveagh gardens. They spent the following week cutting away the dying pansies, clearing out paths and pulling up weeds. Lucy reported on Wednesday 14 June that 'K tired – too much chopping!'

The following day the Porters travelled to Dublin to meet an acquaintance, Mr Murphy.[9] They had tea in the Shelbourne Hotel before starting back for Glenveagh. It was on Saturday 17 June that Kingsley wrote again to Dr Ellis.[10] After all the weeks of waiting for Harvard's decision, two letters had finally arrived from his colleague Edward Forbes. Kingsley, now in cheerful mood, immediately wrote to Ellis, addressing him more as a fond friend than as a physician:

My dear Havelock Ellis,

I want to write you at once that I have two letters from Edward Forbes (Emerson's grandson), director of The Fogg Art Museum, both referring to my being expected back at Harvard next autumn. Therefore at least some of the higher authorities are backing me, and I imagine that he would not have written as he did, were the university officially against me. In another three weeks I shall probably be able to tell rather definitely just how the ground lies. I dread victory almost as much as defeat, for it would entail the moral obligation of sticking out another year, which I doubt whether my nerves could possibly stand. However there is no use worrying over that now: the situation that so troubled me is relieved, and I want to thank you again for your help in our hour of need. Without having seen you, and without having read of your fight against an infinitely more difficult situation I'm not sure I should have weathered the storm ... I dream of getting Æ to lead off with a book against censorship in general.

The letters from Forbes certainly appear to have restored Kingsley's peace of mind, at least for the time being. From his letter to Ellis, it is also clear, however, that Kingsley no longer relished teaching in such a censorious atmosphere.[11] It was more than his nerves could endure to spend another year at Harvard. President Lowell's methods of instilling fear, of demanding secrecy and using subterfuge to control perceived enemies were the antithesis of all that Kingsley held sacred in a hallowed place of learning.

On 19 June, Kingsley wrote to Berenson.[12] The tone of this letter is more like the Kingsley of old, sounding once again like the medieval pilgrim, delighted that his vision for Ireland as a rural land, devoid of industrialization and unspoiled by progress, was still alive and well:

> I feared that the Eucharistic Congress and tourist propaganda might have changed its character, but they haven't; De Valera with his ideal of universal poverty has I think if anything widened the difference between Ireland and the modern world, so that now that traditional air of run-down shiftlessness, general mismanagement and misgovernment that has always given Ireland its charm, is even accentuated. The various attempts to re-establish new industries, open new communications have to my great relief almost universally failed, and the country seems to be slipping back into a state of restless dreaming.

In his letter to Berenson, Kingsley also admitted that they were doing very little entertaining that summer, and that they were: 'camping out in one or two rooms – a measure partly of economy but also actuated by desire, almost need, to be a bit by ourselves'.[13]

During the remainder of June, however, the Porters did entertain Lucy's sisters when they came to visit on Wednesday 21 June, and they also travelled to Dublin to visit Molly Childers.[14] On 23 June they lunched with Mrs Crankshaw but Lucy reported that in the afternoon Kingsley was tired. The following Monday they invited Fr Gallagher to lunch; then on Tuesday Lucy wrote: 'Innisboffin at last.' She reported in her engagement diary that Kingsley was not well and she drew a sad face: 'K tired. Slept at Innisboffin.'

The Porters took a train to Letterkenny on Monday 3 July, having suddenly decided to go to London.[15] On Tuesday they visited Stratford-on-Avon in Warwickshire, presumably to see Alan, but there is no mention in Lucy's diary of whether they travelled to London to meet Dr Ellis. She did note, however, that their cook was to arrive in Glenveagh on Thursday 6 July. Beside this, in very faint writing, Lucy has written: 'Return to Glenveagh; Boat back to Belfast.'

The following day, Friday 7 July, the Porters arrived back in Glenveagh in time for lunch.[16] Lucy again wrote in her diary in very faint print: 'alone'. Their plans for the following day are barely visible: 'Saturday: Æ arrives for month.' Kingsley had invited Æ to Glenveagh before he left Cambridge in May,[17] and Æ wrote to Lucy on 22 June, saying that he would visit them on 8 July.[18] He confirmed this with Kingsley in a letter dated 5 July, writing that he planned to leave Dublin at 12 o'clock on Saturday, to arrive in Strabane at 4.24 and in Letterkenny at 5.35.[19]

Sometime during that Friday the Porters decided to spend the night on Inishbofin. By all accounts it was to be a spectacular night, with a full summer moon sailing above the sea.[20] They drove to Falcarragh and, from McKinley's store, Kingsley sent a cheerful reply to his old friend:

Dear Æ,

On arrival we find your letter with the good news you are coming to-morrow. We have been in England for a day or so and now are going to Inish Bofin for the night if my dear old rain doesn't get so bad as to make it impossible. McCann meets you at Letterkenny at 5.35 to-morrow. Either he will bring you over to Magheraroarty to meet us or take you to Glenveagh directly as you prefer. The distance for the motor is about the same either way – it is simply a question of whether you would rather go straight to Glenveagh and rest until we can get there.

I can't tell you how glad we are you are coming. You and Donegal are, we feel, the best the world has to offer.

Devotedly,

Kingsley[21]

As Kingsley rowed the curragh that afternoon across the foaming sea that never failed to exhilarate him, there were still great challenges that lay ahead. Would he continue to teach at Harvard or would he for the second time tender his resignation? Although he had established great rapport with his students, it was the formality of teaching that did not

40. Map of Donegal coastline and Inishbofin Island, from a mural in Falcarragh, Co. Donegal.
Photograph by Michael Cullen.

suit him. Also, once his homosexual tendencies were suspected by President Lowell, Kingsley would always feel under scrutiny at Harvard. There was also his affair with Alan. Was it likely that this could continue indefinitely? And what of Lucy? What kind of a long-term toll would the affair take on Lucy's emotional well-being? Of course there were endless possibilities as to where Kingsley, now aged 50 and in fine health, could make his home: he could remain in Ireland; he could relocate to his beloved France or Italy; or he could travel much further into the depths of Africa or Asia. Although his fortune had suffered a downturn during the depression years he was still a man of immense wealth who could afford to fulfil any dream imaginable. He could continue his married life with Lucy, or he could travel alone, setting her free to pursue her own adventures. Then he could follow the path of the pilgrim, perhaps on a spiritual quest to attain true awareness and peace.

The account of the remainder of that day and the events of the following day, Saturday 8 July, were later recalled by Lucy at the Coroner's Inquest that was held on 12 September 1933:

> On that day I went onto Inishbofin Island, Co. Donegal, accompanied by Mr Porter who rowed in the curragh. I was accompanied by Owen McGee our boatman who came in a boat. We reached the island about 3pm and landed at a point known as Toberglassan Bay. We entered our cottage on the island, which is situated on its Eastern Peninsula and the only residence on that portion of the island. This cottage was only used on the occasion of periodic visits to the island in the summertime. We visited it about 5 or 6 times during the season. After a short stay in the cottage we returned with Owen McGee in the boat to the island pier which is at the north side of the island. We then returned on foot to the cottage. McGee had beached the boat near the pier. It remained there throughout the night. We both arrived at the cottage after about 6.30pm and remained there throughout the night. We instructed Owen

McGee to come to the cottage at 10am next day. The night passed without incident.

We both had breakfast next morning together about 9.30am and McGee arrived at 10am and had breakfast in the cottage. I went for a walk with McGee after breakfast and on my return Mr Porter who remained at the cottage during my absence said he was going to give Owen a hand with the curragh. The curragh was at this time so placed that it was liable to be washed away as there was a high tide expected. Before leaving he said 'Here are your pencil and paper if you start first.' This had reference to a conversation I had with Mr Porter that morning with effect that it was too rough which meant we would go to write instead. Mr Porter remarked that he was going to write but not letters. We did not arrange to meet at any particular place on the island. I noticed Mr Porter and McGee had left. This would be about 10.30am. After doing work in the house I went out to meet Mr Porter, bringing pencil and paper with me. This was about 10.40am. I went to the Head side of the peninsula towards the Tory Island extremity. I did not meet Mr Porter though I was looking for him. I then came back to the cottage. I don't remember going into the cottage nor meeting Owen. I came close to the cottage and I think I looked in. Mr Porter was not there. I was almost half an hour away from the cottage. As I failed to find him I then went to look for him along the Meenlara side of the peninsula. I went down almost as far as the point known as Cave Arch but found no trace of my husband. I then went back to the cottage and there met Owen. I asked him which way my husband went. We were outside the cottage. He said he didn't know. I again went out to look more carefully at the Meenlara side and went about the same distance as before, but nearer the edge of the caves. I then became anxious and returned to the cottage where I again met Owen. I said 'Owen, I am uneasy about Mr Porter. Come with me at once and we'll look for him.' We went together along the Meenlara side of the

Peninsula. It was then almost 11.45 am or noon. I went out to the point known as Gobrinatroirk and Owen went towards the Ilannamara Point. We met again after a time and separated again, and then went along to the Tory side to a spot where I left a handkerchief. I then searched the Horn Head side and thus completed the search of the shore of the peninsula. Our search was a very thorough one and no trace of Mr Porter was to be found. We continued the search until about 3 pm. Then I asked Owen to get Pat Coll who is a native of the island to help. About 3.45pm Owen returned with Pat and I gave them some water-proofs as there was a heavy thunder storm which continued 'till about 5.30pm. We then went in different directions. I then searched Glenveagh Bay side and I searched the Meenlara side again, and Pat searched the Tory Island side. This continued 'till 7.30 or 8pm. We found nothing of him. I was satisfied that a thorough search was made.[22]

Lucy's account of that fateful day as she frantically searched the island, desperately trying to locate her missing husband all through the day and well into the evening, is indeed harrowing. In the afternoon a thunderstorm developed.[23] The island terrain is rugged and rough, with most of it devoid of pathways. The beaches are strewn with boulders and the caves at the Meenlara side are usually under water. The treacherous cliffs, where Lucy thought that Kingsley had gone to write, are located to the north-east of the Porters' hut. Lucy sought the help of Pat Coll and Owen McGee and the three of them, despite the turbulent conditions, continued to search along the rocks and cliffs.

As the last light faded, Lucy was rowed from the island back to Magheraroarty by Owen McGee.[24] The thunder and the rain had ceased. The fate of Arthur Kingsley Porter was still unknown. Lucy later recounted her journey back that evening, in Æ's Letters to Mínanlábáin:

> Whether it took a longer or a shorter time that night to row in from the island, I do not know. But I did know then, dazed as I

was, that it didn't matter – that the passage of time would never again matter to me now that there was no one to hurry to or to hurry for. We came to the place where the sea is white and you generally steer too much out of your course to avoid the shallows because of the breakers that turn to foam, and hissing and roaring roll their spray swiftly into the land. For the first time I went close to their edge. I had no fear and I knew, dazed as I was, that never again would I be afraid, now that there was no one to shield from danger, nor in case of accident to leave behind.[25]

Æ was standing on the pier at Magheraroarty, expecting to greet Lucy and Kingsley.[26] Lucy later described her arrival that evening at the pier:

> I was only conscious that Fate had granted me this one boon (as if it had been in the plan) that Æ of all the people left in the world was holding out his hand to help me out of the boat on to the land which in a flash had become a stretch of emptiness greater than the sea.

The chauffeur had been waiting with Æ for many hours, wondering what was causing the delay.[27] As they drove off in the car, Lucy turned to Æ and broke the silence: 'Kingsley will not return tonight', she said. 'Kingsley will never return.'

Chapter fifteen

Disappearance and Inquest

The journey back to Glenveagh for Lucy that evening must have been surreal. After all their incredible adventures together, their struggles, triumphs and disappointments, Kingsley had always been by her side. After twenty-one years of marriage, and many unexpected twists and turns, they had always displayed a united front to the world. As she was driven along the dark, lonely road to Glenveagh, Lucy instinctively knew that this was the beginning of a different life. Somehow she managed to keep her composure, unlike the chauffeur whose hands shook with nerves as he swerved along the narrow road, overcome with shock as Kingsley's loss began to sink in.[1] Halfway along the road to Glenveagh, Æ gently took control and persuaded Lucy to turn around so they could report the events to the Civic Guards at Falcarragh Barracks.[2] It had never even occurred to Lucy to report her husband as missing. This they did, before returning to Glenveagh to spend the night.

The following day the Donegal sea patrol went out to search for Kingsley's body without result.[3] That afternoon Lucy was accompanied by Æ to the home of Owen McGee where they had arranged to meet the Civic Guards again. Mrs McGee was overcome with grief but tried to hide it, considering that Lucy displayed a calm exterior. Owen McGee looked shocked and bewildered. All the islanders had been very fond of Kingsley, so his sudden disappearance was very upsetting for everyone.

The Sergeant of the Civic Guards was away that weekend so a subaltern and another guard arrived to fill out the paperwork.[4] They had difficulty with writing and spelling in English, as they were native Irish speakers, so Æ had to take over and write down Lucy's account of the previous day's events. A search of the coastline around Inishbofin went on for several days.[5] No record of any police investigation exists,[6] so in all likelihood Lucy's story was accepted without further questioning. The Porters' status in Donegal in the 1930s was equivalent to royalty. The wife of an eminent Harvard professor and multimillionaire would not have been subjected to any intense grilling about her husband or their life together. The notion that foul play might have been involved was never even considered.

The procedure for dealing with the case today would involve a detailed investigation by the District Garda Superintendent who would begin by taking a full description of Kingsley Porter, as well as details of when and where he was last seen.[7] It is vital that the superintendent collects accurate information and responds quickly in the case of a missing person. In the case of a suspected accident at sea, the Irish Marine Search and Rescue Organization, including the Civil Defence, the Royal National Lifeboat Institution, Search and Rescue Helicopters and sub-aqua would be notified to begin a thorough search of the area. The Missing Person's Bureau would also keep up-to-date records of the case and would liaise with Interpol, the international police organization, if necessary. Interpol was established in 1923 and hence was in operation at the time of Kingsley's disappearance but it does not appear that the Gardaí investigating the Porters' case believed that Kingsley had travelled to Europe. Also, unless there was a suspected crime, the Gardaí would not have pursued Kingsley Porter across Europe. As the investigation progressed, Kingsley's friends, his colleagues in Harvard and his family in Stamford would have been contacted to see if they could shed any light on events.[8] But no such thorough investigation was carried out after Kingsley's disappearance in July 1933. Investigations were also severely hampered by poor telecommunications and the fact that, in bad weather, the island was literally cut off from the mainland.

All through that week Lucy was thankful for Æ's presence.[9] He helped her to send cables and to deal with all the formalities. In the evenings they sat in the library: Lucy lay on the sofa in front of the turf fire while Æ read to her from *The Avatars*. He had hoped to be sitting in that room reading those same pages to Kingsley, but now he read late into the night, perched on the edge of a large armchair, hoping that his words would lull Lucy to sleep.

What is most remarkable about Lucy's own account of her harrowing ordeal is that she gave in so quickly to the belief that Kingsley would never return. It was always possible that Kingsley could have had an accident and was lying injured somewhere on the island. Kingsley was an avid adventurer, so had he, perhaps, indulged an impulsive whim to leave the island with one of the fishermen? Although the seas were choppy that morning, the thunderstorm had not begun until late in the afternoon. Lucy's stoical acceptance that her husband was gone forever, although he had vanished without trace and no body was ever recovered, is indeed peculiar. Her degree of surrender when faced with her husband's uncertain fate can only be understood in one of the following situations: she had indeed reached enlightenment; she was expecting Kingsley's death; she was party to a plan to aid in her husband's contrived disappearance.

In Lucy's engagement pad for that week there is no mention of the visitor who arrived on 10 July.[10] In her hour of need, Alan Campbell travelled from Stratford-on-Avon to Glenveagh to comfort the grieving wife of his recent lover.[11] On 11 July, Alan wrote to Dr Ellis, to acquaint him with the details of Kingsley's tragic disappearance:

> Probably you have read in the newspapers of what has happened – Kingsley and Lucy went over to their island, Friday and Saturday morning. Kingsley was drowned. There was a strong out-going tide, no one saw the body disappear. It is thought he slipped from a high cliff in the wind. He and Lucy had breakfasted together in their cabin – they were going out to write letters and Kingsley went a few minutes ahead to find a sheltered spot.

> Lucy sent a wire to me at Stratford, Sunday morning, and I crossed over that evening.
>
> I am remaining with Lucy as long as she has need of me. Of course just now she can make no plans, but is intending to sail for Elmwood in about ten days. I will cross with her.[12]

Alan went on to describe to Ellis an almost mystical experience that occurred when he was walking with Lucy in Glenveagh: 'Last evening, while walking, we were both able to feel Kingsley has found release & liberation.'[13] Alan obviously believed that Kingsley had died, either from an accident or by his own hand. Either way, he felt that Kingsley was finally free and at peace. Then he went on to tell Ellis about Lucy's incredible strength in the face of such adversity: 'Æ has been here since the accident & I think he has saved Lucy. I thought this might be an unspeakable ordeal; Lucy's courage and understanding are limitless. I only hope I can learn from her.'

Local, national and international newspapers quickly reported various versions of the professor's disappearance. There was a breakdown in telephonic communications in the north-west due to the thunderstorm, so it took some time for accurate information to be gathered by journalists.[14] The main story to circulate was that Kingsley went out in a small boat on Saturday morning and had not been seen since. On Monday 10 July, *The Irish Press* carried the story on the front page: 'Well-Known Professor Drowned in Donegal'. This account told of the professor having gone out in a curragh before the violent thunderstorm, and stated that the boat 'was either struck by lightning or swamped by the heavy seas'. A correspondent for *The Irish Times* reported in Monday's paper: 'Bathing Accident in Donegal'. This article alleged that Kingsley 'was drowned whilst swimming ... It seems that on Saturday he was out in a boat off the island and decided to have a swim. He dived from the boat but was not seen again, and, though a search has been made, the body has not been recovered.'[15] *The Irish Times* account of a boating accident persisted in the Tuesday edition.[16]

The account that Kingsley went out in a small boat was reported in many American papers. The headline in Monday's edition of *The New York Times* stated: 'A. Kingsley Porter Drowned Off Ireland: Archaeologist Lost From Boat in Storm'.[17] The article went on to relate that Kingsley Porter went off in a small boat that morning and that the craft was overturned in a severe thunderstorm. A host of US newspapers carried a similar story.[18] According to *The Brooklyn Daily Eagle* edition of 10 July, 'a cable was received on 9 July from Mrs Arthur Kingsley Porter, reporting that her husband had disappeared last Saturday in a small sailboat and a search since then has failed to reveal any trace of him'.[19]

The New York Evening Post of the same date reported:

> an intensive search for Arthur Kingsley Porter, American archaeologist, who has been missing since he left Inishboffin in a small sailing boat, has thus far proved fruitless ... Five locally owned launches taken over by the Civic Guards and accompanied by fishing boats searched all possible spots where the missing professor might have gone, but all returned without having found a trace of man or boat.[20]

The Irish Press reported on Tuesday 11 July: 'No Trace Of Prof. Porter: Gardaí and Islanders Search Off Coast'.[21] The article stated that despite the intensive search that had been carried out by the guards and islanders on Monday, no trace whatever had been found of the missing professor.

On Wednesday 12 July, *The Irish Press* still carried the story that the Civic Guards were continuing their search for the body of Professor Porter.[22] This was followed up on Thursday 13 July by a report that guards from Falcarragh and Bunbeg were scouring the coastline near Inishbofin in an endeavour to recover the professor's body.[23]

The first newspaper report to place Kingsley's disappearance in the sphere of mystery was printed by a local paper, *The People's Press*, on 15 July.[24] The article was entitled: 'Donegal Sea Mystery: American Professor Missing'. It went on to state: 'Mystery still surrounds the disappearance of Dr Kingsley Porter... Early in the week it was reported that he had gone out in a curragh from Inishbofin Island. This rumour was later discounted, but up to a late hour last night our reporter was unable to glean any further information.'

The disappearance of Arthur Kingsley Porter was about to enter the realm of legend. On the same morning, *The Donegal Democrat* printed an astonishing story entitled 'The Missing Archaeologist'.[25] The report stated: 'On Tuesday, a rumour gained currency in parts of Donegal that he had been found alive and well on an island in Tory Sound, but on inquiry at a number of Civic Guard stations no confirmation of the statement could be had.'

Tory island is 16 kilometres (approximately ten miles) from Magheraroarty on the Donegal coast and 11.7 kilometres (just over seven miles) north-west of Inishbofin. It would have been incredibly dangerous for a small boat to cross that seven-mile stretch of sea in rough conditions, due to the potent mix of Atlantic swell, high wind and strong tides. Even the shorter crossing to one of the uninhabited islands, Inishdooey or Inishbeg, would have been treacherous in a storm but would have been possible in the morning, before the storm broke. No further reports were printed, however, about the appearance of Kingsley on Tory Island.

Whatever Lucy felt about these rumours, she carried on with daily life as best she could. There is no doubt that her sense of loss and pain was acute, as she had lost the great love of her life. She later described how the loss 'was to pierce my spirit with the deepest pain I was ever to know'.[26]

After all her years of entertaining and building up a vast social circle, Lucy's friends and family did not forsake her when she needed them most. From her engagement diary it appears that Louis Porter arrived for his first visit to Glenveagh on 14 July, in an attempt to come to terms with the uncertain fate of his brother.[27] Kingsley's cousin Katherine Merritt visited for a month from 24 July, and Lucy organized a few lunch dates with Mrs Crankshaw and Mrs Rice. Lucy's good friend Rose Dexter travelled from Boston to stay at Glenveagh for a week, from 28 July. Æ stayed for several weeks, helping Lucy to deal with all the practical and official matters. He did not leave until Lucy's sisters were ensconced in Glenveagh to offer comfort and solace. When he returned to London in early August, he wrote to Lucy again:

> I do hope dear Lucy that you have found some peace of mind and that your way of life is now clearer before you. I was so overwhelmed by Kingsley's death that I was not a very consoling companion for you at such a time. Time itself is the only healer, and what is the real name of time? This is only to let you know that you are much in my mind.
> Yours ever,
> Æ.[28]

Lucy continued to be cosseted by friends who wished to help her through the early days of grief and loss. Molly Childers, whose own husband had been executed in 1922, stayed at Glenveagh from 7 to 13 August.[29] It also appears that Kingsley's Harvard colleague Edward Forbes, who had written to him only weeks previously to offer some hope that his reputation was still intact, visited for four day towards the end of August.

Lucy was not ready to return to Cambridge just yet. The inquest into the disappearance of Kingsley was to take place on 12 September.[30] There was also a voyage that she needed to undertake. The Thirteenth International Congress of the History of Art was scheduled to take place in Stockholm during the first week of September.[31] Kingsley had already agreed to represent the US at the conference, along with Dr C.R. Morey of Princeton.[32] Lucy decided to attend the conference in her husband's place, and on Monday 28 August she left Glenveagh and travelled to London.[33] She boarded a ship for Stockholm on 31 August and arrived on 2 September; the conference began the following day.

By 12 September, Lucy was back in Donegal, ready to face the official inquest into Kingsley's disappearance.[34] It was the first inquest without a body to be held in Ireland.[35] Lucy was represented by a

Dublin solicitor, Mr A. Cox. The Guards were represented by Superintendent Glynn of Dungloe. The inquest was conducted in Gortahork by the Coroner, Dr Joseph P. McGinley.[36] Lucy was first to take the stand and to be sworn in. She began by stating: 'I am widow of Professor Kingsley Porter and reside at Glenveagh Castle, Co. Donegal, and Elmwood, Cambridge, Massachusetts, USA. He was aged 50 years and was a Professor of Fine Arts at Harvard University.'

Lucy began by giving her account of their journey to the island on Friday 7 July; of their evening spent together on the island; of their decision to delay their journey back to Magheraroarty due to strong currents on Saturday 8 July; of Kingsley's subsequent disappearance and her frantic search to find him all through that day.[37] She ended the deposition with the following account of her husband's general state of mind:

> Mr Porter was in his usual health on the day of his disappearance. He was always in good health. Our married life was a happy one and Mr Porter had no troubles, financial or otherwise. He was accustomed to explore the caves or may have gone down to a sheltered spot amid the cliffs to write. The tide was going out all the time about the time he disappeared and was coming in when we were searching in the evening. I think that Mr Porter must have been on top of one of the cliffs and slipped and have fallen into the sea and that his body was carried out to sea. There was no reason whatsoever why he should want to leave the island. Mr Porter had arranged with Mr George Russell (Dublin) (Æ) to meet him at Glenveagh on Magheraroarty Pier next evening. I left the island about 8 pm and reported the matter at Falcarragh barracks the same evening.

Owen McGee was then sworn in.[38] He gave the following account of the two days in question:

> I am a farmer fisherman being of Magheraroarty and looked after Mr Porter's boats. I remember the 7th July 1933. I went

41. Cliffs on Inishbofin.

Michael Cullen.

onto the island with Mr and Mrs Porter. They rowed the curragh and I sailed the boat. I am a native of the island. All the boats on the island are kept near the pier. I left Mr Porter's boat near the pier on 7/7/33 and beached the curragh on Toberglassan Strand. I stayed on the island that night and returned to Mr Porter's cottage at 10am next day where I had breakfast. Immediately after Professor Porter and I went down to the shore and pulled up the curragh to a secure position. It was then almost 11am and the Professor walked away in the direction of the cottage and did not tell me where he was going. I then went back to the cottage and found nobody in it, but when I was coming out I met Mrs Porter and I asked her was her husband in and she said no, and asked me in what direction did he go and I said I didn't know. She went off to look for him in the Meenlara side of the island – came back in a short time after. I accompanied her on a search of the island until 3pm. I then went for Pat Coll who assisted us in the search till about 8pm. We searched the island thoroughly from Curragh Bay to Toberglassan Bay but failed to find Mr Porter. There was a very strong gale blowing from the land in the morning. Mrs Porter said to me that she was afraid that something had happened to her husband after the first search. While searching I had a view of the sea around the peninsula. There was no boat to be seen. I saw no boat leaving the island and heard of none. There was no boat near that part of the island that morning. There was no boat around the island by which Mr Porter could have gone and a landing or departure from the island could only be made from the pier on Toberglassan bay. It is not possible to thoroughly examine the cliffs of Curragh Bay as the sea at that point is always rough. Mr and Mrs Porter were always on good terms and he was in good spirits. It would have been impossible for him to have left the island on that day. In my opinion he must have fallen over the cliffs. I never saw him since. If he had landed on the mainland I would have heard of it.

James McGinley was the next to be questioned.[39] He was a fisherman living on the island. He gave the following account of the day that Kingsley was lost:

> I live beside the pier and can see where all the boats are beached. I knew Professor Porter. I was at my house on the day he was missing. Mr Porter did not leave the island on any boat from the pier that day. All the island boats were at the pier and there was no other means of getting off the island. The only boat that left the island was James Ferry's. Mr Porter wasn't on his boat. I am living on the island since and I have not seen nor heard of Professor Porter. The islanders were anxious to locate his body and were searching for it. They used the drift-net when fishing around the island.

Pat Coll, the fisherman who had helped Lucy to search for Kingsley, was also called to give testimony:

> I am a fisherman living on Inishbofin island and look after Professor Porter's cottage. I remember the day he was reported missing. About 3 pm I went looking for him accompanied by Mrs Porter and Owen McGee. We searched the peninsula but found no trace of him. I never saw him since. If he was on the island I would have heard of it.[40]

James Ferry, also a fisherman on the island was the last person to give his version of events: 'I left the island about 11 am and crossed to Magheraroarty Pier. I had a boy named Tom Coll there with me. I had nobody else on the boat. I never saw or heard of him since.'[41]

From the transcript of the inquest it appears that no further questioning took place. Lucy had once again protected Kingsley's reputation with the statement: 'Our married life was a happy one and Mr Porter had no troubles, financial or otherwise.'[42] His near-expulsion from Harvard, his homosexual tendencies and his recent financial losses were not mentioned. Above all else, Kingsley had feared the kind of sexual scandal that had plagued his boyhood years. Lucy would go to great lengths indeed to protect the character of the husband she idolized.

Likewise, the testimony of Owen McGee went unchallenged. The discrepancy between his statement and Lucy's concerning their journey to the island was somehow overlooked. Lucy had stated that Kingsley rowed the curragh while she travelled in the small boat with Owen McGee, their boatman.[43] McGee maintained that he sailed the boat alone while Lucy and Kingsley went together in the curragh. It was a minute discrepancy but in a Coroner's Court it is such tiny disparities that may lead to major inferences and further questioning. The discrepancy probably told more about McGee's awareness of social etiquette – that Lucy and Kingsley should have been together in the curragh – and the fact that he did not want any aspersions being cast upon himself or his employers, rather than there being any great intrigue involved. Perhaps Lucy felt that the boat was more comfortable to travel in, although many fishermen deem the curragh to be a safer craft.[44]

The other interesting testament was made by James Ferry, a fisherman on the island.[45] He told the Coroner that he rowed a boat, along with a young boy, Tom Coll, from Inishbofin to Magheraroarty Pier at 11 a.m. on 8 July, at a time very close to that given by Lucy for Kingsley leaving the hut, at 10.30 a.m. It was therefore possible for a boat to travel safely to the mainland at that time. James McGinley, another fisherman on the island that day, confirmed Ferry's account. McGinley also stated that no other boat had left the island that day.

The fact remains that if Kingsley Porter, a man of enormous wealth and superb intellect, had really wanted to make a secret escape from Inishbofin on that morning there were plenty of options he could have chosen. It is also an interesting detail that a story persisted for many weeks, and was published in newspapers on a daily basis, that Professor Porter had left the island in a small boat and had subsequently disappeared. The tiny cracks that remained hidden during the inquest would soon gain visibility, becoming deep fissures where facts, rumours and fables began to merge and grow. There was nothing further required from any of the witnesses. Lucy sat in the Coroner's Court, still looking as composed as ever, awaiting the inquest's verdict.

Chapter sixteen

Verdict

The Coroner, Dr Joseph P. McGinley, finally read out the verdict:

> Good and lawful men of the County aforesaid, who being sworn
> and charged to enquire when, where, how and after what
> manner the said came to his death, do upon their Oaths say that
> I find that the deceased Arthur Kingsley Porter came by his
> death on 8th July 1933 at Inishbofin island, Co. Donegal and that
> the cause of death was misadventure.[1]

The Coroner agreed with Lucy's version of events, that Kingsley
must have slipped off the cliffs, fallen into the sea and been carried away
by the strong tides.[2] In conclusion, Dr McGinley spoke highly of the
professor, saying that he was extremely cultured, kindly and charitable
with the islanders, and that his mainland friends of the literary world
would miss a man of international repute.[3]

Lucy had succeeded in suppressing any mention of Kingsley's
history of depression, his visits to Dr Ellis or his involvement with Alan
Campbell. She must indeed have been relieved to leave the Coroner's
Court on that autumn afternoon, knowing that Kingsley's reputation
was still intact. When Lucy rowed from the island on the day that
Kingsley vanished, there is every likelihood that she believed that her
husband had jumped from the cliffs. Her grave declaration to Æ, when
she met him on Magheraroarty Pier, that 'Kingsley will never return',[4]
was the lament of a woman whose hope had died of ever seeing her
husband alive.

Since Grosskurth (1980) revealed Kingsley's hitherto unknown letters to Ellis and his homosexual affair, many writers have assumed that Kingsley did indeed commit suicide to save himself and Lucy from a scandal that was about to break at Harvard.[5] According to Shorter and Healy (2007), Kingsley Porter had committed suicide, 'torn, as were so many gay individuals in those days, between the desire to live as a gay male and the necessity of maintaining the façade of a heterosexual marriage'.[6]

There is, in fact, as much evidence to postulate that Kingsley's death was an accident: that he slipped from the cliffs and hit his head on the rocks beneath, and that his body was dragged out to sea by the swirling currents. For on the morning of Kingsley's disappearance, the Porters had planned to travel back to the mainland and were waiting to see if it would be safe to cross later in the day.[7] Also, Kingsley was looking forward to seeing his closest friend Æ, who was waiting for the Porters on the mainland.[8]

The greatest comfort that Lucy had when she arrived back at Magheraroarty Pier that evening was the presence of Æ. In her account of that nightmarish evening, she mentioned her gratitude that Æ was there to take her hand, 'as if it had been in the plan'.[9] On first reading, this may seem to be a reference to Kingsley's predetermined plan to take his own life on Inishbofin and then to have Æ meet Lucy that evening to console her. However, the letter written by Kingsley to Æ before rowing to the island on 7 July[10] was indecisive, as it allowed Æ to choose whether he wished to wait for their arrival at the castle or to travel to Magheraroarty to meet them the following day. Therefore, there was no predetermined plan on Kingsley's part to arrange for Æ to meet Lucy after her terrible ordeal. There was, in fact, no premeditated scheme – often a factor in suicides – on Kingsley's part to take his own life on Inishbofin on 8 July, as the Porters had planned to travel back to the mainland after breakfast.[11] It was only the sudden incoming storm that forced them to change their plans.

Kingsley had told Lucy he was going to help Owen McGee to pull up the boat and then to spend time writing, presumably near the cliffs where he often walked.[12] Lucy was to follow after him, sometime later. It is difficult to believe that Kingsley would have willingly thrown himself from the cliffs, knowing that Lucy was following close behind him. Could Kingsley have inflicted such an agonizing drama on his wife, knowing that she would have to search all over the island long into the evening, without ever finding him?

Despite the fact that Kingsley had taken a young lover, there is little doubt that Lucy was the love of his life. For all their married life they hardly spent a night apart. Friends and relations constantly remarked on the goodness and kindness of both husband and wife, and on how remarkably suited they were to each other. Even in the darkest days of depression and in the euphoric episodes experienced with Campbell, Kingsley's closest confidante was always Lucy.

Kingsley's problems may have been considerable but at least he had been given a recent respite by the letter from Forbes, stating that he was expected back at Harvard to teach during the autumn term.[13] From his letter to Ellis on 17 June 1933, it is clear that Kingsley considered resigning from Harvard because he felt that he did not have the strength to continue teaching. His resignation would have severed his connection with Harvard without scandal and would have given him back his precious freedom to write and study wherever he chose. Although there had been a downturn in his finances,[14] he still had enormous resources at his disposal: two magnificent homes on each side of the Atlantic; an illustrious career that would have assured him of another teaching position anywhere in Europe or the US; a remarkable ability to research and to write, so that he could become engrossed in any amount of fulfilling projects; a loving, intelligent companion who would always remain by his side.

The Porters' friend Nicky Mariano had no difficulty in believing that Kingsley had drowned by accident, having fallen from the slippery cliffs in stormy conditions: 'For us who knew Kingsley's love of dangerous climbs combined with his so easily being lost in a dream nothing seemed more likely than his absent-minded attempt to climb from one rock to another in spite of the violent storm. Swept away by a wave his body was carried off by the strong current and never found again.'[15]

There were many, however, who remained dissatisfied with the verdict. Rumours continued unabated that Kingsley Porter used to secretly visit his wife in the castle at night.[16] There were also darker, more sensational stories, recklessly told and embellished by people who knew nothing about the Porters. One account told how Kingsley had been murdered by locals because he was having an affair with one of the young ladies.[17] This tale may have been a gross exaggeration of the rumour that had been circulating among servants in local country houses since 1930, that Kingsley was having an affair.[18] There was also idle gossip that Mrs Porter had had her husband killed to inherit his estate.[19]

There was no shortage of superstitious explanations to account for the professor's sudden disappearance. Although Catholicism was the religion of the large majority of Irish people, superstition was rife, particularly in rural areas. Stories of ghosts and haunted houses were commonplace, passed down from one generation to another.[20] Eddie Heron, born in Ardlaghan, Cloghan, Co. Donegal in 1913, recalled the supernatural beliefs of his neighbourhood when he was a youth, including sightings of fairies, and the cry of the banshee that signalled death or misfortune: 'I heard the Banshee myself. I heard her, her lonely crying. It was a sign that someone was going to die.'[21]

It was not surprising that a local myth was resurrected to account for Kingsley's disappearance, telling how a jealous rival had turned the cursing stones of Innishmurray against him, presumably for all his delving into Irish archaeological matters.[22] The curse that had been put on Black Jack Adair and the future owners of Glenveagh Castle was also said to have resulted in Kingsley's sudden demise.[23] There were also more romantic stories of Kingsley being smuggled off the island and travelling to Paris, where he made a new life.[24] This rumour persisted and is still recounted today by the descendants of some Inishbofin islanders.[25]

For those who insisted on a supernatural explanation for Kingsley's demise, then his disturbance of the tomb at Sahagún in 1926, the subsequent onset of his depression and his mysterious disappearance would have been fodder for their belief in a medieval curse that had been unleashed on the unwary archaeologist. There was still one fact to emerge, involving the infamous sarcophagus slab, that was certainly uncanny. The negotiations that had been ongoing for two years between the Spanish government and representatives of the Fogg Art Museum, to return the burial artefact that Kingsley had brought to Harvard, were finally concluded.[26] The sarcophagus lid that had enclosed the tomb of Alfonso Ansúrez in 1093 was finally returned to its rightful place on 8 July 1933 – the day of Kingsley's disappearance. On that Saturday, the Fogg Art Museum received great praise from the Office of Museums of the League of Nations for returning such a venerated monument to the Spanish nation. The Director of the Museo Arqueologico Nacional de Madrid had good reason to remember 8 July with elation: 'The arrival of such a valuable stone shall mark a memorial date for the culture friendship between the museums of the world.'

The date of the return of the coffin slab would surely have struck Lucy as being deeply ironic. She returned to Elmwood on Friday 22 September,[27] and the following Monday she noted in her engagement diary: 'College opens.' Two days later, on 26 September, Kingsley's will was filed for probate at East Cambridge.[28] Under Kingsley's will, Elmwood was given to Lucy for the duration of her life, but would pass into the hands of Harvard after her death, with the hope that the university 'will preserve and maintain the house as a historical monument'. The will also provided a trust fund for Lucy of $100,000, the income of which was to go to her for life. On Lucy's death, the principal was to go to the President and fellows of Harvard for the maintenance of Elmwood, or, if this was unnecessary, for the purchase of works of art for the Fogg Art Museum.

The rest of Kingsley's estate went to Lucy, who was named co-executor with Louis Porter.[29] After Kingsley's personal difficulties with Harvard, his will is testament to his belief in Harvard as a university of excellence, and to his hope that in a more enlightened era, prejudice against individuals for their colour, creed or sexual orientation would cease.

Then, in early October, an incredible story gained currency in Inishbofin: that the professor's bones had been discovered.[30] The report was printed widely in local, national and international newspapers. The most detailed account was reported by *The Leitrim Observer* on Saturday 7 October.[31] A young boy, Ned Herrity, from Inishbofin had been walking along the strand when he saw bones buried in the sand. According to the article, 'Two of them were visible and to the boy they looked like the bones of a human shoulder. He reported the matter to adults who presumed them to be those of Professor Kingsley Porter. Falcarragh Guards are awaiting a suitable tide to investigate the find.'

Far from solving the mystery of the professor's disappearance, however, the story of the bones only compounded the enigma. *The Irish Times* carried a further report that on the previous Tuesday, 3 October, Superintendent Glenn and Sergeant Baker of Falcarragh visited the Island, as the tide was considered favourable to investigate the alleged discovery made by the Inishbofin boy.[32] The guards were shown the place where the bones were supposed to have been seen. Although a thorough search was made, no trace of any bones could be found.

The Irish Times article concluded: 'It was believed possible when the boy told the story that they were the remains of Professor Kingsley Porter, whose death by drowning was presumed.'[33] Yet again, Kingsley's fate was inconclusive: the bones had also vanished without trace.

Chapter seventeen

Aftermath

In October 1933, Lucy set about establishing a scientific fellowship for research into homosexuality.[1] Lucy contacted Dr Ellis on 19 October to ask if he could recommend a colleague who would be interested in receiving a scholarship to study homosexuality:

> My plan now is to make a short will (which will be as you suggest a provisional will) leaving the bulk of Kingsley's money to his brother. Then in a sealed letter to him, requesting him to use a stipulated amount of this money to forward a trust the interest of which is to be used to pay a firstclass scientist, doctor, or professor... My object would be:
> 1. to help homosexuals to understand themselves
> 2. to have society to understand them with the hope that they may lead happy and useful lives in society. Mr Louis Porter will not be bound legally but morally he will, which is sufficient. Probably I shall live to take the matter in hand, so as to make serious, and I hope adequate investigations.

Lucy had learned from first-hand experience just how mistreated and misunderstood people with homosexual tendencies were in the America of the 1930s. It was also apparent that she believed that Kingsley's demise, and that of many other sensitive and brilliant people, was caused by society's harsh and disparaging judgement. To no one but Ellis could Lucy admit that she was very relieved to have escaped appearing before the Probate Court in Massachusetts, unlike the situation in which she had been questioned at the Irish inquest: 'The Court of the Commonwealth of Massachusetts admitted Kingsley's will for probation (I am never sure my legal prepositions are correct) without my ever having to appear before the Judge in chambers. So I am pleased I have not had to talk and have kept my peace about so much concerning Kingsley.[2]

In her letter to Dr Ellis, Lucy also mentioned Alan.[3] She was obviously still corresponding with Alan as she knew he was working on his book and writing articles about his travels in India.

Lucy's sponsorship of the research was to remain anonymous. So, on Lucy's behalf, Ellis contacted an American psychiatrist, Dr Joseph Wortis from New York.[4] Wortis believed that Kingsley Porter had committed suicide because he had been rejected by his gay lover.[5] Lucy again wrote to Ellis on 9 February 1934, stating her hope that Wortis's work would be beneficial in moving society towards a more sympathetic view of homosexuality.[6] She also mentioned her own goal: 'that he may help and save a life of value before the breaking point'.

In her letter to Ellis,[7] Lucy also enclosed a letter written by Æ and addressed to Ellis,[8] in which he discussed the doctor's philosophy of sex and the causes of sexual aberrations. Æ wished to discuss the subject of sex in the context of eastern mystical literature, the study of eros and its natural and cosmic aspects. He stated his beliefs that the fire element sometimes strays and becomes incorrectly channelled through the system, creating sexual abnormalities.

Wortis never wanted to become a sexologist or to concentrate on the study of homosexuality.[9] Nevertheless, he agreed to accept the money from Lucy under the following condition: 'it allowed me to pursue my general psychiatric training, with a view to later turning my interests to special studies in the field of sex'. Wortis also requested to undergo analysis with Freud before studying homosexuality.

During 1934, Lucy compiled *The Writings of A. Kingsley Porter (1883–1933): A Bibliography,* that included references for her husband's collection of books and articles.[10] It was published by the Fogg Art Museum.

Lucy still kept up a correspondence with Æ. During the summer of 1934, Lucy returned to Glenveagh with her two sisters while Æ rented a cottage in Ballymore, Co. Donegal.[11] Lucy asked Æ to visit Glenveagh but reluctantly he refused, as he was caught up in writing a book for Macmillan on his reminiscences and he needed to return to Dublin in July.[12] He still recalled his special fondness for Glenveagh: 'It must be lovely at Glenveagh now. I see a misty sun here and imagine what it must be on the lakes and hills in Donegal.'

On 21 September 1934, Lucy wrote to Ellis, outlining her misgivings about financing Dr Wortis's studies with Freud, due to a drop in her finances caused by another slump in the American stock markets.[13] However she finally consented to pay $1,600 for Wortis's four-month analysis with Freud and also agreed to pay him a stipend for seven years to study homosexuality.[14] Wortis never did study what Lucy had requested.[15] He did not agree with Lucy's view that homosexual tendencies were innate. He refused to use science to come to the defence of homosexuals[16] and he concluded his research by deciding that homosexuality was conditioned and not inherent, a result that was contradictory to the beliefs of both Lucy and Havelock Ellis.[17]

Lucy still continued to attend lectures on Irish antiquities and medieval archaeology.[18] So much of Kingsley's world had seeped into her own being that she found herself socializing with his Harvard colleagues, exhibiting his medieval art collection at various events and publishing his remaining works in a number of volumes.

Just after Thanksgiving that year, on 28 November, the Porter family suffered another tragedy when Louis's youngest daughter, 24-year-old Beatrice, died after an illness.[19] Lucy had always been close to both Joyce and Beatrice so this must have been another bitter blow to her and the whole Porter family.

Lucy continued to spend several months each year at Glenveagh. On 23 April 1935, Æ wrote to Lucy, saying he would love to accept her invitation to stay at Glenveagh but he was feeling unwell due to an inflammation of the colon.[20] He wrote to Lucy again on 2 June: 'I have no more now to say except to thank you for your letter and hope to see you sometime when I am recovered. Yours ever, Æ.'[21]

It was the last letter that Æ ever sent to Lucy. After a long battle with cancer, he died in Bournemouth, Dorset, on 17 July 1935.[22] Æ, the great poet, orator, mystic and economist, was mourned throughout Ireland and the US. His death was yet another sad loss for Lucy to bear.

The following summer, Lucy returned to Glenveagh. On 29 June, Kingsley's old friend Peter Teigen, artist and professor of drawing at Princeton, came to visit.[23] From the beginning of his holiday he appeared to be ill, and his condition worsened on Tuesday 11 August, but he refused to accept medical treatment as he was a Christian Scientist.[24] He continued to weaken but would not see a doctor. In desperation, Lucy contacted a male nurse in London who was also a Christian Scientist, in the hope that Teigen would see him. Her plan was to have the nurse transport Teigen to London for specialist treatment if he was fit to travel. By the time Nurse Hugh James Thomas arrived at Glenveagh, Teigen was already dying. He suffered heart failure on Thursday 13 August and died in Glenveagh Castle.[25] He was just 42 years old.[26]

Lucy was called as a witness at the inquest into the death of her friend and had to obtain the representation of her solicitor, Mr Cox.[27] A verdict of natural causes due to tuberculosis that had brought on the heart attack was returned.[28] The death of Professor Teigen revived the newspapers' interest in Kingsley Porter's disappearance. They reminded readers that just three years previously, Lucy's husband had disappeared in mysterious circumstances and that his body had never been found.[29]

The recent deaths that Lucy had experienced must have been difficult to deal with. Still, she had been reared to believe in the restorative power of work so she threw herself into several important projects in memory of Æ and Kingsley. In February 1937, *Æ's Letters To Mínanlábáin* was published.[30] It is a record of Æ's letters to Kingsley and Lucy from December 1930 to June 1936, just before Æ's death. Lucy wrote the introduction to the book that includes a beautifully written but poignant description of that final, fateful day when

Kingsley disappeared on Inishbofin. Lucy's last lines describe the freedom that she had finally found, now that all fear had passed: 'And now that the sea had become his sepulchre I was released from the dread of it which had haunted me... This fear which had always hung upon me suddenly dropped and let me free.'[31]

In February 1937, an American visitor to Glenveagh, Una Jeffers, wrote to a friend, telling her that Lucy planned to visit Italy on an archaeological trip.[32] Mrs Jeffers described Lucy as 'a busy, keen, energetic woman – devoted to the husband who drowned from their house on Inishbofin Is. 4 yrs ago. We found ourselves very sympathetic.'

Later that year, Lucy also published *Glenveagh Castle: Visitors' Book 1931–1937*, recalling happier times when Æ spent the summer of 1931 at Glenveagh, sketching, painting, and discussing literature and economics with Kingsley, well into the small hours of the morning.[33] Just when Lucy must have felt that she was getting her life back on track, however, another catastrophe occurred. In July 1937, Lucy's chauffeur, Thomas McCann, was transporting guests to Glenveagh when a cyclist failed to stop at a crossroads.[34] The driver put on the brakes and swerved but the car went into a skid. The 70-year-old cyclist, John Mitchell, was struck and fatally injured, and he was pronounced dead on arrival at Lifford hospital. Yet another inquest was held involving Lucy and Glenveagh Castle. It was found that the chauffeur had only been driving at thirty miles an hour and that the brakes were in perfect working order. The verdict was returned in accordance with the medical evidence and the driver was exonerated.

It was as though Lucy's once charmed life was slowly disintegrating and she was powerless to stop the destructive forces that threatened to annihilate her world. Neither Lucy nor Kingsley had practised organized religion, yet even the greatest sceptic might have begun to question whether some curse from the days of Black Jack Adair[35] or from the disturbed sarcophagus slab was being fulfilled. Lucy's feelings at the time are unknown but what is certain is that she immediately began to look for a buyer for Glenveagh.

The perfect candidate to buy the castle and magnificent estate was Henry McIllhenny, art collector and curator at the Philadelphia Museum of Art. McIllhenny had already stayed at Glenveagh and had been a former student of Kingsley's at Harvard.[36] McIllhenny was described in *The Irish Independent* as 'a typical square-shouldered, good-looking and rich American bachelor from Philadelphia'.[37] Apparently he was so enamoured with Glenveagh and Donegal that he wrote to a friend in raptures about the beauty of the county: 'No summer in this country (USA) can measure up to a few months in Donegal.'

On a curious note, McIllhenny was also homosexual and was quite open about his tendencies.[38] Not surprisingly, he never married and remained childless. Lucy sold Glenveagh to McIllhenny for £5,000 in 1937.[39] Before leaving Ireland, Lucy presented over 1,000 of Kingsley's books and 500 of his pamphlets to the National Museum of Ireland.[40]

On her return to Elmwood, Lucy maintained a correspondence with Dr Ellis. On 12 May 1939 she wrote to him while visiting England, saying she hoped to meet him.[41] She told him of her plans to visit Italy, 'to continue studying and photographing the Lombard Churches'. Her secretary, Natalie Hoyt, accompanied her. It was a way of reliving those joyous days in the mid-1920s when she stood beside Kingsley, writing her copious diary entries and photographing Romanesque church interiors. While Lucy was in Italy that summer, *Medieval Studies in Memory of A. Kingsley Porter* was published in two volumes by Harvard University Press.[42] Lucy had written the introduction to this well-received work.

Havelock Ellis died on 8 July 1939. When Lucy returned to Elmwood in December, she wrote to his mistress, Françoise Lafitte-Cyon, offering sympathy on the death of a truly great physician.[43] Lucy also mentioned that she was living quietly at Elmwood, working and studying. She wrote of the horrors of yet another world war, recalling her days with Kingsley in Paris during the final days of the First World War.

Lucy lived out the remainder of her days at Elmwood, becoming the Grand Dame of Cambridge, a renowned patron of the arts and a generous organizer of fundraising events for many charities and social causes.

She continued to hold dinner parties at Elmwood and to entertain distinguished guests, but much of the sparkle and adventure of her years with Kingsley also vanished on that fateful July morning at Inishbofin.

In his memoirs, Austin Warren described Mrs Porter in the late 1930s as 'neither beautiful nor elegant nor brilliant; nor in any other way stylized. It was her husband who had created the setting, the world, the ritual which she, proud of him and of his books and his international circle of friends–art historians and artists–felt it her obligation to continue.'[44] It is surprising that Warren could not decipher Lucy's intelligence and charm that had so captivated Kingsley Porter and many of his Harvard Colleagues at the height of those glittering years at Elmwood. Perhaps Lucy was growing tired and lacklustre as the days, months and years dragged on. Gone was the zest and thrill that had once possessed her whenever Kingsley was near, suggesting another quest that would fill every moment with breathless zeal.

In June 1939, Lucy loaned some of Kingsley's collection of Italian paintings, including a Jacopo di Cione, to the exhibition of New England Art Collectors at the Museum of Fine Arts, Boston.[45] For the medieval art exhibition that took place in Boston in the spring of 1940, Lucy loaned Italian sculptures, including one of the highlights of the exhibition, a marble statue dated 1300 AD, *The Adorning Angel*, that had once occupied the Duomo in Florence.[46] In April 1941 she was one of the distinguished guests at the Pan-American Society of Massachusetts reception that was held at the Fogg Art Museum.[47]

During the war years, Lucy was involved in many fundraising events on behalf of the Cambridge Women's War Finance Committee.[48] She also continued to sponsor musical events, including a concert at the Cambridge Teachers' Club.[49] Lucy was also a committee member for the grand victory ball that was organized by the Massachusetts Federation of the Polish Women's Club, held in Statler in November 1945.[50]

Throughout the 1940s and 1950s, Lucy continued to champion the cause of international students studying in Boston,[51] women's groups and artists,[52] musicians, and various fundraising events.[53] Lucy also continued to entertain guests for dinner and musical events at Elmwood.[54]

In 1949, Lucy wrote a book on the history of the occupants of Elmwood, entitled *The Owners of Elmwood: A History & Memoir*,[55] that was published by Cambridge Historical Society.

In Kingsley's memory, Lucy still kept Elmwood open to students and Harvard professors.[56] In her senior years she adopted many of Kingsley's traits, particularly his desire to live without modern conveniences as he had done in the fisherman's hut on Inishbofin. Elmwood became dilapidated as Lucy chose to live in flickering candlelight and without proper sewage connections. *The Harvard Crimson* described the elderly Mrs Porter:

> [the] widow of a Harvard professor of Fine Arts and a strong-willed woman who brooked no meddling with her crumbling mansion. Shunning modern comforts, she lived by 19th Century candlelight that masked the rotting timbers in shadow and made her appear so formidable that even the City of Cambridge dared not violate her wishes by installing sewer connections. The great elms which gave the house its name had grown up into the sort of forest one finds in Grimm tales, and inside, each of the twelve large rooms was done up in gloomy Victorian style – a sad fate for what was once a bright, airy Colonial country house.[57]

One by one the central players in the life she had shared with Kingsley met their demise. Louis Porter died on 18 January 1946, at the age of 71.[58] His wife Marion died only five months later, on 29 June, aged 73 years.[59] Just three offspring remained: Joyce (Arneill), Louise and Louis Junior. The Porter homestead in Darien was sold later that year to the Daycroft School.[60]

Alan Campbell fulfilled his dream when the Paris publishers Obelisk Press accepted his novel *Starborn* (1938), under the pseudonym Arion.[61] He finally settled in San Francisco, where he opened a bookshop and art gallery, Studio Forty-Four, on Filmore Street. In November 1959 he was injured in a bar. Later that evening he tripped while going downstairs and died on the landing below. He was just 49 years old.

42. Man wading and man in rowboat, Inishbofin shore,
photograph, c. 1929.
Harvard University Archives, HUG 1706.125 (12).

Alone in Elmwood with her books, letters and photographs, Lucy
must have often relived those golden days in Paris just after the war, and
those glorious summer afternoons at Glenveagh when she walked with
Kingsley across the purple hills. Lucy kept everything – photos, letters,
journals – and later bequeathed the collection to Harvard.[62] Only the
letters from Dr Ellis and Alan Campbell were destroyed. Among that
vast collection there is one photo that shows Kingsley striding towards
a boat. There is an unidentified person already inside, waiting.
Kingsley's back is turned and he is just seconds away from getting into
the boat and rowing across the sea to the mainland.

In *Medieval Studies* (1939), Lucy eloquently wrote her final farewell
to her beloved Kingsley:

> And here, at Inish Bofin, he was drowned (July 8, 1933)...The
> gentle bearing of this tall, self-effacing man contrasted strangely
> with the daring ruggedness of his mind. In Ireland his originality

reveled in handling in unexpected ways the pagan and Christian sagas, as is shown in 'Columcille Goes', a play based on the life of that gentle-stormy Irish saint...And in Ireland, his own life – a silent shining flame – for the last time curved upwards, suddenly to drop like a rocket into the sea.[63]

Lucy died at Elmwood on 19 September 1962, at the age of 86.[64] If indeed Lucy knew anything further of her husband's fate, then she carried the secret to her grave.

Chapter eighteen

Legend and Legacy

The legend that Arthur Kingsley Porter was still alive and had relocated to some exotic city in Europe or Asia continued for many years. Although the Coroner recorded death by misadventure at the inquest held on 12 September 1933, still the speculation continued. Later there were reports that Kingsley had been seen in Paris, while others said they saw him in Brussels.[1] A group of American archaeologists swore they saw Kingsley Porter at Silos.[2] Kingsley had written about the Abbey of Santo Domingo de Silos in northern Spain in *Romanesque Sculpture of the Pilgrimage Roads* (1923). He had considered the architectural brilliance of the abbey to be at 'a level equal with, if not superior, to that of the best contemporary work in Europe'.[3] It would have been fitting indeed if Kingsley had relocated to northern Spain after his devotion to the study of Spanish sculpture for over a decade.

Speculation as to the fate of Kingsley Porter continued unabated for many years. Lucy's grand-niece, Ellen, was the wife of Adlai Stevenson, who later ran for the US Presidency. Ellen had visited Glenveagh on several occasions. Her husband mentioned in a talk that he gave to the Wayfarer's Club in Chicago on 20 November 1941 that Kingsley Porter had disappeared because he knew 'too much about the little people, that inhabit the dangerous, obscure nooks and crannies of the wild ancient country'.[4]

Professor Harbison reported hearing or reading somewhere that Kingsley Porter had been seen at the quay at Marseille in France, and also in a Buddhist monastery in India.[5] Morton Vose, Harvard graduate and art historian, was an acquaintance of Kingsley's at Harvard.[6] In an oral interview with Robert F. Brown in 1986, Vose described Professor Porter and the rumours that followed his disappearance – that he had in fact faked his death in order to start a new life: 'He was a very ethereal sort of man. As I remember he had a strange mysterious end. He was drowned off the coast of Ireland, sailing. There were strange rumours that he wanted to get away from it all and staged the thing, and that he was somewhere else. I don't know about that.'[7]

Rumours that Kingsley often returned at night to Glenveagh Castle to visit Lucy are still recalled today.[8] Descendants of the families who lived on the island at the time of the Porters still speak kindly of the wealthy Americans who gave their ancestors two pounds for the privilege of having access to the best beach on the island.[9] To the islanders at the time of Kingsley's disappearance, it was more than possible that the Harvard gentleman had found a way off the island and had kept on travelling. Such was the extent of Kingsley's wealth that it would have been entirely possible for him to relocate to any country of his choosing.

There are still two questions that remain unanswered: was Kingsley rowed to the mainland from Inishbofin before the storm took hold, with or without Lucy's knowledge? Could he have continued his studies and travels as the medieval pilgrim he had always yearned to be, leaving behind a life that was no longer tenable?

Kingsley was an intrepid traveller, having explored the Middle East, North Africa and Asia on his world tour in 1902.[10] From August 1918 to August 1921 he had lived almost full-time in Europe, traversing France, Italy and Spain, exploring tiny villages and embracing many conditions and landscapes, including sunny sandstone valleys and sloping vineyards, bleak icy mountains and hot arid plains. He had travelled widely throughout the US and, at the age of 50, he was still fit, adventurous and craving the freedom to carve out a new life, away from prying eyes. His knowledge and experience of world travel was impressive. He had the time and the means to plan his disappearance meticulously. This was an era when no identification was required to open bank accounts and there was little likelihood that any questions would be asked if a wealthy gentleman deposited large amounts of cash anywhere in the world.

What is highly unlikely, however, is that Lucy Porter had any part in staging Kingsley's disappearance. The story is still told by islanders today, of Lucy running into the village, distraught and dishevelled, looking for help to search for her missing husband.[11] Lucy Porter would have gone to great lengths to please her husband, but putting on such a bizarre, prolonged performance that involved an entire island would not have been in her character. If indeed Kingsley left the island and travelled abroad, it must have been without Lucy's knowledge. There is, however, always the possibility that Kingsley contacted her at some future time. They may have even met again, perhaps on her 1939 archaeological tour of Italy, but this is all mere conjecture.

In Woodland Cemetery in Stamford, Connecticut, each member of the Porter and Hoyt families share a shaded plot of ground, finally united in death, the conflicts and disputes of the past all laid to rest. The small, simple footstones lie side by side. The large stone monument contains an entry for Kingsley:

Arthur Kingsley Porter

February 6 1883

Drowned at sea

July 8 1933[12]

On the other side of the Atlantic, the hut that Kingsley built on Inishbofin has almost disintegrated and is now little more than a pile of rubble. Lucy never set foot on the island again after her traumatic ordeal on that July day, so that the hut slowly decayed. The island is now deserted, except for a few islanders who return to their old homesteads every summer. Luckily, Elmwood and Glenveagh Castle continue to be well maintained. After Lucy's death, Elmwood became the residence of the President of Harvard; a bequest of over one million dollars was also willed by Lucy to Harvard, to maintain a chair that was to be called the A. Kingsley Porter Professorship.[13] In 1975, Henry McIllhenny sold the

43. Woodland Cemetery, Stamford, CT, USA.

Michael Cullen.

Glenveagh Estate to the Irish State and it became known as Glenveagh National Park. In 1983 he bestowed Glenveagh Castle and gardens to the Irish nation.[14]

44. Inishbofin Island showing ruined hut.
Michael Cullen.

Throughout the decades many academics and archaeologists have concentrated on Kingsley's legacy, on all that he brought to the study of medieval sculpture and monuments. His brilliance as a writer and original researcher is undisputed and his work is still studied today, despite the great technological advances in research techniques that Kingsley foretold would come to pass. His ability as a teacher to inspire his students had lasting and substantial effects, as several of his protégés followed in his footsteps and made their mark on the study of architecture and art history. Kenneth Conant went on to teach at Harvard and carried out extensive excavations of the medieval abbey at Cluny;[15] Walter Muir Whitehill developed Kingsley's ideas of the importance of Spanish sculpture over a Franco-centric model; Russell Hitchcock became a renowned teacher, historian and author.[16]

The Committee of the Faculty of Arts and Sciences of Harvard described Kingsley Porter thus:'Pre-eminent among his many distinctions as a scholar was the union that he attained of broad erudition and scientific method, with the nature of a poet.'[17]

Kingsley's great friend, the Harvard historian Bernard Berenson, dedicated his book, *Aesthetics and History* (1954), to his favourite sparring partners, Denman Ross and Arthur Kingsley Porter:'May we meet there [in Elysium] and quarrel there as merrily as we have here on earth.'[18]

The preface to Kingsley's three plays, written by Walter Muir Whitehill, depicts an almost Indiana Jones-type character, who fused scholarly archaeologist with maverick adventurer:

> Those who shared his friendship and confidence in Elmwood, in Ireland, or on the Continent, felt the man was greater than the scholar, and that his most characteristic thoughts were so far removed from conventional archaeology that they were more appropriate for walks by the Charles, through Irish bogs, or in a Spanish Plaza Mayor, than for the pages of his learned works.[19]

The fact that Kingsley's theories are still discussed today at symposiums on medieval architecture throughout the world confirms his rightful place in the annals of architectural studies. His writings total 274 works, published in 526 publications, in seven languages.[20] His photographic collection contains 35,000 photographs and 11,700 negatives, pertaining to every aspect of medieval art.[21] Perhaps his greatest legacy is his explanation for the gradual evolution of Romanesque art and sculpture through France and Spain, citing the influence of monasticism and pilgrimage in the sharing of knowledge.[22]

Despite such an illustrious legacy, the legend still remains. For it is the legends and stories of heroes, villains, gods and magicians that have always intrigued the human imagination. The person who would have loved this legend most of all was Kingsley himself. It would have given him great delight that people believed him to be travelling the world, continuing his research and studies. Kingsley, the romantic and idealist, would have revelled in the vision of an eccentric multimillionaire, now exiled from his home and family, wandering from one medieval ruin to another, perhaps carrying little more than a satchel on his back that contained all his worldly goods, free and unfettered to pursue his studies and adventures, dwelling in primitive conditions, sleeping in caves or in open fields beneath the stars.

45. Arthur Kingsley Porter,
Courtesy of Glenveagh Castle Archives.

Notes

The Search: Inishbofin, Co. Donegal, 8 July 1933

1. Main chapter source: National Archives of Ireland, Coroner's Inquest, Co. Donegal, 1933, IC/83/117.
2. Harvard University Archives, HUG 1706.114, Porter Family Correspondence, Correspondence of A.K. Porter and Lucy W. Porter, c. 1914–19, Box 1, Letter from Kingsley to Lucy, from Dijon, undated.
3. Harvard University Archives, HUG 1706.114, Correspondence of Arthur Kingsley Porter and Lucy W. Porter, 1911–25, 1918, Letters from A. Kingsley Porter in Rome to Lucy W. Porter in Paris, undated.
4. L.K. Porter, 'Introduction', in Æ (George Russell), *Æ's Letters to Mínanlábáin* (New York: Macmillan, 1937), p.16.

Early Life: The Scandal That Shook Darien

1. Stamford Vital Records, 1875 to 1906, Page: 133: Births 1883 O–P.
2. M. Hart, 'Darien: A Brief History', Darien Historical Society (2009), http://www.darienct.gov/content/108/415/423/default.aspx.
3. J. Beckwich, 'Kingsley Porter: Blazing the Trail in Europe', *Apollo* (December 1970), pp.494–7.
4. Yale University, Obituary Record: Graduates of Yale University, Deceased from June 1900 to June 1910, vol. 1900 to 1910 (New Haven, CT).
5. Ibid.
6. 'Died', *New York Times*, 28 December 1861.
7. 'Widow of a Millionaire', *Sun* (Baltimore), 4 February 1901.
8. D.W. Hoyt, *The Hoyt Family Meeting: Held at Stamford Connecticut, 20–1 June 1866* (Boston, MA: Henry Hoyt, 1866).
9. E.W. Forbes, 'Arthur Kingsley Porter (1883–1933)', *Proceedings of the American Academy of Arts and Sciences*, 69, 13 (February 1935), p.537.
10. 'Married', *New York Times*, 10 November 1870.
11. Stamford Historical Society website: http://www.stamfordhistory.org/.
12. *Gracious Living in Stamford, Late 19th and 20th Early Centuries* (Stamford Historical Society, c. 1892).
13. Rootsweb: http://wc.rootsweb.ancestry.com/.
14. Harvard University Archives, HUG 1706.110, Family Correspondence 1880–99,

Correspondence and papers of Porter Family, Folder 1882–83, Letter from Louisa to Timothy H., undated.

15. Ibid.

16. Ibid.

17. Harvard University Archives, HUG 1706.110, Family Correspondence 1880–99, Correspondence and papers of Porter Family, Folder 1882–83, Letter from Timothy H. Porter to Blachley Porter, undated.

18. Harvard University Archives, HUG 1706.110, Family correspondence and papers of Porter Family 1880–99, Letter from Timothy H. to Kingsley, undated.

19. Harvard University Archives, HUG 1706.110, Family correspondence 1880–99, Letter from Timothy H. to Louise, undated.

20. Harvard University Archives, HUG 1706.110, Family correspondence and papers of Porter Family 1880–99, Folder 1892–93, Letter from Louis to Kingsley, 9 April 1893.

21. Harvard University Archives, HUG 1706.110, Family correspondence and papers of Porter Family 1880–99, Correspondence and papers of Porter Family, 1892–93, Letter from Blachley to Kingsley, 17 April 1892.

22. Harvard University Archives, HUG 1706.110, Family correspondence and papers of Porter Family 1885–86, Folder 1892–93, Letter from Timothy H. Porter to Kingsley, 15 July 1886.

23. Harvard University Archives, HUG 1706.110, Family correspondence and papers of Porter Family 1880–99, Folder 1892–93, Letter from Blachley to Kingsley, 17 April 1892.

24. Harvard University Archives, HUG 1706.110, Family correspondence and papers of Porter Family 1880–99, Poems written to Kingsley's mother by her husband on her birthdays, 1866–76.

25. Rootsweb: http://wc.rootsweb.ancestry.com/.

26. Yale University, Obituary Record: Graduates of Yale University, Deceased from June 1900 to June 1910, vol. 1900 to 1910 (New Haven, CT).

27. The dates of birth and death for many of the Porter and Hoyt clan were obtained by the author from the monument at Woodland Cemetery, Fairfield County Stamford, Connecticut, USA. The Porter/Hoyt plot at Woodland Cemetery contains a central monument in Section D and twenty-nine footstones, arranged in a circular pattern around the monument. The monument is inscribed on four faces: Central Face: Porter/Arthur Kingsley Porter/February 6 1883/Drowned at sea/July 8 1933/His Wife/Lucy Wallace Porter/January 23, 1876/September 19, 1962/Timothy Hopkins Porter/Born Feb. 16 1826/Died Jan. 1 1901/Edmund L. Hoyt/Dec. 8th 1882, Aug. 25th 1883/Louise/Daughter of Joseph B. Hoyt/And wife of/Timothy H. Porter/Born May 6th 1847/Died Dec. 13th 1891/Blachley Hoyt Porter/Feb. 27 1876, Aug 1 1895.
Right Face: Joseph Blachley Hoyt/Died Dec. 27, 1888/Aged 75 years, and 1 Mon and 5 days/Catherine/Wife of/Joseph B. Hoyt/Died Dec. 7th 1862/Aged 46 years 9 Mons and 11 days/Edward Hoyt/Died Oct 8th 1853/Aged 1 year and 14 days.
Right face+1: Porter/Louis Hopkins Porter/March 10 1874/January 18 1946 Ellen Marion Porter/September 7 1872/June 29 1946/Their children/Beatrice Sept. 6 1910/Nov. 28 1934/Louise Hoyt Porter/January 1 1904/July 31

1980/Buried at Henfield Cemetery/Sussex, England/Louis Hopkins Porter, Jr./Dec. 19 1904/Nov. 27 1984/Mary C. Hoyt/Died July 26 1877/Aged 59 Yrs and 10 Mos/Susan Evans/Wife of Joseph B. Hoyt/Born Oct 20 1837/Died Aug 21 1907/JOSEPH B. HOYT/Jane Forby /Wife of/Frederick M. Hoyt/Born Feb 28 1881/Died July 17 1932/Frederick M. Hoyt/Sept 15 1873/July 5 1940.

Right Face+2: Joseph Hoyt/Died Dec. 25 1854/Aged 67 years and 10 mos/Maria B. Hoyt/

Died Sept 28th 1854/Aged 63 years and 6 mos/Sylvester Hoyt/Died Sept 10th 1847/Aged 10 years and 10 mos/Alvah Hoyt/Died March 31st 1853/Aged 23 years and 11 mos.

Layout of twenty-nine footstones in Porter/Hoyt plot at Woodland Cemetery (reproduced by kind permission of researcher Barbara Kaye):

Emily M. [Emily M. Hoyt, daughter of Joseph Blachley Hoyt & Mary Blachley Weed]; Sylvester [Sylvester Hoyt, son of Joseph Blachley Hoyt & Mary Blachley Weed]; Maria B. [Mary Blachley Weed, daughter of Eliphalet Weed & Mary Hoyt]; Joseph [Joseph Blachley Hoyt, son of Joseph Hoyt & Sarah Weed]; Alvah [Hoyt, Alvah, daughter of Joseph B. Hoyt & Mary B. Weed]; Mary; Marion [Ellen Marion Hatch, wife of Louis H. Porter]

Louis H. [Louis Hopkins Porter, son of Timothy Hopkins Porter & Maria Louisa Hoyt]; Beatrice [daughter of Louis H. Porter & Ellen Marion Hatch]; Louis H., Jr. [Louis Hopkins Porter, Jr., son of Louis Hopkins Porter & Ellen Marion Hatch]; Louise Hoyt [Louise Hoyt Porter, daughter of Louis Hopkins Porter & Ellen Marion Hatch]; Kingsley [Arthur Kingsley Porter, son of Louis Hopkins Porter & Ellen Marion Hatch]; Lucy [Lucy Bryant Wallace, wife of Arthur Kingsley Porter]; Edmund [Edmund L. Hoyt, son of Joseph Blachley Hoyt & Susan S. Evans]; Edward [Edward Hoyt, son of Joseph Blachley Hoyt & Mary Blachley Weed]; Catherine [Catherine Krom, 1st wife of Joseph Blachley Hoyt]; Joseph B. [Joseph Blachley Hoyt]; Susan E. [Susan S. Evans, second wife of Joseph Blachley Hoyt]; Louise; Blachley; Joanna Krom, born Jan. 1, 1838, died Jan. 2, 1920; Timothy H. Porter, born Feb. 16, 1828, died Jan. 1, 1901; Jane; Fred; Emily; Samuel; Ellen; Susie; Lucy; Edwina.

28. 'Mr Merritt's Statement: What He Has to Say about the Fayerweather and Hoyt Wills', *New York Times*, 10 January 1891.

29. 'Timothy H. Porter Dead: Well-Known Trustee of the J.B. Hoyt Estate Passes Away', *Sun* (New York), 3 January 1901.

30. 'Died', *Evening Post* (New York), 14 December 1891.

31. 'Mr Porter's Love Letters, Some of the Copies that One of the Millionaires Sons Made', *Sun* (New York), 12 January 1894.

32. United States Federal Census, 1870.

33. United States Patents, Oscar T. Earle, 10 January 1865; 9 March 1880; 9 September 1873; 14 June 1870; 9 March 1880.

34. *Sun* (New York), 4 October 1891.

35. United States Federal Census, 1880.

36. *Sun* (New York), 4 October 1891.

37. 'His Registration Accepted: Pastor McNeille's Dress Suit and Patent Leathers Lose the Day', *New York Times*, 30 March 1893.

38. 'Barred Doors to Bridal Couple: But Mr and Mrs Timothy H. Porter Effected an Entrance through a Rear Window: Third Wife on the Stand', *New York Herald*, 13 January 1897.
39. 'Millionaire Porter Claims Conspiracy', *New York Times*, 15 July 1894.
40. 'Porter Conspiracy Quashed', *New York Times*, 6 January 1898.
41. 'Mr Porter's Love Letters', *Sun* (New York), 12 January 1894.
42. Ibid.
43. Ibid.
44. Ibid.
45. Ibid.
46. Ibid.
47. Ibid.
48. Ibid.
49. Ibid.
50. Ibid.
51. Ibid.
52. 'Porter Conspiracy Quashed', *New York Times*, 6 January 1898.
53. 'Mr Porter's Lovemaking', *Sun* (New York), 11 January 1894.
54. 'Mr Porter's Love Letters', *Sun* (New York), 12 January 1894.
55. Ibid.
56. Forbes, 'Arthur Kingsley Porter', p.537.
57. 'Porter Conspiracy Quashed', *New York Times*, 6 January 1898.
58. 'Charges of Insanity Withdrawn', *New York Times*, 27 March 1894.
59. *Hudson Daily Evening Register* (New York), 19 March 1894.
60. 'Porter-Earle', *New York Times*, 30 March 1894.
61. 'Mr Porter Marries Miss Earle: He is the Eccentric Millionaire Whose Love Letters Became Public Recently', *Sun* (New York), 30 March 1894.
62. 'Timothy H. Porter's Estate: Contest of the Will Began and prolonged Litigation Likely', *Sun* (New York), 16 January 1901.
63. 'Mr Porter Marries Miss Earle', *Sun* (New York), 30 March 1894.
64. *Hudson Daily Evening Register* (New York), 19 March 1894.
65. 'Timothy H. Porter Dead: Well-Known Trustee of the J.B. Hoyt Estate Passes Away', *Sun* (New York), 3 January 1901.
66. 'Millionaire Porter Claims Conspiracy', *New York Times*, 15 July 1894.
67. Ibid.
68. 'Timothy Porter's Troubles: Answer of the Defendants Against Whom the Aged Bridegroom Brought Suit for $200,000', *New York Times*, 8 January 1895.
69. 'Barred Doors to Bridal Couple', *New York Herald*, 13 January 1897.
70. Ibid.
71. Ibid.
72. Ibid.
73. Ibid.
74. Ibid.
75. Ibid.
76. Ibid.
77. Ibid.

78. Ibid.
79. 'Bolt Fells Twenty People', *Arcadian Weekly Gazette*, 5 August 1895.
80. Ibid.
81. *Dictionary of Art Historians*, ed. Lee Sorensen (Durham, NC: Duke University), www.dictionaryofarthistorians.org.
82. 'Fight Over The Hoyt Estate Settled', *New York Tribune*, 29 July 1896.
83. 'Timothy H. Porter Suit Fails', *New York Tribune*, 14 March 1897.
84. Ibid.
85. Ibid.
86. 'Porter Conspiracy Quashed', *New York Times*, 6 January 1898.
87. 'Weddings', *New York Tribune*, 28 September 1901.
88. R. Keyser, *History of the First Company Governor's Foot Guard, Hartford, Connecticut, 1771–1901* (Hartford, CT: Case, Lockwood L. Brainard, 1901).
89. 'Quality not Quantity', *Bridgeport Herald*, 11 March 1900.
90. Ibid.
91. R. Johnson, *Twentieth Century Biographical Dictionary of Notable Americans* (Boston, MA: Biographical Society, 1904).

Coming of Age: Freedom and Vocation

1. 'Charges Against a Banknote Company', *New York Times*, 31 October 1902.
2. 'Timothy H. Porter Dead', *Sun* (New York), 3 January 1901.
3. 'Timothy H. Porter's Will', *Hartford Courant*, 14 January 1901.
4. 'Timothy H. Porter's Estate: Contest of the Will Began and Prolonged Litigation Likely', *Sun* (New York), 16 January 1901.
5. 'Timothy H. Porter Dead', *Sun* (New York), 3 January 1901.
6. 'Timothy H. Porter's Will', *Hartford Courant*, 14 January 1901.
7. 'Timothy H. Porter's Estate', *Sun* (New York), 16 January 1901.
8. Ibid; 'Timothy H. Porter's Will', *Hartford Courant*, 14 January 1901.
9. 'Timothy H. Porter's Estate', *Sun* (New York), 16 January 1901.
10. 'Settlement of Estate of Rev. Timothy H. Porter', *Hartford Courant*, 13 April 1901, p.2.
11. 'Widow of a Millionaire', *Sun* (Baltimore), 4 February 1901.
12. Maryland Historical Trust, Lambdin House, Survey Number T-253.
13. 'Weddings', *New York Tribune*, 28 September 1901.
14. 'Louis Porter Ill: Was Conspicuous Recently because of Litigation against His Father', *New York Tribune*, 2 December 1901.
15. Ibid.
16. United States Department of Immigration and Naturalization Archives, Passport Application of Arthur Kingsley Porter, 8 January 1902.
17. Forbes, 'Arthur Kingsley Porter', pp.537–41.
18. *Dictionary of American Biography* (New York: Charles Scribner's Sons, 1944), p.601; 'A. Kingsley Porter 1883–1933', *The Bulletin of the Fogg Art Museum*, 3 (November 1933), p.3.
19. Forbes, 'Arthur Kingsley Porter', pp.537–41; 'A. Kingsley Porter 1883–1933', *The Bulletin of the Fogg Art Museum*, p.4.
20. *A Cruise To The Orient: Auguste Victoria*, Hamburg-American Line, 1901 (leaflet).

21. Harvard University Archives, HUG 1706.150, selection of photos from Kingsley and Louis Porter's world tour of 1902.
22. *Utica Herald Dispatch*, 27 June 1904.
23. Ibid.
24. Ibid.
25. *Dictionary of American Biography*, p.600.
26. *Dictionary of Art Historians*, ed. Sorensen.
27. Ibid.
28. W.P. Koehler (ed.), *Medieval Studies in Memory of A. Kingsley Porter* (Cambridge: MA: Harvard University Press, 1939), cited in Beckwich, 'Kingsley Porter', p.494.
29. Ibid.
30. *Dictionary of Art Historians*, ed. Sorensen.
31. Ibid.
32. Forbes, 'Arthur Kingsley Porter', p.537.
33. *New York Times*, 4 December 1906.
34. Yale College Class Book 1904 (Dorman Lithographing, 1904), http://books. google.com/books?id=nkA4AAAAYAAJ&dq=blakeman+quintard+meyer&sites ec=reviews.
35. G.E. Parks (ed.), *Sexennial Record of the Class of 1904* (New Haven: CT, Yale University Press, 1911), p.204, cited in J. Mann, *Romanesque Architecture and its Structural Decoration in Christian Spain 1000–1200: Exploring Frontiers and Defining Identities* (Toronto: University of Toronto Press, 2009).
36. A.K. Porter, *Medieval Architecture: Its Origins and Development, with Lists of Monuments and Bibliographies*, 2 vols (New York: Baker & Taylor, 1909).
37. Mann, *Romanesque Architecture*, p.20.
38. Beckwich, 'Kingsley Porter', p.494.
39. 'A. Kingsley Porter 1883–1933', *The Bulletin of the Fogg Art Museum*, p.1.
40. A.K. Porter, *Medieval Architecture*, vol. 2, p.253, cited in Mann, *Romanesque Architecture*, p.20.
41. *Sun* (New York), 17 February 1909.
42. 'American Scholarship', *Washington Times*, 18 July 1908.
43. 'Among the Authors', *New York Times*, 2 January 1909.
44. A.K. Porter, *Beyond Architecture* (Boston, MA: Marshall Jones, 1918).
45. Ibid.
46. Harvard University Archives, HUG 1706.104, Letter from William Henry Goodyear to A. Kingsley Porter, 8 November 1909, cited in Mann, *Romanesque Architecture*, p.26.
47. *New York Times*, 17 April 1909.
48. Mann, *Romanesque Architecture*, p.20.
49. A.K. Porter, *Construction of Lombard and Gothic Vaults* (New Haven, CT: Yale University Press, 1911).

Establishing Roots: Marriage and Yale

1. P. Petro, *The Slow Breath of Stone* (London: Fourth Estate, 2005), p.20.
2. 'Mrs A. Kingsley Porter Dead: Widow of Harvard Medievalist', *New York Times*, 21 September 1962.

3. Thomas Wallace was born in 1826 in England. He married Ellen Bryant (born in 1832 in Massachusetts) in 1857. Thomas Wallace died on 1 January 1916, aged 88. They had seven children (United States Federal Census 1880, cited in 'Ancestry of Lucy (Bryant Wallace) Porter', babcockancestry.com):
Thomas Wallace was born in 1861;
Elizabeth Wallace was born in 1863 and married James. B. Waller from Chicago. They had at least one daughter, Ellen. Elizabeth Wallace Waller died in May 1919 (Monroe: 1919). Daughter, Ellen, married John Borden 2 February 1907 (*Chicago Tribune*, 2 July 1933). They were divorced on 12 December 1924 (*New York Times*, 11 January 1933). Ellen then married John Alden Carpenter on 30 January 1933 (*New York Times*, 30 January 1933).
Frederick Wallace was born in 1866;
Eleanor Bryant Wallace was born in August 1867. She died in New York on 13 October 1952 (*New York Times*, 15 October 1952);
Ruth M. Wallace was born on 24 January 1874 and died in New York, in February 1967 (US Social Security Death Index);
Lucy Bryant Wallace was born on 23 January 1876. Lucy married Arthur Kingsley Porter on 1 June 1912 (*New York Tribune*, 2 June 1912, p.9). She died in Cambridge, MA, on 19 September 1962 (*New York Times*, 21 September 1962);
Harold S. Wallace was born in April 1877.
4. United States Federal Census 1880, cited Ancestry of Lucy (Bryant Wallace) Porter, in babcockancestry.com; United States Federal Census 1880; 'Mrs A. Kingsley Porter Dead', *New York Times*, 21 September 1962.
5. For the origins of Wallace & Sons, established by Thomas Wallace, father of Lucy (Bryant Wallace) Porter, see 'A Brief Historical Profile of Wallace & Sons', The Lampworks, http://www.thelampworks.com/lw_companies_wallace.htm.
6. H. Monroe (ed.), *A Magazine of Verse* (543 Cass Street, Chicago, IL), 14, 6 (April–September 1919).
7. 'Events In Chicago Society', *Chicago Tribune*, 19 February 1903.
8. Newberry Library, Inventory of the Waller Family Papers 1803–1938 (bulk 1803–1888), Roger and Julie Baskes Department of Special Collections, 60 West Walton Street, Chicago, IL.
9. Harvard University Archives, HUG 1706.114, Correspondence of Arthur Kingsley Porter and Lucy W. Porter, 1911–25; 1911: Before Engagement, Letter from Kingsley to Lucy, 15 June 1911.
10. Ibid.
11. Harvard University Archives, HUG 1706.114, Correspondence of Arthur Kingsley Porter and Lucy W. Porter, 1911–25; 1911: Before Engagement, Letter from Kingsley to Lucy, 24 July 1911.
12. Ibid.
13. Ibid.
14. Harvard University Archives, HUG 1706.114, Correspondence of Arthur Kingsley Porter and Lucy W. Porter, 1911–25; 1911: Before Engagement, Letter from Kingsley to Lucy, undated.
15. Harvard University Archives, HUG 1706.114, Correspondence of Arthur

Kingsley Porter and Lucy W. Porter, 1911–25; 1911: Before Engagement, Letter from Kingsley to Lucy, on headed paper, Hotel Schenley, Pittsburgh, Pennsylvania, undated.

16. Harvard University Archives, HUG 1706.114, Correspondence of Arthur Kingsley Porter and Lucy W. Porter, 1911–25; 1911: Before Engagement, Letter from Kingsley to Lucy, undated.

17. Harvard University Archives, HUG 1706.114, Correspondence of Arthur Kingsley Porter and Lucy W. Porter, 1911–25; 1911: 1911–12: After engagement, Letter from Lucy to Kingsley, from 346 West 71st, 13 December 1911.

18. Harvard University Archives, HUG 1706.114, Correspondence of Arthur Kingsley Porter and Lucy W. Porter, 1911–25; 1911: 1911–12: After engagement, Letter from Lucy to Kingsley, undated.

19. Harvard University Archives, HUG 1706.114, Correspondence of Arthur Kingsley Porter and Lucy W. Porter, 1911–25; 1911–12: After engagement, Letter from Lucy to Kingsley, 26 December 1911.

20. Harvard University Archives, HUG 1706.114, Correspondence of Arthur Kingsley Porter and Lucy W. Porter, 1911–25; 1911–12: After engagement, Letter from Kingsley to Lucy, on headed paper, Hotel Schenley, Pittsburgh, Pennsylvania, 28 December 1911.

21. Harvard University Archives, HUG 1706.114, Correspondence of Arthur Kingsley Porter and Lucy W. Porter, 1911–25; 1911–12: After engagement, Letter from Kingsley to Lucy, 13 January 1912.

22. W. Lord, *A Night to Remember* (London: Penguin Books , 1976), p.197.

23. Ibid., pp.209–10.

24. Harvard University Archives, HUG 1706.114, Correspondence of Arthur Kingsley Porter and Lucy W. Porter, 1911–25; 1911–12: After engagement, Letter from Lucy to Kingsley, May 1912.

25. 'June Brides A-Plenty', *New York Tribune*, 2 June 1912.

26. 'New of the Society World: Personal Notes', *Chicago Sunday Tribune*, 26 May 1912.

27. 'June Brides A-Plenty', *New York Tribune*, 2 June 1912.

28. Yale University Library, Records of Arthur Twining Hadley as President of Yale University, 1899–1921, Letter to Mr Hadley, from A. Kingsley Porter, 450 West End Avenue, New York, 28 January 1916, courtesy of Digital Collections (Image numbers 45040 and 45041), New Haven, CT.

29. Harvard University Archives, HUG 1706.114, Correspondence of Arthur Kingsley Porter and Lucy W. Porter, 1911–25; 1911–12: After engagement, Letter from Lucy to Kingsley, 23 October 1912.

30. D.A. Willey, 'Bathing Facilities of the Modern Steamship – 1913', *Modern Sanitation*, 10, 9, (September 1913).

31. S. Hall and B. Beveridge, *Olympic and Titanic: The Truth behind the Conspiracy* (Haverford, PA: Infinity, 2004), p.8.

32. Lady Decies, *King Lehr* (1935), p.167, cited in R. Davenport-Hines, *Titanic Lives: Migrants and Millionaires, Conmen and Crew* (London: Harper Press, 2012), p.155.

33. Rollin Van N. Hadley (ed.), *The Letters of Bernard Berenson and Isabella Stewart Gardner, 1887–1924: With Correspondence by Mary Berenson* (Boston, MA: Northeastern University Press, 1987), pp.450, 458, cited in Davenport-Hines, *Titanic Lives*, p.156.

34. R.W.B Lewis and N. Lewis, *Letters of Edith Wharton* (New York: Scribner, 1988), pp.312–13, cited in Davenport-Hines, *Titanic Lives*, p.156.

35. 'Panniers Reign Supreme in Paris Fashion World', *Philadelphia Inquirer*, 21 April 1912, cited in Davenport-Hines, *Titanic Lives*, p.157.

36. Davenport-Hines, *Titanic Lives*, p.157

37. Harvard University Archives, HUG 1706.114, Arthur Kingsley Porter Family Correspondence, Correspondence of A.K. Porter and Lucy W. Porter c. 1914–19, Box 1, Letter from Kingsley to Mrs Wallace, from Florence, 3 February 1913.

38. Harvard University Archives, HUG 1706.127, Appointment Diary, 1923.

39. 'Passengers For Europe', *New York Times*, 9 December 1913.

40. 'Architecture: Important Results of Mr Goodyear's Researchers, by A. Kingsley Porter', *New York Times*, 5 April 1914.

41. The following is an outline of the family members of Louis H. Porter:
Louis Hopkins Porter was born on 10 March 1874 (Woodland Cemetery, Stamford, CT, records). He married Ellen Marion Hatch from New York, who was born on 7 September 1872 (Woodland Cemetery, Stamford, CT, records) on 3 October 1901. Louis died on 19 January 1946, aged 71 (*New York Times*, 20 January 1946). Ellen Marion Porter died on 29 June 1946, aged 73 (*New York Times*, 1 July 1946). They had five children:
Louise Hoyt Porter was born on 1 January 1904. She died on 31 July 1980, aged 76. She is buried in Henfield Cemetery, Sussex, England (Woodland Cemetery, Stamford, CT, records);
Joyce Porter Arneill was born on 10 June 1908 (United States Social Security Death Index**).** Joyce married James Arneill of Denver, Colorado on 23 June 1929. Mrs Joyce Porter Arneill had two children: James R. Arneill 111, born on 18 March 1930 and died on 1 December 2005 (United States Social Security Death Index); Bruce Porter Arneill, born on 1 May 1934 in New York City (*American Architects Directory*, 3rd Edition, 1970, R.R. Bowker LLC). Joyce died on 4 June 1990 in Colorado, aged 81; (United States Social Security Death Index).
Louis Hopkins Porter Jnr. was born on 19 December 1904 (United States Social Security Death Index). He married Regina F. McKinney on 1 July 1946 (*New York Times*, 1 July 1946, Page 24). They had one daughter, Gail Porter, born on 16 April 1941, died on 10 September 2008. Gail also had one daughter, Melanie Porter Torres. Louis Hopkins Porter Jnr. died on 27 November 1984, aged 79 (Woodland Cemetery, Stamford, CT, records);
Beatrice Porter was born on 6 September 1910. She died on 28 November 1934, aged 24;
Arthur Kingsley Porter apparently died soon after birth (Woodland Cemetery, Stamford, CT, records).

42. 'Jewels Lost In Fire', *New York Times*, 31 March 1915.

43. D. Preston, *Lusitania: An Epic Tragedy* (Berkeley, CA: Berkeley Books, 2003), p.91.

44. Ibid.

45. Ibid., p.378.

46. Ibid.

47. A. Kingsley Porter of the Yale School of Fine Arts, 'Art Collections at Yale Finest of All Universities', *Yale Daily News* (New Haven, CT), 23 January 1917.

48. Ibid.
49. 'Died', *New York Times*, 4 January 1916.
50. Yale University Library, Records of Arthur Twining Hadley as President of Yale University, 1899–1921, Letter to Mr Hadley, from A. Kingsley Porter, 450 West End Avenue, New York, 28 January 1916, courtesy of Digital Collections (Image numbers 45040 and 45041), New Haven, CT.
51. Ibid.
52. Harvard University Archives, HUG 1706.115, Family Correspondence, Correspondence of A.K. Porter with Louis Porter (his brother) 1916–33, Letter from Kingsley to Louis from 450 West End Avenue, New York, 1 March 1916.
53. ' "Cupid and Psyche"Will Start Pageant Festivities', *Yale Daily News* (New Haven, CT), 19 October 1916.
54. 'Davanzati Art Sale now near $1,000,000', *New York Times*, 28 November 1916.
55. 'December Social Gayeties', *New York Times*, 3 December 1916.
56. 'Corporation Makes Several Important Appointments', *Yale Daily News* (New Haven, CT), 20 March 1917.
57. A.K. Porter, *Lombard Architecture*, 4 vols (New Haven, CT:Yale University Press, 1917).
58. 'Notable Books in Brief Review: Lombard Architecture', *New York Times*, 22 July 1917.
59. Mann, *Romanesque Architecture*, p.21.
60. 'Notable Books In Brief Review: Lombard Architecture', *New York Times*, 22 July 1917.
61. A.K. Porter, *Lombard Architecture, vol 1*, p.7.
62. 'Notable Books in Brief Review: Lombard Architecture', *New York Times*, 22 July 1917.
63. Forbes, 'Arthur Kingsley Porter', p.537.
64. E. Mâle, 'L'architecture et la sculpture en Lombardie a l'Epoque Romane', *Gazette des Beaux-Arts* (Paris), 60 (1918), cited in Mann, *Romanesque Architecture*, p.21.
65. Beckwich, 'Kingsley Porter', pp.494–7.
66. A.K. Porter, 'The Rise of Romanesque Sculpture', *American Journal of Archaeology* 22 (1918), pp.399–427.
67. Mann, *Romanesque Architecture*, p.21.
68. J. Mann, 'Romantic Identity, Nationalism, and the Understanding of the Advent of Romanesque Art in Christian Spain', *Gesta* (International Centre of Medieval Art, New York), 36, 2 (1997), pp.156–64.
69. E. Samuels and J.N. Samuels, *Bernard Berenson:The Making of a Legend* (Cambridge, MA: Belknap Press, 1987).
70. Ibid.
71. Brooklyn Museum Archives, New York, William Henry Goodyear Archival Collection SRG, Correspondence with Arthur Kingsley Porter.
72. Princeton University Library, Princeton, NJ, Allan Marquand Papers, 1858–1951 (bulk 1878–1950), Correspondence with Arthur Kingsley Porter, 1918–20: Box 17, Folder 38.
73. Glenvairn Museum Archives, Bryn Athyn, PA, Letter from A.K. Porter to Raymond Pitcairn, 24 October 1917.

74. 'Loan Exhibition of Italian Primitives for War Relief: Art at Home and Abroad', *New York Times*, 11 November 1917.
75. 'The Week's Free Lectures', *New York Times*, 11 November 1917.
76. 'Old Italian Table Cover Brings $4,000', *New York Times*, 19 December 1917.
77. 'French Architecture Lecture at 8.15', *Harvard Crimson*, 13 March 1918.
78. 'Italian Paintings on Exhibition', *Harvard Crimson*, 15 March 1918.
79. Forbes, 'Arthur Kingsley Porter', p.539.
80. A.K. Porter, *Beyond Architecture*, p.ix.
81. Ibid., p.11.
82. Ibid., p.30.
83. Ibid., p.31–2.
84. Ibid., p.75–6.
85. Harvard University Archives, HUG 1706.127, Appointment Pad, 1918.
86. Ibid.
87. Koehler (ed.), *Medieval Studies*, cited in Beckwich, 'Kingsley Porter', p.496.
88. *Dictionary of Art Historians*, ed. Sorensen.
89. Harvard University Archives, HUG 1706.127, Appointment Pad, 1918.
90. Ibid.
91. Ibid.
92. Ibid.
93. Ibid.

War and Separation

1. Harvard University Archives, HUG 1706.127, Appointment Pad, 1918.
2. Ibid.
3. Harvard University Archives, HUG 1706.114, Family Correspondence, Correspondence of A.K. Porter and Lucy W. Porter c. 1914–19, Letter from Robert Lansing to A. Kingsley Porter, 21 August 1918.
4. Harvard University Archives, HUG 1706.127, Appointment Pad, 1918.
5. Ibid.
6. Ibid.
7. Harvard University Archives, HUG 1706.114, Correspondence of Arthur Kingsley Porter and Lucy W. Porter 1911–25, 1918: Letters from A. Kingsley Porter in Rome to Lucy W. Porter in Paris, from Grand Hôtel de la Cloche, Dijon, 26 October 1918.
8. Harvard University Archives, HUG 1706.127, Appointment Pad, 1918.
9. Ibid.
10. Ibid.
11. Harvard University Archives, HUG 1706.114, Correspondence of Arthur Kingsley Porter and Lucy W. Porter 1911–25, 1918: Letters from A. Kingsley Porter in Rome to Lucy W. Porter in Paris, from Grand Hôtel de la Cloche, Dijon, 26 October 1918.
12. Harvard University Archives, HUG 1706.114, Correspondence of Arthur Kingsley Porter and Lucy W. Porter 1911–25, 1918: Letters from A. Kingsley Porter in Rome to Lucy W. Porter in Paris, from Grand Hôtel de L'Europe, Bourg-en-Breuse, 28 October 1918.

13. Harvard University Archives, HUG 1706.114, Correspondence of Arthur Kingsley Porter and Lucy W. Porter 1911–25, 1918: Letters from A. Kingsley Porter in Rome to Lucy W. Porter in Paris, from Grand Hôtel de la Cloche, Dijon, 26 October 1918.

14. Harvard University Archives, HUG 1706.114, Porter Family Correspondence, Correspondence of A.K. Porter and Lucy W. Porter c. 1914–19, Box 1, Letter from Kingsley to Lucy, from Dijon, undated.

15. Harvard University Archives, HUG 1706.114, Correspondence of Arthur Kingsley Porter and Lucy W. Porter 1911–25, 1918: Letters from A. Kingsley Porter in Rome to Lucy W. Porter in Paris, from Grand Hôtel de L'Europe, Bourg-en-Breuse, 28 October 1918.

16. Ibid.

17. Harvard University Archives, HUG 1706.114, Correspondence of Arthur Kingsley Porter and Lucy W. Porter 1911–25, 1918: Letters from Lucy W. Porter in Paris to A. Kingsley Porter, 28 October 1918.

18. Harvard University Archives, HUG 1706.114, Correspondence of Arthur Kingsley Porter and Lucy W. Porter 1911–25, 1918: Letters from A. Kingsley Porter in Rome to the Ambassador, from Rome Grand Hotel, 31 October 1918.

19. Harvard University Archives, HUG 1706.127, Appointment Pad, 1918.

20. Harvard University Archives, HUG 1706.114, Correspondence of Arthur Kingsley Porter and Lucy W. Porter 1911–25, 1918: Letters from Lucy W. Porter in Paris to A. Kingsley Porter in Rome, 2 November 1918.

21. Harvard University Archives, HUG 1706.114, Correspondence of Arthur Kingsley Porter and Lucy W. Porter 1911–25, 1918: Letters from A. Kingsley Porter in Rome to Lucy W. Porter in Paris, undated.

22. Harvard University Archives, HUG 1706.114, Correspondence of Arthur Kingsley Porter and Lucy W. Porter 1911–25, 1918: Letters from A. Kingsley Porter in Rome to Lucy W. Porter in Paris, Rome Grand Hotel, 5 November 1918.

23. Harvard University Archives, HUG 1706.114, Correspondence of Arthur Kingsley Porter and Lucy W. Porter 1911–25, 1918: Letters from A. Kingsley Porter in Rome to the Ambassador, from Rome Grand Hotel, 4 November 1918.

24. Ibid.

25. Harvard University Archives, HUG 1706.114, Correspondence of Arthur Kingsley Porter and Lucy W. Porter 1911–25, 1918: Letters from A. Kingsley Porter in Rome to Lucy W. Porter in Paris, undated.

26. Harvard University Archives, HUG 1706.114, Correspondence of Arthur Kingsley Porter and Lucy W. Porter 1911–25, 1918: Letters from Lucy W. Porter in Paris to A. Kingsley Porter in Rome, 2 November 1918.

27. Harvard University Archives, HUG 1706.114, Correspondence of Arthur Kingsley Porter and Lucy W. Porter 1911–25, 1918: Letters from A. Kingsley Porter in Rome to the Ambassador, from Rome Grand Hotel, 3 November 1918.

28. Harvard University Archives, HUG 1706.114, Correspondence of Arthur Kingsley Porter and Lucy W. Porter 1911–25, 1918: Letters from A. Kingsley Porter in Rome to Lucy W. Porter in Paris, Rome Grand Hotel, 6 November 1918.

29. Harvard University Archives, HUG 1706.114, Correspondence of Arthur Kingsley Porter and Lucy W. Porter 1911–25, 1918: Letters from A. Kingsley Porter in Rome to Lucy W. Porter in Paris, Rome Grand Hotel, 5 November 1918.
30. Ibid.
31. Harvard University Archives, HUG 1706.114, Correspondence of Arthur Kingsley Porter and Lucy W. Porter 1911–25, 1918: Letters from A. Kingsley Porter in Rome to Lucy W. Porter in Paris, Rome Grand Hotel, 6 November 1918.
32. Harvard University Archives, HUG 1706.114, Correspondence of Arthur Kingsley Porter and Lucy W. Porter 1911–25, 1918: Letters from A. Kingsley Porter in Rome to the American Ambassador in Paris; Rome Grand Hotel, 7 November 1918.
33. Harvard University Archives, HUG 1706.114, Correspondence of Arthur Kingsley Porter and Lucy W. Porter 1911–25, 1918: Letters from A. Kingsley Porter in Rome to Lucy W. Porter in Paris, 7 November 1918.
34. Ibid.
35. Harvard University Archives, HUG 1706.127, Appointment Pad, 1918.
36. Harvard University Archives, HUG 1706.114, Correspondence of Arthur Kingsley Porter and Lucy W. Porter 1911–25, 1918: Letters from A. Kingsley Porter in Rome to Lucy W. Porter in Paris, 13 November 1918.
37. Harvard University Archives, HUG 1706.127, Appointment Pad, 1918.
38. Harvard University Archives, HUG 1706.114, Correspondence of Arthur Kingsley Porter and Lucy W. Porter 1911–25, 1918: Letters from Lucy W. Porter to A. Kingsley Porter, from Hotel Alexandra, Nice, 18 November 1918.
39. Harvard University Archives, HUG 1706.127, Appointment Pad, 1918.
40. Ibid.
41. Ibid.

Travels in France
1. Harvard University Archives, HUG 1706.127, Appointment Pad, 1918.
2. Ibid.
3. A.K. Porter, *Romanesque Sculpture of the Pilgrimage Roads*, vol. 1 (Boston, MA: Marshall Jones Co., 1923), p.130.
4. Ibid., p.259.
5. Harvard University Archives, HUG 1706.127, Appointment Pad, 1918.
6. A.E. Cornebise, *Soldier-Scholars: Higher Education in the AEF, 1917–1919* (Philadelphia, PA: American Philosophical Society, 1997), p.1.
7. Ibid., p.110.
8. Harvard University Archives, HUG 1706.127, Appointment Diary, 1919.
9. Harvard University Archives, HUG 1706.105, Correspondence: 1916–24, Letter from Kingsley Porter to Joseph Breck, from Hôtel De France & Choiseul, 239–241 Rue St Honore, Place Vendome, Paris, 20 February 1919.
10. Ibid.
11. Ibid.
12. Harvard University Archives, HUG 1706.127, Appointment Correspondence of

Lucy Porter, Appointment Diaries 1919–23; 1927–29, Appointment pads 1918, 1927–33.

13. Harvard University Archives, HUG 1706.127, Appointment Diary, 1919.
14. Ibid; Petro, *Slow Breath of Stone*, p.6.
15. Ibid; Petro, *Slow Breath of Stone*, p.6.
16. Harvard University Archives, HUG 1706.127, Appointment Diary, 1919.
17. Harvard University Archives, HUG 1706.114, Correspondence of Arthur Kingsley Porter and Lucy W. Porter 1911–25, 1919: Letters from Lucy W. Porter to Miss Ruth Wallace containing enclosures from others, 27 April 1919.
18. 'A. Kingsley Porter 1883–1933', *The Bulletin of the Fogg Art Museum*, p.3.
19. Monroe (ed.), *Magazine of Verse*, 14, 6 (April–September 1919).
20. Harvard University Archives, HUG 1706.127, Appointment Diary, 1919.
21. A.K. Porter, *Romanesque Sculpture of the Pilgrimage Roads*, vol. 1, p.142.
22. Harvard University Archives, HUG 1706.127, Appointment Diary, 1919.
23. Ibid.
24. Ibid.
25. Ibid.
26. Ibid.
27. Ibid.
28. Ibid.
29. Samuels and Samuels, *Bernard Berenson*.
30. Ibid., p.262.
31. Petro, *Slow Breath of Stone*, p.47.
32. A.K. Porter, *Romanesque Sculpture of the Pilgrimage Roads*, vol, 1, p.177.
33. Petro, *Slow Breath of Stone*, p.47.
34. A.K. Porter, *Three Plays* (Portland, ME: Anthoensen Press, 1952), p.vi.
35. A.K. Porter, *The Seven Who Slept* (Boston, MA: Marshall Jones, 1919).
36. 'Poetry and Drama', *New York Times*, 26 July 1919.
37. Ibid.
38. Ibid., p.16–18.
39. Ibid., p.14.
40. Harvard University Archives, HUG 1706.127, Appointment Diary, 1919.
41. Ibid.
42. Petro, *Slow Breath of Stone*, p.74; Samuels and Samuels, *Bernard Berenson*.
43. Harvard University Archives, HUG 1706.127, Appointment Diary, 1919.
44. J. Ackermann, 'The Visual Arts Collection: Manifold Resources', in L. Todd and M. Banta (eds), *The Invention of Photography and Its Impact of Learning: Photographs from Harvard University and Radcliff College and from the Collection of Harrison D. Horblit,* (Cambridge, MA: Harvard University Library, 1989), p.170, cited in Mann, *Romanesque Architecture*.
45. Petro, *Slow Breath of Stone*, p.74
46. Samuels and Samuels, *Bernard Berenson*, p.262.
47. Harvard University Archives, HUG 1706.127, Appointment Diary, 1919.
48. A.K. Porter, *Romanesque Sculpture of the Pilgrimage Roads*, vol. 1, p.131.
49. Ibid., p.xvii.
50. Ibid., p.300.

51. Harvard University Archives, HUG 1706.127, Appointment Diary, 1919.
52. Ibid.
53. Ibid.
54. Ibid.

European Travels

1. M. Frank, *Denman Ross and American Design Theory* (Lebanon, NH: University Press of New England, 2011), p.195.
2. Petro, *Slow Breath of Stone*, p.76.
3. 'Notes of Coming Books', *Brooklyn Daily Eagle*, 27 March 1920.
4. Ibid.
5. Harvard University Archives, HUG 1706.185, Kingsley Porter to Bernard Berenson, 9 January 1920, cited in J. Mann, 'Georgina Goddard King and A. Kingsley Porter Discover the Art of Spain', in R. Kagan (ed.), in *Spain in America: The Origins of Hispanism in the United States* (Chicago, IL: University of Illinois Press, 2002), p.190.
6. Petro, *Slow Breath of Stone*, p.91.
7. Harvard University Archives, HUG 1706.127, Appointment Diary, 1920.
8. A.K. Porter, *Romanesque Sculpture of the Pilgrimage Roads*, vol. 1, p.21.
9. Harvard University Archives, HUG 1706.127, Appointment Diary, 1920.
10. A.K. Porter, *Romanesque Sculpture of the Pilgrimage Roads*, vol. 1, p.xxv.
11. Harvard University Archives, HUG 1706.127, Appointment Diary, 1920.
12. Ibid.
13. Samuels and Samuels, *Bernard Berenson*, p.265.
14. Harvard University Archives, HUG 1706.127, Appointment Diary, 1920.
15. Ibid.
16. Ibid.
17. Ibid; Petro, *Slow Breath of Stone*, p.1.
18. Harvard University Archives, HUG 1706.127, Appointment Diary, 1920.
19. Ibid.
20. Ibid; Petro, *Slow Breath of Stone*, p.3.
21. Ibid; Petro, *Slow Breath of Stone*, p.3.
22. Harvard University Archives, HUG 1706.127, Appointment Diary, 1920.
23. A.K. Porter, *Romanesque Sculpture of the Pilgrimage Roads*, vol. 1, p.8.
24. Harvard University Archives, HUG 1706.127, Appointment Diary, 1920.
25. Forbes, 'Arthur Kingsley Porter', p.538.
26. Harvard University Archives, HUG 1706.127, Appointment Diary, 1920.
27. A.K. Porter, *Romanesque Sculpture of the Pilgrimage Roads*, vol. 1, p.180.
28. Ibid., p.203.
29. Harvard University Archives, HUG 1706.127, Appointment Diary, 1920.
30. Mann, 'Georgina Goddard King and A. Kingsley Porter', p 21.
31. Harvard University Archives, HUG 1706.185, letter from Kingsley Porter to Bernard Berenson, 14 January 1920; cited in Mann, 'Georgina Goddard King and A. Kingsley Porter', p 21.
32. Harvard University Archives, HUG 1706.127, Appointment Diary, 1920.

33. A.K. Porter, *Romanesque Sculpture of the Pilgrimage Roads*, vol. 1, p.53.

34. Ibid., p.269.

35. A.K. Porter quoted from the twelfth-century guidebook that was used by pilgrims on their way to Santiago de Compostela, in his lecture, 'The Sculpture of the West', given at the Metropolitan Museum of Art, New York, on 3 December 1921: 'There are four roads which lead to St James. These unite at Puente la Reina in the land of Spain. The first leads through St Gilles and Montpellier and Toulouse and the Port d'Aspe; the second through Notre Dame of Le Puy and Ste Foy of Conques and St Pierre of Moissac; the third through Ste Marie Madeleine of Vézelay and St Léonard near Limoges and the city of Périgueux; the fourth through St Martin of Tours and St Hilaire of Poitiers and St Jean d'Angély and St Eutrope of Sainters and the city of Bordeaux. The roads that pass through Ste Foy and St Léonard and St Martin unite at Ostabat, and passing the Port de Cize join Puente la Reina, the road which passes by the Port d'Aspe. Thence one road leads to St James.' The lecture was later published as *The Sculpture of the West* (Boston, MA: Marshall Jones, 1921).

36. Mann, *Romanesque Architecture*, p.23.

37. Ibid., p.24.

38. Harvard University Archives, HUG 1706.127, Appointment Diary, 1920.

39. Ibid.

40. Ibid.

41. Ibid.

42. A.K. Porter, *Romanesque Sculpture of the Pilgrimage Roads*, vol. 1, p.253.

43. Harvard University Archives, HUG 1706.127, Appointment Diary, 1920.

44. Mann, *Romanesque Architecture*, p.36.

45. Ibid., p.4.

46. Harvard University Archives, HUG 1706.127, Appointment Diary, 1920.

47. Mann, *Romanesque Architecture*, p.33.

48. Ibid.

49. Ibid., p.25.

50. Harvard University Archives, HUG 1706.127, Appointment Diary, 1920.

51. A.K. Porter, *Romanesque Sculpture of the Pilgrimage Roads*, vo;. 1, p.195.

52. Ibid., p.382.

53. Ibid.

54. Harvard University Archives, HUG 1706.127, Appointment Diary, 1920.

55. Petro, *Slow Breath of Stone*, p.67.

56. Ibid.

57. Harvard University Archives, HUG 1706.127, Appointment Diary, 1920.

58. R.E. Lentz II, *W.R. Trivett, Appalachian Pictureman: Photographs of a Bygone Time* (Jefferson, NC: McFarland, 2001), p.25–6.

59. Harvard University Archives, HUG 1706.127, Appointment Diary, 1920.

60. Ibid.

61. Petro, *Slow Breath of Stone*, p.73.

62. Ibid.

63. E.N. Emery, *Romancing the Cathedral: Gothic Architecture in Fin-de-Siècle French Culture* (Albany, NY: New York Press, 2001), pp.166–7.

64. Ibid.
65. Harvard University Archives, HUG 1706.127, Appointment Diary, 1920.
66. Ibid.
67. Ibid.
68. Ibid.
69. Ibid.
70. Ibid.
71. Ibid.
72. Petro, *Slow Breath of Stone*, p.76.
73. Frank, *Denman Ross and American Design Theory*, p.244.
74. N. Mariano, *Forty Years with Berenson* (New York: Knopf, 1966), p.34, cited in Beckwich, 'Kingsley Porter', pp.494–7.
75. Petro, *Slow Breath of Stone*, p.116.
76. Letter to Bernard Berenson from Kingsley Porter, cited in Petro, *Slow Breath of Stone*, p.116.
77. F.L. Allen, *Only Yesterday: An Informal History of the Nineteen Twenties* (New York: Harper & Row, 1989), first published 1931.
78. S.S. Kallen, *The Roaring Twenties* (Farmington Hills, MI: Greenhaven Press, 2001); Allen, *Only Yesterday*.
79. Allen, *Only Yesterday*, p.93.
80. Harvard University Archives, HUG 1706.127, Appointment Diary, 1921.
81. A. Warren, *Becoming What One Is* (Detroit, MI: University of Michigan, 1995), p.139.
82. '33 Elmwood', *Harvard Crimson*, 14 October 2001.
83. Harvard University Archives, HUG 1706.127, Appointment Diary, 1921.
84. Ibid.
85. Ibid.
86. Ibid.

Elmwood, Harvard and Further Travels

1. Harvard University Archives, HUG 1706.127, Appointment Diary, 1921; Frank, *Denman Ross and American Design Theory*, p.195.
2. 'Art Course For Children', *New York Times*, 25 September 1921.
3. A.K. Porter, *Sculpture of the West*, p.5.
4. 'Art Societies and Individuals', *New York Times*, 20 November 1921.
5. 'Art Watercolour and Art', *New York Times*, 27 November 1921.
6. *New York Tribune*, 1 October 1922.
7. Harvard University Archives, HUG 1706.105, Arthur Kingsley Porter Papers Correspondence, Correspondence re. Purchases of Elmwood, Letter from Dr Francis L. Burnett, 205 Beacon Street, Boston, MA, 1 February 1923, re. the letting of Elmwood.
8. Harvard University Archives, HUG 1706.105, Arthur Kingsley Porter Papers Correspondence, Correspondence re. Income Tax 1922 (Return).
9. *New York Tribune*, 1 October 1922.
10. '33 Elmwood', *Harvard Crimson*, 14 October 2001.

11. Ibid.
12. 'A. Kingsley Porter 1883–1933', *The Bulletin of the Fogg Art Museum*.
13. Ibid.
14. R.F. Brown, oral history interview with Frederick A. Sweet, 13–14 February 1976, in Sargentville, ME, for the Archives of American Art, Smithsonian Institution, Washington DC, http://www.aaa.si.edu/collections/interviews/oral-history-interview-frederick-sweet-12866.
15. Forbes, 'Arthur Kingsley Porter', p.538.
16. R.F. Brown, oral history interview with S. Morton Vose, 24 July 1986 to 28 April 1987, at his home in Brookline, MA, for the Archives of American Art, Smithsonian Institution, Washington DC, http://www.aaa.si.edu/collections/interviews/oral-history-interview-s-morton-vose-12367.
17. R.F. Brown, oral history interview with Frederick A. Sweet, 13–14 February 1976.
18. R.F. Brown, oral history interview with S. Morton Vose, 24 July 1986 to 28 April 1987.
19. R.F. Brown, oral history interview with Frederick A. Sweet, 13–14 February 1976.
20. Ibid.
21. Ibid.
22. United States Federal Census 1930.
23. Brown, oral history interview with Frederick A. Sweet, 13–14 February 1976.
24. Harvard University Archives, HUG 1706.127, Appointment Diary, 1922.
25. Forbes, 'Arthur Kingsley Porter', p.538.
26. Harvard University Archives, HUG 1706.127, Appointment Diary, 1923.
27. Ibid.
28. Ibid.
29. Beckwich, 'Kingsley Porter', p.496.
30. Harvard University Archives, HUG 1706.127, Appointment Diary, 1923.
31. Ibid.
32. Ibid.
33. Beckwich, 'Kingsley Porter', p.496.
34. Harvard University Archives, HUG 1706.127, Appointment Diary, 1923.
35. Ibid.
36. Ibid.
37. Ibid.
38. Ibid.
39. Ibid.
40. C. Newman de Vegvar, 'In the Shadow of the Sidhe: Arthur Kingsley Porter's Vision on an Exotic Ireland', *Irish Arts Review Yearbook*, 17 (2001), p.54.
41. Harvard University Archives, HUG 1706.127, Appointment Diary, 1923.
42. 'A Pilgrimage to the Land Of Romanesque Art: New Chronology Established for Medieval Monuments', *New York Times*, 12 August 1923.
43. A.K. Porter, *Romanesque Sculpture of the Pilgrimage Roads*, vol. 1, p.3–4.
44. Ibid. p.5.
45. 'Pilgrimage To The Land Of Romanesque Art', *New York Times*, 12 August 1923.
46. A.K. Porter, *Romanesque Sculpture of the Pilgrimage Roads*, vol. 1, p.53.

47. Ibid., pp.21, 205, 257, 301.
48. Ibid., pp.56, 119.
49. Ibid., p.43.
50. Ibid.
51. Beckwich, 'Kingsley Porter', p.496.
52. 'Pilgrimage To The Land Of Romanesque Art', *New York Times*, 12 August 1923.
53. Harvard University Archives, HUG 1706.127, Appointment Diary, 1923.
54. Ibid.
55. Ibid.
56. Ibid.
57. 'Other Changes in Faculty', *Harvard Crimson*, 31 January 1924; Forbes, 'Arthur Kingsley Porter', p.538.
58. Forbes, 'Arthur Kingsley Porter'.
59. Mann, *Romanesque Architecture*, p.150.
60. S. Freud, *The Interpretation of Dreams* (New York: Macmillan, 1913).
61. Mann, *Romanesque Architecture*, p.150.
62. Ibid., p.81.
63. Ibid., p.82.
64. Ibid.
65. Harvard University Archives, HUG 1706.105, Arthur Kingsley Porter Papers Correspondence, Folders not included in main file (1916–24), The Route Deluxe to Italy: SS *Duilio*.
66. 'New York: It's Big Income', *New York Times*, 25 October 1924.
67. Harvard University Archives, HUG 1706.103, Arthur Kingsley Porter Papers, Carbon copies of letters sent; some letters and memos, Folder: 1924–25, H/J Letters sent, Invitations for musicale, 9 November 1924.
68. '33 Elmwood', *Harvard Crimson*, 14 October 2001.
69. *Chicago Tribune*, 2 July 1933.
70. 'John Borden Marries', *New York Times*, 15 March 1925.
71. *New York Times*, 11 January 1933.
72. 'John Borden Marries', *New York Times*, 15 March 1925.
73. 'Harvard Advances Edgell and Morize', *Daily Boston Globe*, 28 February 1925.
74. 'Table Gossip', *Daily Boston Globe*, 11 January 1925.
75. *New York Evening Post*, 21 March 1925.
76. 'SS Martha Washington Takes 235 From Boston', *Daily Boston Globe*, 3 June 1925.
77. *Dictionary of Art Historians*, ed. Sorensen.
78. K. McComb (ed.), *The Selected Letters of Bernard Berenson* (Boston, MA: Houghton Mifflin, 1964), cited in Beckwich, 'Kingsley Porter', p.496.
79. Forbes, 'Arthur Kingsley Porter', pp.538–9; Beckwich, 'Kingsley Porter', p.497.
80. Beckwich, 'Kingsley Porter', p.497.
81. Andrew T. Weil, 'Fords Occupy Restored Elmwood: Gerry Lowell Lived In Old Fame House', *Harvard Crimson*, 23 September 1963.
82. Harvard University Archives, HUG 1706.185, Kingsley Porter to Bernard Berenson, 11 November 1925, cited in Mann, *Romanesque Architecture*, p.169.
83. There are several journal articles listed, that Kingsley Porter had published during 1926, in *The Writings of A. Kingsley Porter (1883–1933): A Bibliography*, compiled

under the direction of Lucy Kingsley Porter, with an introduction by Lucy Kingsley Porter (Cambridge, MA: Fogg Art Museum, 1934).

84. Harvard University Archives, HUG 1706.185, letter from Kingsley Porter to Bernard Berenson, 25 June 1926.

85. Letter to Bernard Berenson from Kingsley Porter, cited in Petro, *Slow Breath of Stone*, p.116.

86. *Official Register of Harvard University, Containing Report of the President of Harvard College and Reports of Departments for 1925, 1926*, 24, 8 (9 March 1927), p.272.

87. 'Collections and Critiques', *Harvard Crimson*, 12 December 1935.

88. A.K. Porter, 'The Tomb of Doña Sancha and the Romanesque Art of Aragon', *Burlington Magazine*, October 1924.

89. B.F. Reilly, *Santiago, Saint-Denis, and Saint Peter: The Reception of the Roman Liturgy in León-Castile in 1080* (New York: Fordham University Press, 1985); H. Richardson, 'Preface', in Françoise Henry, *Studies in Early Christian and Medieval Irish Art, Volume III: Sculpture and Architecture* (London: Pindar Press, 1985), p.65.

90. M.F. Hearne, *Romanesque Sculpture: The Revival of Monumental Stone Sculpture in the Eleventh and Twelfth Centuries* (Ithaca, NY: Cornell University Press, 1981), p.65; D. Hassig, 'He Will Make Alive Your Mortal Bodies: Cluniac Spirituality and the Tomb of Alfonso Ansúrez', *Gesta* (International Centre of Medieval Art, New York), 30, 2 (1991) pp.140–53.

91. S. Moralejo, 'The Tomb of Alfonso Ansúrez (1093): Its Place and the Role of Sahagún in the Beginnings of Spanish Romanesque Sculpture', in Bernard F. Reilly (ed.), *Santiago, Saint-Denis, and Saint Peter: The Reception of the Roman Liturgy in León-Castile in 1080* (New York: Fordham University Press, 1985); Walter Muir Whitehill, *Spanish Romanesque Architecture of the Eleventh Century* (Oxford: Oxford University Press, 1941); Hassig, 'He Will Make Alive', pp.140–53.

92. Hassig, 'He Will Make Alive', pp.140–53.

93. Collections and Critiques, *Harvard Crimson*, 12 December 1935.

94. *Official Register of Harvard University, Containing Report of the President of Harvard College and Reports of Departments for 1932, 1933*, 31, 3 (5 February 1934), p.309.

95. Hearne, *Romanesque Sculpture*, p.65–6.

96. Ibid., p.66.

97. *Official Register of Harvard University, Containing Report of the President of Harvard College and Reports of Departments for 1923, 1924*, 23, 2 (20 January 1926), p.260.

98. S. Hendrickx, R.F. Friedman, K.M. Cialowicz and M. Chlodnicki (eds), *Egypt at its Origins: Studies in Memory of Barbara Adams* (Louvain, Belgium: Peeters, 2004), p.622.

99. *Official Register of Harvard University, Containing Report of the President of Harvard College and Reports of Departments for 1925, 1926*, 24, 8 (9 March 1927), p.272.

100. Harvard University Archives, HUG 1706.103, Carbon copies of letters sent; some letters and memos, Folder: 1925–26, A–Z, Party at Elmwood for Joyce and Beatrice Porter, 4 December 1926 at 8 o'clock.

Accolades and New Horizons

1. Harvard University Archives, HUG 1706.127, Appointment Diary, 1927.

2. Ibid.
3. Ibid.
4. Ibid.
5. Ibid.
6. Beckwich, 'Kingsley Porter', p.497.
7. Ibid.
8. Ibid.
9. Mariano, *Forty Years with Berenson*, p.154, cited in Beckwich, 'Kingsley Porter', p.496.
10. Harvard University Archives, HUG 1706.127, Appointment Pad, 1927.
11. Ibid.
12. P. Cummings, oral history interview with Fairfield Porter, 6 June 1968, for the Archives of American Art, Smithsonian Institution, Washington DC, http://www.aaa.si.edu/collections/interviews/oral-history-interview-fairfield-porter-12873.
13. Warren, *Becoming What One Is*, p.139.
14. Ibid., p.140.
15. Ibid.
16. Harvard University Archives, HUG 1706.127, Appointment Pad, 1927.
17. Ibid.
18. Ibid.
19. Harvard University Archives, HUG 1706.127, Appointment Diary, 1928.
20. A.K. Porter, *Spanish Romanesque Sculpture* (Florence: Pantheon, 1928).
21. *Dictionary of American Biography* (New York: Charles Scribner's Sons, 1944), p.601
22. A.K. Porter, *Spanish Romanesque Sculpture*.
23. Ibid., cited in Mann, *Romanesque Architecture*, p.28.
24. A.K. Porter, *Spanish Romanesque Sculpture*.
25. Harvard University Archives, HUG 1706.127, Appointment Diary, 1928.
26. 'Special to New York Times: Princeton, NJ', *New York Times*, 15 August 1936.
27. Harvard University Archives, HUG 1706.127, Appointment Diary, 1928.
28. Newman de Vegvar, 'In the Shadow of the Sidhe', p.50.
29. H. Richardson, 'The Fate of Kingsley Porter', *Donegal Annual*, 45 (1993), pp.83–7.
30. P. Harbison, 'Arthur Kingsley Porter 1883–1933: Résumé of His Life' (unpublished), Glenveagh Castle Archives (Donegal), Document No. 31 (22 October 1985).
31. Forbes, 'Arthur Kingsley Porter', p.539.
32. Harvard University Archives, HUG 1706.127, Appointment Diary, 1928.
33. Newman de Vegvar, 'In the Shadow of the Sidhe', p.60.
34. Harvard University Archives, HUG 1706.102, Letter from Charles S. Bird of Bective House, Co. Meath, to Kingsley Porter, 9 March 1928.
35. Harvard University Archives, HUG 1706.127, Appointment Diary, 1928.
36. Ibid.
37. Ibid.
38. Ibid.
39. Ibid.
40. Ibid.
41. Ibid.

42. Ibid.
43. Ibid.
44. Warren, *Becoming What One Is*, p.138.
45. Harvard University Archives, HUG 1706.127, Appointment Diary, 1928.
46. Ibid.
47. Ibid.
48. Ibid.
49. Ibid.
50. M.O. Anderson, *Adomnán's Life of Columba*, rev. edn (Oxford: Clarendon Press, 1991).
51. Harvard University Archives, HUG 1706.127, Appointment Diary, 1928.
52. Ibid.
53. Ibid.
54. Ibid.
55. Ibid.

Depression and Confession

1. Forbes, 'Arthur Kingsley Porter', p.539.
2. Harvard University Archives, HUG 1706.127, Appointment Diary, 1928.
3. Ibid.
4. Harvard University Archives, HUG 1706.115, Family Correspondence, Correspondence of A.K. Porter with Louis Porter (his brother) 1916–33; Letter from Kingsley to Louis, Shepherd's Hotel, Cairo, 18 November 1928.
5. Harvard University Archives, HUG 1706.115, Family Correspondence, Correspondence of A.K. Porter with Louis Porter (his brother) 1916–33; 10 November 1928, cited in Mann, *Romanesque Architecture*, p.37.
6. Harvard University Archives, HUG 1706.115, Family Correspondence, Correspondence of A.K. Porter with Louis Porter (his brother) 1916–33; Letter from Kingsley to Louis, Shepherd's Hotel, Cairo, 18 November 1928.
7. Harvard University Archives, HUG 1706.127, Appointment Diary, 1928.
8. Ibid.
9. Ibid.
10. Ibid.
11. Harvard University Archives, HUG 1706.115, Family Correspondence, Correspondence of A.K. Porter with Louis Porter (his brother) 1916–33; Letter from Kingsley to Louis, 7 June 1929.
12. Harvard University Archives, HUG 1706.127, Appointment Diary, 1929; 'Six Ships Sale Today for Foreign Ports', *New York Times*, 30 January 1929.
13. Harvard University Archives, HUG 1706.127, Appointment Diary, 1929.
14. Ibid.
15. Harvard University Archives, HUG 1706.115, Family Correspondence, Correspondence of A.K. Porter with Louis Porter (his brother) 1916–33; Letter from Kingsley to Louis, 3 April 1929.
16. Ibid.
17. Ibid.

18. Ibid.
19. Harvard University Archives, HUG 1706.115, Family Correspondence, Correspondence of A.K. Porter with Louis Porter (his brother) 1916–33; Letter from Kingsley to Louis, 7 June 1929.
20. Ibid.
21. Harvard University Archives, HUG 1706.127, Appointment Diary, 1929.
22. Harvard University Archives, HUG 1706.115, Family Correspondence, Correspondence of A.K. Porter with Louis Porter (his brother) 1916–33; 23 June 1929, cited in Mann, *Romanesque Architecture*, p.37.
23. Kingsley Porter's library at Glenveagh Castle, Co. Donegal, still contains two books on psychoanalysis written by Charles Baudouin and signed on the frontispiece: A. Kingsley Porter, *Studies in Psychoanalysis* (1922) and *Psychoanalysis and Aesthetics* (1924).
24. N. Woloch, *Women and the American Experience: A Concise History* (New York: McGraw-Hill, 2002), p.274.
25. C. Baudouin, *Studies in Psychoanalysis: An Account Of Twenty-Seven Concrete Cases Preceded by a Theoretical Exposition* (London: George Allen & Unwin, 1922).
26. Ibid., pp.85–6.
27. Ibid., p.86.
28. Ibid., p.102.
29. Ibid.
30. D. Shand-Tucco, *Ralph Adams Cram: An Architect's Four Quests: Medieval, Modernist, American, Ecumenical* (Amherst, MA: University of Massachusetts Press, 2005), p.237–8.
31. A.K. Porter, *Beyond Architecture*, pp.75–6.
32. W.L. Anderson and D.W. Little, 'All's Fair: War and other Causes of Divorce from a Beckerian Perspective', *American Journal of Economics and Sociology*, 58, 4 (October 1999), pp.901–22.
33. A.R. Palcy, 'The Secret Court of 1920', *Harvard Crimson*, 21 November 2002.
34. G. Chauncey, N.F. Cott, J. D'Emilio, E.B. Freedman, T.C. Holt, J. Howard, L. Hunt, M. Jordan, D. Lapovsky, E. Kennedy and L.P. Kerber, 'The Historians' Case Against Gay Discrimination', George Mason University's History News Network (Seattle, WA), pp.1–2, http://hnn.us/articles/1539.html.
35. A.K. Porter, *An Egyptian Legend in Ireland*, Verlag des Kunstgeschichtlichen Seminars (Marburg, Germany: Phillips University, 1929), p.2.
36. 'Miss Joyce Porter Completes Plans For June Wedding', *New York Evening Post*, 23 May 1929.
37. Harvard University Archives, HUG 1706.127, Appointment Diary, 1929.
38. Ibid.
39. Frank, *Denman Ross and American Design Theory*, p.202.
40. Harvard University Archives, HUG 1706.127, Appointment Diary, 1929.
41. Harvard University Archives, Porter to Edward Forbes and Paul Sachs, 29 August 1929, cited in Mann, *Romanesque Architecture*, p.36.
42. Mann, *Romanesque Architecture*, p.36.
43. L.K. Porter, 'Introduction', in Æ (George Russell), *Æ's Letters to Mínanlábáin*, pp.2–3.

44. Ibid.
45. The Pond Bureau, Publicity sheet for Æ's lecture tour in the USA, 23 October 1930.
46. L.K. Porter, 'Introduction', in Æ (George Russell), *Æ's Letters to Mínanlábáin*, pp.2–3.
47. Larner (ed.), *Glenveagh Castle & Gardens* (Donegal: Glenveagh National Park, 2003).
48. G. Moriarty, 'Where Eagles Dare', *Irish Times*, 5 September 2011.
49. Larner (ed.), *Glenveagh Castle & Gardens*.
50. M. Harmon, 'The Era of Inhibitions: Irish Literature 1920–1960', in Masaru Sekine (ed.), *Irish Writers and Society at Large* (Totowa, NJ: Barnes & Noble, 1985), pp.31–41.
51. A. Haggerty, 'Stained Glass and Censorship: The Suppression of Harry Clarke's Geneva Window, 1931', *New Hibernia Review/Iris Eireannach Nua*, 3, 4 (1999), pp.99–117.
52. Harvard University Archives, HUG 1706.127, Appointment Diary, 1929.
53. *Irish Times*, 27 October 1980.
54. Larner (ed.), *Glenveagh Castle & Gardens*, p.10.
55. I. Knox, *The Houses of Steward from 1500* (2003), http://knoxthedonegalroutes.net/.
56. Harvard University Archives, HUG 1706.127, Appointment Diary, 1929.
57. Ibid.
58. Harvard University Archives, HUG 1706.127, Appointment Pad, 1929.
59. A.K. Porter, *The Virgin and the Clerk* (Boston, MA: Marshall Jones, 1929).
60. Ibid.

Glenveagh Castle & Inishbofin

1. Harvard University Archives, HUG 1706.127, Appointment Pad, 1929.
2. Harvard University Archives, HUG 1706.115, Family Correspondence, Correspondence of A.K. Porter with Louis Porter (his brother) 1916–33, Letter to Louis from Kingsley, 18 December 1929.
3. Ibid.
4. Harvard University Archives, HUG 1706.127, Appointment Pad, 1930.
5. B. Berenson and A.K. McComb, *Selected Letters of Bernard Berenson* (London: Hutchinson, 1965), p.109, cited in Beckwich, 'Kingsley Porter', p.497.
6. P. Clavin, *The Great Depression in Europe 1929–1939* (New York: St Martin's Press, 2000).
7. Warren, *Becoming What One Is*, p.141.
8. Harvard University Archives, HUG 1706.185, letter from Kingsley Porter to Bernard Berenson, 13 June 1933; HUG 1706.185, 19 June 1933, cited in Newman de Vegvar, 'In the Shadow of the Sidhe', p.58.
9. A.K. Porter, *The Crosses and Culture of Ireland: Five Lectures Delivered at the Metropolitan Museum of Art, New York* (February and March 1930) (New Haven, CT: Yale University Press, 1935).
10. Ibid., p.16.
11. Ibid., p.18.
12. Harvard University Archives, HUG 1706.127, Appointment Pad, 1930.

13. 'Second Lecture by Porter', *Harvard Crimson*, 18 March 1930.
14. Harvard University Archives, HUG 1706.127, Appointment Pad, 1930.
15. Ibid.
16. M.D. McDougal, *The Letters of 'Norah' on her Tour through Ireland, Being a Series of Letters to the Montreal 'Witness' as Special Correspondent to Ireland* (Montreal: Private subscription, 1882; ebook, Project Gutenberg, 2004). A visitor to Donegal in 1882, known as Norah, wrote an account of the devastation that occurred to the tenants of Glenveagh due to the cruelty of the infamous landlord.
17. Moriarty, 'Where Eagles Dare', *Irish Times*, 5 September 2011.
18. Harvard University Archives, HUG 1706.127, Appointment Pad, 1930.
19. Forbes, 'Arthur Kingsley Porter', p.540.
20. Moriarty, 'Where Eagles Dare', *Irish Times*, 5 September 2011.
21. Transcribed by the author from the monument to St Columcille, located in Gartan, Co. Donegal.
22. Lucy Kingsley Porter, 'Introduction', in Koehler (ed.), *Medieval Studies*, cited in Harbison, 'Arthur Kingsley Porter 1883–1933'.
23. L.K. Porter, 'Introduction', in Æ (George Russell), *Æ's Letters to Mínanlábáin*, p.4.
24. Harvard University Archives, HUG 1706.127, Appointment Pad, 1930.
25. Larner (ed.), *Glenveagh Castle & Gardens*.
26. L.K. Porter, 'Introduction', in Æ (George Russell), *Æ's Letters to Mínanlábáin*, p.4.
27. Harvard University Archives, HUG 1706.127, Appointment Pad, 1930.
28. L.K. Porter, 'Introduction', in Æ (George Russell), *Æ's Letters to Mínanlábáin*.
29. A.K. Porter, *Crosses and Culture of Ireland*.
30. A.K. Porter, *Three Plays*, p.7.
31. Ibid.
32. Harvard University Archives, HUG 1706.127, Appointment Pad, 1930.
33. Harvard University Archives, HUG 1706.107, Letters and papers re. estate in Donegal, Ireland (Glenveagh); Inishbofin. c. 1930–38; Letter to Kingsley from Joseph McCarthy of Falcarragh, Co.Donegal, Ireland, 21 November 1930.
34. From Inishbofin, (Co. Donegal (website), http://www.irelandbyways.com/top-irish-peninsulas/irelands-northwest/co-donegals-offshore-islands/inishbofin-co-donegal/.
35. C. Duff, *On Celtic Tides* (New York: St Martin's Griffin, 2000).
36. W.M.Whitehill, *Analecta Biografica: A Handful of New England Portraits* (Brattleboro, VT: Stephen Greene Press, 1969).
37. Harvard University Archives, HUG 1706.107, Letters and papers re. estate in Donegal, Ireland (Glenveagh); Inishbofin. c. 1930–38; Letter to Kingsley from Joseph McCarthy of Falcarragh, Co. Donegal, Ireland, 21 November 1930.
38. L.K.Porter, 'Introduction', in Æ (George Russell), *Æ's Letters to Mínanlábáin*, pp.8–9.
39. Harvard University Archives, HUG 1706.127, Appointment Pad, 1931.
40. Ibid.
41. Ibid.
42. 'Collections and Critiques', *Harvard Crimson*, 12 December 1935.
43. Harvard University Archives, HUG 1706.127, Appointment Pad, 1931.
44. 'Dublin Weddings', *Weekly Irish Times*, 25 April 1931.

45. Harvard University Archives, HUG 1706.127, Appointment Pad, 1931.

46. Glenveagh Castle Archives, *Agreement Kingsley Porter and Daniel Sweeney, Re. Fence, Document* No. 44, 26 May 1931.

47. L.K. Porter, 'Introduction', in Æ (George Russell), *Æ's Letters to Mínanlábáin*, p.6.

48. Harvard University Archives, HUG 1706.127, Appointment Pad, 1931.

49. Harvard University Archives, HUG 1706.107, Letters and papers re. estate in Donegal, Ireland (Glenveagh); Inishbofin. c. 1930–38; Letter to Kingsley from Edward Dixon of Meenlaragh, Gortahork, Co. Donegal, 13 May 1931.

50. L.K. Porter, 'Introduction', in Æ (George Russell), *Æ's Letters to Mínanlábáin*, p.6.

51. Ibid., p.5.

52. Ibid., p.6.

53. Harvard University Archives, HUG 1706.127, Appointment Pad, 1931.

54. Ibid.

55. L.K. Porter, 'Introduction', in Æ (George Russell), *Æ's Letters to Mínanlábáin*, p.8.

56. Ibid., p.21.

57. Harvard University Archives, HUG 1706.127, Appointment Pad, 1931.

58. Ibid.

59. 'Social and Personal', *Irish Independent*, 17 August 1931; 'Court and Personal', *Irish Times*, 17 August 1931.

60. Æ (George Russell), *Æ's Letters to Mínanlábáin*, p.23.

61. Ibid., p.26.

62. Harvard University Archives, HUG 1706.127, Appointment Pad, 1931.

63. *Polar Record*, 16, 102 (1972), pp.445–53.

64. L.K. Porter, *Glenveagh Castle: Visitors' Book: 1931–1937*, 1937.

65. 'Royal Society of Antiquaries: Professor Kingsley Porter's Paper', *Irish Times*, 30 September 1931.

66. Newman de Vegvar, 'In the Shadow of the Sidhe', pp.49–61; Harbison, 'Arthur Kingsley Porter 1883–1933'.

67. A.K. Porter, *Crosses and Culture of Ireland*, p.105.

68. Forbes, 'Arthur Kingsley Porter', p.541.

69. Newman de Vegvar, 'In the Shadow of the Sidhe', pp.50.

70. Richardson, 'Fate of Kingsley Porter', p.83–7.

71. Æ (George Russell), *Æ's Letters to Mínanlábáin*, pp.29–30.

72. Harvard University Archives, HUG 1706.127, Appointment Pad, 1931.

73. Glenveagh Castle Archives, *Diary of Visitor in Mrs Porter's Time*, Document No. 36 (1–4 August), p.111.

74. Larner (ed.), *Glenveagh Castle & Gardens*.

75. Ibid.

76. Ibid.

77. Glenveagh Castle Archives, *Diary of Visitor in Mrs Porter's Time*, Document No. 36 (1–4 August), p.112–13.

Ellis and the Ménage à Trois

1. Harvard University Archives, HUG 1706.127, Appointment Pad, 1931.

2. P. Grosskurth, *Havelock Ellis: A Biography* (London: Allen Lane, 1981).

3. Ibid., p.418.
4. J. Karman, *The Collected Letters of Robinson Jeffers, with Selected Letters of Una Jeffers, Volume 2, 1931–1939* (Stanford, CA: Stanford University Press: 2011).
5. Grosskurth, *Havelock Ellis*, p.418.
6. Harvard University Archives, HUG 1706.127, Appointment Pad, 1931.
7. British Library Department of Manuscripts, No. ADD70553, Havelock Ellis Papers, 1039B, letter from A. Kingsley Porter to Dr Ellis, Glenveagh, 1 November 1931.
8. Ibid.
9. Ibid.
10. Harvard University Archives, HUG 1706.127, Appointment Pad, 1931.
11. British Library Department of Manuscripts, No. ADD70553, Havelock Ellis Papers, 1039B, letter from A. Kingsley Porter to Dr Ellis, Glenveagh, December 1931.
12. Ibid.
13. Harvard University Archives, HUG 1706.127, Appointment Pad, 1931.
14. Æ (George Russell), *Æ's Letters to Mínanlábáin*, p.34.
15. Ibid., p.37.
16. Harvard University Archives, HUG 1706.127, Appointment Pad, 1932.
17. Ibid.
18. Æ (George Russell), *Æ's Letters to Mínanlábáin*, p.38.
19. British Library Department of Manuscripts, No. ADD70553, Havelock Ellis Papers, 1039B, letter from A. Kingsley Porter to Dr Ellis, Elmwood, 22 April 1932.
20. Ibid.
21. Ibid; 'New York Youth a Suicide in West: Peter K. Stockton, Harvard Sophomore, Shot Himself Jan. 16 in Michigan Hotel', *New York Times*, 30 January 1932.
22. British Library Department of Manuscripts, No. ADD70553, Havelock Ellis Papers, 1039B, letter from A. Kingsley Porter to Dr Ellis, Elmwood, 22 April 1932.
23. Æ (George Russell), *Æ's Letters to Mínanlábáin*, p.47.
24. British Library Department of Manuscripts, No. ADD70553, Havelock Ellis Papers, 1039B, letter from A. Kingsley Porter to Dr Ellis, Elmwood, 15 June 1932.
25. 'Gets Honorary Degree', *New York Times*, 21 June 1932.
26. Harvard University Archives, HUG 1706.127, Appointment Pad, 1932.
27. British Library Department of Manuscripts, No. ADD70553, Havelock Ellis Papers, 1039B, letter from A. Kingsley Porter to Dr Ellis, 2 July 1932.
28. Harvard University Archives, HUG 1706.127, Appointment Pad, 1932.
29. British Library Department of Manuscripts, No. ADD70553, Havelock Ellis Papers, 1039B, letter from A. Kingsley Porter to Dr Ellis, Glenveagh, 10 July 1932.
30. Annie McIntyre was aged 99 years in April 2012. The author corresponded with Annie's son, Danny, who interviewed his mother about her recollections of Kingsley Porter.
31. British Library Department of Manuscripts, No. ADD70553, Havelock Ellis Papers, 1039B, letter from A. Kingsley Porter to Dr Ellis, Glenveagh, 10 July 1932.
32 Æ (George Russell), *Æ's Letters to Mínanlábáin*, p.51.
33. Ibid., p.52.
34. Harvard University Archives, HUG 1706.127, Appointment Pad, 1932.

35. Ibid.
36. Ibid.
37. Harvard University Archives, HUG 1706.115, Family Correspondence, Correspondence of A.K. Porter with Louis Porter (his brother) 1916–33: 10 November 1928, cited in Mann, *Romanesque Architecture*, p.37.
38. British Library Department of Manuscripts, No. ADD70553, Havelock Ellis Papers, 1039B, letter from A. Kingsley Porter to Dr Ellis, Glenveagh, 31 July 1932.
39. Harvard University Archives, HUG 1706.127, Appointment Pad, 1932.
40. Ibid.
41. Ibid.
42. British Library Department of Manuscripts, No. ADD70553, Havelock Ellis Papers, 1039B, letter from A. Kingsley Porter to Dr Ellis, Glenveagh, 20 September 1932.
43. Ibid.
44. Harvard University Archives, HUG 1706.127, Appointment Pad, 1932.
45. British Library Department of Manuscripts, No. ADD70553, Havelock Ellis Papers, 1039B, letter from A. Kingsley Porter to Dr Ellis, Glenveagh, 2 October 1932.
46. Ibid.
47. British Library Department of Manuscripts, No. ADD70553, Havelock Ellis Papers, 1039B, letter from A. Kingsley Porter to Dr Ellis, Glenveagh, 12 October 1932.
48. 'Two Men Found Shot in Flat here: Suicide Pact Seen', *The Paris Herald* (Paris), 4 October 1932.
49. British Library Department of Manuscripts, No. ADD70553, Havelock Ellis Papers, 1039B, letter from A. Kingsley Porter to Dr Ellis, Glenveagh, 12 October 1932.
50. Ibid.
51. Harvard University Archives, HUG 1706.127, Appointment Pad, 1932.
52. Æ (George Russell), *Æ's Letters to Mínanlábáin*, p.60–1.
53. Ibid.
54. Harvard University Archives, HUG 1706.127, Appointment Pad, 1932.
55. Harvard University Archives, HUG 1706.127, Appointment Pad, 1933.
56. Æ (George Russell), *Æ's Letters to Mínanlábáin*, p.68.
57. Harvard University Archives, HUG 1706.127, Appointment Pad, 1933.
58. British Library Department of Manuscripts, No. ADD70553, Havelock Ellis Papers, 1039B, letter from A. Kingsley Porter to Dr Ellis, Glenveagh, 3 January 1933.
59. Ibid.
60. Harvard University Archives, HUG 1706.127, Appointment Pad, 1933.
61. British Library Department of Manuscripts, No. ADD70553, Havelock Ellis Papers, 1039B, letter from A. Kingsley Porter to Dr Ellis, Glenveagh, 12 January 1933.
62. Harvard University Archives, HUG 1706.127, Appointment Pad, 1933.
63. British Library Department of Manuscripts, No. ADD70553, Havelock Ellis Papers, 1039B, letter from A. Kingsley Porter to Dr Ellis, Glenveagh, 12 January 1933.

Harvard Witch-Hunt

1. Harvard University Archives, HUG 1706.127, Appointment Pad, 1933.
2. 'Mrs Waller Borden Wed', *New York Times*, 31 January 1933.
3. Harvard University Archives, HUG 1706.127, Appointment Pad, 1933.
4. 'Mrs Waller Borden Wed', *New York Times*, 31 January 1933.
5. 'John Borden Marries', *New York Times*, 15 March 1925.
6. 'Mrs Waller Borden Wed', *New York Times*, 31 January 1933.
7. Harvard University Archives, HUG 1706.127, Appointment Pad, 1933.
8. Æ (George Russell), *Æ's Letters to Mínanlábáin*, pp.75–6.
9. Ibid.
10. Harvard University Archives, HUG 1706.127, Appointment Pad, 1933.
11. Ibid.
12. Ibid.
13. Ibid.
14. British Library Department of Manuscripts, No. ADD70553, Havelock Ellis Papers, 1039B, letter from Alan Campbell to Dr Ellis, Elmwood, 22 February 1933.
15. Ibid.
16. Ibid.
17. Ibid.
18. Harvard University Archives, HUG 1706.127, Appointment Pad, 1933.
19. British Library Department of Manuscripts, No. ADD70553, Havelock Ellis Papers, 1039B, letter from Alan Campbell to Dr Ellis, Elmwood, 7 March 1933.
20. Ibid.
21. Harvard University Archives, HUG 1706.127, Appointment Pad, 1933.
22. Æ (George Russell), *Æ's Letters to Mínanlábáin*, pp.78–80.
23. 'Collections and Critiques', *Harvard Crimson*, 12 December 1935.
24. Ibid; *Official Register of Harvard University, Containing Report of the President of Harvard College and Reports of Departments for 1932, 1933*, 31, 3 (5 February 1934), p.309.
25. 'Collections and Critiques', *Harvard Crimson*, 12 December 1935.
26. Harvard University Archives, HUG 1706.127, Appointment Pad, 1933.
27. British Library Department of Manuscripts, No. ADD70553, Havelock Ellis Papers, 1039B, letter from A. Kingsley Porter to Dr Ellis, Elmwood, 6 April 1933.
28. Ibid.
29. Ibid.
30. Ibid.
31. Ibid.
32. Ibid.
33. Harvard University Archives, HUG 1706.127, Appointment Pad, 1933.
34. British Library Department of Manuscripts, No. ADD70553, Havelock Ellis Papers, 1039B, letter from Alan Campbell to Dr Ellis, Elmwood, 11 April 1933.
35. Ibid.
36. Ibid.
37. Harvard University Archives, HUG 1706.127, Appointment Pad, 1933.
38. Ibid.
39. Ibid.

40. 'Old Cambridge Houses Opened in Aid of Architects' Emergency Relief Drive', *Daily Boston Globe*, 11 May 1933.
41. Harvard University Archives, HUG 1706.127, Appointment Pad, 1933.
42. Ibid.
43. Ibid.

Rendezvous On Inishbofin

1. Harvard University Archives, HUG 1706.127, Appointment Pad, 1933.
2. British Library Department of Manuscripts, No. ADD70553, Havelock Ellis Papers, 1039B, letter from A. Kingsley Porter to Dr Ellis, Glenveagh, 17 June 1933.
3. Petro, *Slow Breath of Stone*, p.236.
4. Harvard University Archives, HUG 1706.127, Appointment Pad, 1933.
5. Dr Havelock Ellis lived for many years at Herne Hill. Source: 'The Ward Names of Cane Hill', The Time Chamber 2007–2011, http://www.thetimechamber.co.uk/Sites/Hospital/Cane%20Hill/WardNames.php
6. Harvard University Archives, HUG 1706.127, Appointment Pad, 1933.
7. British Library Department of Manuscripts, No. ADD70553, Havelock Ellis Papers, 1039B, letter from A. Kingsley Porter to Dr Ellis, Shelbourne Hotel, Dublin, 9 June 1933.
8. Harvard University Archives, HUG 1706.127, Appointment Pad, 1933.
9. Ibid.
10. British Library Department of Manuscripts, No. ADD70553, Havelock Ellis Papers, 1039B, letter from A. Kingsley Porter to Dr Ellis, Glenveagh, 17 June 1933.
11. Ibid.
12. Harvard University Archives, HUG 1706.185, Kingsley Porter to Bernard Berenson, 13 June 1933; HUG 1706.185, 19 June 1933; cited in Newman de Vegvar, 'In the Shadow of the Sidhe', p.58.
13. Harvard University Archives, HUG 1706.185, letter from Kingsley Porter to Bernard Berenson, 19 June 1933; Petro, *Slow Breath of Stone*, p.232.
14. Harvard University Archives, HUG 1706.127, Appointment Pad, 1933.
15. Ibid.
16. Ibid.
17. Æ (George Russell), *Æ's Letters to Mínanlábáin*, p.82.
18. Ibid., p.84.
19. Ibid., p.85.
20. R. Sterner, *Full Moon Dates Between 1900 and 2100* (Baltimore, MD: Applied Physics Laboratory Laurel, Johns Hopkins University, 2000), http://home.hiwaay.net/~krcool/Astro/moon/fullmoon.htm.
21. A.K. Porter, 'Letter to Æ', in Æ (George Russell), *Æ's Letters to Mínanlábáin*, p.86.
22. National Archives of Ireland, Coroner's Inquest, Co. Donegal, 1933, IC/83/117.
23. Ibid.
24. Ibid.
25. L.K. Porter, 'Introduction', in Æ (George Russell), *Æ's Letters to Mínanlábáin*, pp.15–16.
26. Ibid., p.16.
27. Ibid.

Disappearance and Inquest

1. L.K. Porter, 'Introduction', in Æ (George Russell), *Æ's Letters to Mínanlábáin*, p.16.
2. Ibid., p.17.
3. Ibid.
4. Ibid.
5. 'Searchers Look In Vain For Harvard Archaeologist, Feared Drowned', *New York Evening Post*, 10 July 1933.
6. Records pertaining to the disappearance of Arthur Kingsley Porter on 8 July 1933 were consulted at the Garda Museum Archives, at the Record Tower, Dublin Castle, Dublin 1, but no relevant records were found.
7. Missing Persons Review and Recommendation (Ireland: Garda Inspectorate, March 2009).
8. Missing Person Investigations: Guidelines and Curriculum (California Commission on Peace Officer Standards and Training, December 2011).
9. L.K. Porter, 'Introduction', in Æ (George Russell), *Æ's Letters to Mínanlábáin*, p.18.
10. Harvard University Archives, HUG 1706.127, Appointment Pad, 1933.
11. British Library Department of Manuscripts, No. ADD70553, Havelock Ellis Papers, 1039B, letter from Alan Campbell to Dr Ellis, Glenveagh, 11 July 1933.
12. Ibid.
13. Ibid.
14. 'Well-Known Professor Drowned in Donegal: Curragh Caught in Thunderstorm', *Irish Press*, 10 July 1933.
15. 'Bathing Accident in Donegal: Mr J. Kingsley Porter Drowned: From Our Correspondent, Letterkenny', *Irish Times*, 10 July 1933.
16. 'Late Dr Kingsley Porter: Letterkenny', *Irish Times*, 11 July 1933.
17. 'A. Kingsley Porter Drowned off Ireland: Archaeologist Lost from Boat in Storm', *New York Times*, 10 July 1933.
18. 'Porter Archaeologist Feared Lost in Storm Dublin, Irish Free State', *Poughkeepsie New York Daily*, 10 July 1933; 'Porter, Noted Archaeologist Reported Lost', *Schenectady New York Gazette*, 9 July 1933; 'Scientist Lost at Sea in Small Boat', *Rochester Democrat and Chronicle*, 10 July 1933; 'A. Kingsley Porter Is Missing Abroad: Archaeologist Feared Lost in Storm off Ireland', *Daily Boston Globe*, 10 July 1933; 'Porter Still Unheard of after Violent Storm', *Harvard Crimson*, 11 July 1933.
19. 'A. Kingsley Porter, Archaeologist, 50, Believed Drowned Is Missing in Stormy Sea off Irish Coast', *Brooklyn Daily Eagle*, 10 July 1933.
20. 'Searchers Look in Vain for Harvard Archaeologist, Feared Drowned', *New York Evening Post*, 10 July 1933.
21. 'No Trace of Prof. Porter: Gardai and Islanders Search off Coast', *Irish Press*, 11 July 1933.
22. 'Donegal Coast Tragedy', *Irish Press*, 12 July 1933.
23. *Irish Press*, 13 July 1933.
24. 'Donegal Sea Mystery: American Professor Missing: Cause of Death Unknown', *People's Press* (Donegal), 15 July 1933.
25. 'The Missing Archaeologist', *Donegal Democrat*, 15 July 1933.
26. L.K. Porter, 'Introduction', in Æ (George Russell), *Æ's Letters to Mínanlábáin*, p.15.

27. Harvard University Archives, HUG 1706.127, Appointment Pad, 1933.
28. Æ (George Russell), *Æ's Letters to Mínanlábáin*, pp.87–8.
29. Harvard University Archives, HUG 1706.127, Appointment Pad, 1933.
30. National Archives of Ireland, Coroner's Inquest, Co. Donegal, 1933, IC/83/117.
31. Harvard University Archives, HUG 1706.127, Appointment Pad, 1933.
32. 'A Swedish Art Congress', *New York Times*, 4 June 1933.
33. Harvard University Archives, HUG 1706.127, Appointment Pad, 1933.
34. Ibid.
35. 'Inquest Without A Body', *Irish Times*, 23 September 1933.
36. National Archives of Ireland, Coroner's Inquest, Co. Donegal, 1933, IC/83/117.
37. Ibid.
38. Ibid.
39. Ibid.
40. Ibid.
41. Ibid.
42. Ibid.
43. Ibid.
44. J. Hornell, 'The Curraghs of Ireland', *Mariner's Mirror: The Quarterly Journal of the Society for Nautical Research* (Greenwich, London), 14, 1 (January 1938).
45. National Archives of Ireland, Coroner's Inquest, Co. Donegal, 1933, IC/83/117.

Verdict

1. National Archives of Ireland, Coroner's Inquest, Co. Donegal, 1933, IC/83/117.
2. 'Coroner's Tribute', *Irish Times*, 15 September 1933.
3. Ibid.
4. L.K. Porter, 'Introduction', in Æ (George Russell), *Æ's Letters to Mínanlábáin*, p.16.
5. Richardson, 'Fate of Kingsley Porter', p.86; Petro, *Slow Breath of Stone*, p.236; G. Greenburg, *Manufacturing Depression: The Secret History of a Modern Disease* (New York: Simon & Schuster, 2010), p.133.
6. E. Shorter and D. Healy, *Shock Therapy: A History of Electroconvulsive Treatment in Mental Illness* (New Brunswick, NJ: Rutgers University Press, 2007).
7. National Archives of Ireland, Coroner's Inquest, Co. Donegal, 1933, IC/83/117.
8. A.K. Porter, 'Letter to Æ', in Æ (George Russell), *Æ's Letters to Mínanlábáin*, p.86.
9. L.K. Porter, 'Introduction', in Æ (George Russell), *Æ's Letters to Mínanlábáin*, p.16.
10. A.K. Porter, 'Letter to Æ', in Æ (George Russell), *Æ's Letters to Mínanlábáin*, p.86.
11. National Archives of Ireland, Coroner's Inquest, Co. Donegal, 1933, IC/83/117.
12. Ibid.
13. British Library Department of Manuscripts, No. ADD70553, Havelock Ellis Papers, 1039B, Letter from A. Kingsley Porter to Dr Ellis, Glenveagh, 17 June 1933.
14. Petro, *Slow Breath of Stone*, p.236.
15. Mariano, *Forty Years with Berenson*, p.218.
16. A tour guide in Glenveagh Castle during the author's visit on 9 June 2011 told of the local rumour that Kingsley Porter continued to visit his wife at the castle in secret at night.

17. The rumour that Kingsley Porter was murdered by locals because of an affair was reported on the following website: http://www.geocities.ws/glenveaghnationalpark/owners.html.

18. Reference to this rumour was made by Annie McIntyre, aged 99 years in April 2012. Ms McIntyre passed on her memories of Kingsley Porter to the author through her son, Danny.

19. Duff, *On Celtic Tides*.

20. Warren, *Becoming What One Is*, p.143.

21. A. McMenamin, *When We Were Young: Stories and Photographs* (Balleybofey, Co. Donegal: Voice Publications, 2000), p.41.

22. J.M. Feehan, *The Secret Places of Donegal* (Cork: Royal Carbery Books, 1988).

23. The closing verses of the local ballad, 'Five Hundred Thousand Curses on Cruel John Adair', describes the curse inflicted on Adair and the future owners of Glenveagh Castle:

> Beside the lake in sweet Glenveigh, his tall white castle stands,
> With battlement and tower high, fresh from the mason's hands;
> It's built of ruined hearth stones, its cement is bitter tears,
> It's a monument of infamy to all the future years,
> He is written childless, for of his blood no heir
> Shall inherit land or lordship from cruel John Adair.
>
> . . . The silver birches of Glenveigh when stirred by summer air
> Shall whisper of the curse that hangs o'er cruel John Adair.

24. Larner (ed.), *Glenveagh Castle & Gardens*, p.10.

25. The story that Kingsley Porter made a new life in Paris was told to the author on Inishbofin Island on 10 June 2011, by a descendant of a family who lived on the island when Kingsley disappeared.

26. 'Collections and Critiques', *Harvard Crimson*, 12 December 1935.

27. Harvard University Archives, HUG 1706.127, Appointment Pad, 1933.

28. 'Old Lowell House Is Left to Harvard: Arthur Kingsley Porter's Will Provides for Memorial after Death of Widow', *New York Times*, 26 September 1933.

29. Ibid.

30. 'Believe Bones on an Island May Be Those of Porter: Dublin, Irish Free State', *Schenectady Gazette* (New York), 3 October 1933; 'Donegal Mystery: Grim Clue to Tragedy, USA Professor', *Donegal Vindicator*, 7 October 1933.

31. 'Donegal Boy's Find: Bones on Strand Recall Recent Tragedy', *Leitrim Observer*, 7 October 1933.

32. 'The Innisboffin Bones: Guards Find no Trace: From Our Correspondent Letterkenny', *Irish Times*, 6 October 1933.

33. Ibid.

Aftermath

1. British Library Department of Manuscripts, No. ADD70553, Havelock Ellis Papers, 1039B, Letter from Lucy Kingsley Porter to Dr Ellis, Elmwood, 19 October 1933.

2. Ibid.
3. Ibid.
4. Ibid.
5. Greenburg, *Manufacturing Depression*, p.133.
6. British Library Department of Manuscripts, No. ADD70553, Havelock Ellis Papers, 1039B, Letter from Lucy Kingsley Porter to Dr Ellis, Elmwood, 9 February 1934.
7. Ibid.
8. British Library Department of Manuscripts, No. ADD70553, Havelock Ellis Papers, 1039B, Enclosed letter from Æ to Dr Ellis, 9 February 1934.
9. J. Wortis, *Fragments of an Analysis with Freud* (New York: Simon & Schuster, 1954), p.1, cited in Greenburg, *Manufacturing Depression*, p.134.
10. A.K. Porter, *Writings of A. Kingsley Porter*.
11. Æ (George Russell), *Æ's Letters to Mínanlábáin*, p.94.
12. Ibid., p.98.
13. British Library Department of Manuscripts, No. ADD70553, Havelock Ellis Papers, 1039B, Letter from Lucy Kingsley Porter to Dr Ellis, Elmwood, 21 September 1934.
14. Wortis, *Fragments of an Analysis*, p.5, cited in Greenburg, *Manufacturing Depression*, p.135; Grosskurth, *Havelock Ellis*, p.419.
15. Glenveagh Castle Archives, *Gave Lecture at Visitor Centre 1991 on Kingsley Porter: Dr Joseph Wortis*, Document No. 43, unpublished, 1991.
16. T. Dufresne, *Against Freud* (Palo Alto, CA: Stanford University Press, 2007), p.15, cited in Greenburg, *Manufacturing Depression*, p.134.
17. Glenveagh Castle Archives, *Gave Lecture at Visitor Centre 1991 on Kingsley Porter: Dr Joseph Wortis*, Document No. 43, unpublished, 1991.
18. 'Mrs Kingsley Porter's Valuable Work: A Woman Archaeologist', *Irish Independent*, 12 October 1934.
19. *Brooklyn Daily Eagle*, 30 November 1934.
20. Æ (George Russell), *Æ's Letters to Mínanlábáin*, p.99.
21. Ibid., p.101.
22. R.M. Kain and J.H. O'Brien, *George Russell (Æ)* (Cranbury, NJ: Bucknell University Press, 1976), p.12.
23. 'Donegal', *Sunday Independent*, 16 August 1936.
24. 'Three Tragic Deaths: Donegal Inquest US Visitor's Ban on Doctors', *Irish Press*, 17 August 1936.
25. 'Special to New York Times: Princeton, NJ', *New York Times*, 15 August 1936.
26. *Irish Independent*, 17 August 1936.
27. 'Three Tragic Deaths', *Irish Press*, 17 August 1936.
28. 'Donegal', *Sunday Independent*, 16 August 1936.
29. Ibid; *Irish Independent*, 17 August 1936; 'Three Tragic Deaths', *Irish Press*, 17 August 1936.
30. 'Books Received', *Irish Independent*, 28 February 1937.
31. L.K. Porter, 'Introduction', in Æ (George Russell), *Æ's Letters to Mínanlábáin*, p.17.
32. 'Una Jeffers Correspondence: The Luhan Letters, Excerpts, 1937', *Robinson Jeffers Newsletter*, 37 (Summer 1993).

33. L.K. Porter, *Glenveagh Castle: Visitors' Book: 1931–1937*.
34. 'Fatal Collision, Septuagenarian Cyclist's Tragic Death', *Irish Press*, 3 July 1937, p.15.
35. Moriarty, 'Where Eagles Dare', *Irish Times*, 5 September 2011.
36. *Dictionary of Art Historians*, ed. Sorensen.
37. 'Philadelphia Owner', *Irish Independent*, 1 October 1941.
38. *Dictionary of Art Historians*, ed. Sorensen.
39. *Irish Times*, 27 October 1980.
40. The Arthur Kingsley Porter Bequest Collection is housed in the National Museum of Ireland in Dublin. According to the museum's catalogue, 'A collection of over 1,000 monographs and 500 pamphlets from the library of the Harvard architectural historian, Arthur Kingsley Porter (1883–1933), were donated to the National Museum of Ireland by his wife Lucy. The emphasis within this collection is on medieval European architecture and to a lesser extent Irish archaeology. This collection is held at the Main Library, Collins Barracks, and also at the Irish Antiquities library, Kildare Street. To-date 800 items have been catalogued.' See http://www.museum.ie/en/info/library.aspx.
41. British Library Department of Manuscripts, No. ADD70553, Havelock Ellis Papers, 1039B, Letter from Lucy Kingsley Porter to Dr Ellis, Elmwood, 12 May 1939.
42. L.K. Porter, 'Introduction', in Koehler (ed.) *Medieval Studies*.
43. British Library Department of Manuscripts, No. ADD70553, Havelock Ellis Papers, 1039B, Letter from Lucy Kingsley Porter to Dr Ellis, Elmwood, 22 December 1939.
44. Warren, *Becoming What One Is*.
45. 'New England Art Collectors Show Excellent Taste', *Daily Boston Globe*, 11 June 1939.
46. 'Medieval Art Exhib Opens at Museum here', *Daily Boston Globe*, 18 February 1940.
47. 'Reception Planned at Fogg Museum by Pan-American Society of Massachusetts', *Daily Boston Globe*, 6 April 1941.
48. 'Cambridge Women's War Finance Committee Plans Book and Author War Bond Rally', *Daily Boston Globe*, 5 September 1943; 'War Time: Society', *Daily Boston Globe*, 26 January 1944.
49. 'Cambridge Concert', *Daily Boston Globe*, 9 April 1944.
50. 'Federation to Hold Victory Ball', *Daily Boston Globe*, 25 November 1945.
51. 'International Student Association Spring Festival at "Elmwood" in Cambridge', *Daily Boston Globe*, 22 May 1949.
52. 'Society: Flower Portraits', *Daily Boston Globe*, 1 November 1950.
53. 'Society: Experts to Lecture for Benefit of Mt Auburn Hospital', *Daily Boston Globe*, 12 December 1951.
54. 'Society: Here from New York', *Daily Boston Globe*, 29 June 1957.
55. L.K. Porter, *The Owners of Elmwood: A History & Memoir* (Cambridge, MA: Cambridge Historical Society, 1949).
56. Andrew T. Weil, 'Fords Occupy Restored Elmwood/Gerry Lowell Lived in Old Fame House', *Harvard Crimson*, 23 September 1963.

57. Ibid.

58 'L.H. Porter Dead: Noted Lawyer, 71', *New York Times*, 20 January 1946.

59. 'Mrs Louis H. Porter: Widow of Corporation Lawyer a Leader in Stamford Clubs', *New York Times*, 1 July 1946.

60. 'Stamford School Buys: Daycroft Gets Main House and Part of Porter Acreage', *New York Times*, 18 December 1946.

61. Karman, *Collected Letters of Robinson Jeffers, with Selected Letters of Una Jeffers, Volume 2, 1931–1939.*

62. 'Mrs A. Kingsley Porter Dead: Widow of Harvard Medievalist', *New York Times*, 21 September 1962.

63. L.K. Porter, 'Introduction', in Koehler (ed.), *Medieval Studies.*

64. 'Mrs A. Kingsley Porter Dead', *New York Times*, 21 September 1962.

Legend and Legacy

1. Beckwich, 'Kingsley Porter', p.497.

2. Ibid.

3. A.K. Porter, *Romanesque Sculpture of the Pilgrimage Roads*, vol. 1, p.40.

4. W. Johnson (ed.), *The Papers of Adlai Stevenson: Volume 1, Beginnings of Education 1900–1941* (Boston, MA: Little, Brown, 1972), p.516, cited in Newman de Vegvar, 'In the Shadow of the Sidhe', p.59.

5. Harbison, 'Arthur Kingsley Porter 1883–1933'. In correspondence with the author during January 2012, Professor Harbison stated that he did not recall who had sighted Kingsley Porter at either location.

6. R.F. Brown, oral history interview with S. Morton Vose, 24 July 1986 to 28 April 1987.

7. Ibid.

8. A tour guide at Glenveagh Castle during the author's visit on 9 June 2011 told of the local rumour that Kingsley Porter continued to visit his wife at the castle in secret at night.

9. The story that Kingsley Porter made a new life in Paris was told to the author on Inishbofin Island on 10 June 2011, by a descendant of a family who lived on the island when Kingsley disappeared.

10. *A Cruise To The Orient: Auguste Victoria*, Hamburg-American Line, 1901.

11. Duff, *On Celtic Tides.*

12. The Porter/Hoyt plot at Woodland Cemetery Monument, Stamford, Fairfield County Connecticut, contains a central monument in Section D and twenty-nine footstones, arranged in a circular pattern around the monument. The monument is inscribed on four faces. The central face contains the reference to Arthur Kingsley Porter: Porter/Arthur Kingsley Porter/February 6 1883/Drowned at sea/July 8 1933.

13. 'Widow of Archaeologist Wills Million to Harvard', *New York Times*, 7 November 1962.

14. Larner (ed.), *Glenveagh Castle & Gardens.*

15. T. Marquardt and A.A. Jordan, *Medieval Art and Architecture after the Middle Ages* (Newcastle Upon Tyne: Cambridge Scholars, 2009), p.8.

16. Frank, *Denman Ross and American Design Theory*, p.202.

17. 'A. Kingsley Porter 1883–1933', *The Bulletin of the Fogg Art Museum*, p.3.

18. B. Berenson, *Aesthetics and History* (New York: Doubleday, 1954).

19. A.K. Porter, *Three Plays*, p.v.

20. 'Porter, Arthur Kingsley 1883–1933', Worldcat Identities, http://www.worldcat.org/identities/lccn-n50-23212.

21. Ackermann, 'Visual Arts Collection', p.170.

22. C. Rudolph (ed.), *A Companion to Medieval Art: Romanesque and Gothic in Northern Europe* (Boston, MA: Blackwell, 2006).

Bibliography

Archive Sources

British Library (London), Department of Manuscripts, No. ADD 70553, Havelock Ellis Papers 1039B

Letter from A. Kingsley Porter to Dr Ellis, Glenveagh, 1 November 1931.

Letter from A. Kingsley Porter to Dr Ellis, Glenveagh, December 1931.

Letter from A. Kingsley Porter to Dr Ellis, Elmwood, 22 April 1932.

Letter from A. Kingsley Porter to Dr Ellis, Elmwood, 15 June 1932.

Letter from A. Kingsley Porter to Dr Ellis, 2 July 1932.

Letter from A. Kingsley Porter to Dr Ellis, Glenveagh, 10 July 1932.

Letter from A. Kingsley Porter to Dr Ellis, Glenveagh, 31 July 1932.

Letter from A. Kingsley Porter to Dr Ellis, Glenveagh, 20 September 1932.

Letter from A. Kingsley Porter to Dr Ellis, Glenveagh, 2 October 1932.

Letter from A. Kingsley Porter to Dr Ellis, Glenveagh, 12 October 1932.

Letter from A. Kingsley Porter to Dr Ellis, Glenveagh, 3 January 1933.

Letter from A. Kingsley Porter to Dr Ellis, Glenveagh, 12 January 1933.

Letter from Alan Campbell to Dr Ellis, Elmwood, 22 February 1933.

Letter from Alan Campbell to Dr Ellis, Elmwood, 7 March 1933.

Letter from A. Kingsley Porter to Dr Ellis, Elmwood, 6 April 1933.

Letter from Alan Campbell to Dr Ellis, Elmwood, 11 April 1933.

Letter from A. Kingsley Porter to Dr Ellis, Shelbourne Hotel, Dublin, 9 June 1933.

Letter from A. Kingsley Porter to Dr Ellis, Glenveagh, 17 June 1933.

Letter from Alan Campbell to Dr Ellis, Glenveagh, 11 July 1933.

Letter from Lucy Kingsley Porter to Dr Ellis, Elmwood, 19 October 1933.

Letter from Lucy Kingsley Porter to Dr Ellis, Elmwood, 9 February 1934.

Enclosed letter from Æ to Dr Ellis, 9 February 1934.

Letter from Lucy Kingsley Porter to Dr Ellis, Elmwood, 21 September 1934.

Letter from Lucy Kingsley Porter to Dr Ellis, Elmwood, 12 May 1939.

Letter from Lucy Kingsley Porter to Dr Ellis, Elmwood, 22 December 1939.

Harvard University Archives (Cambridge, MA)

HUG 1706.102, Letter from Charles S. Bird of Bective House, Co. Meath, to Kingsley Porter, 9 March 1928.

HUG 1706.103, Arthur Kingsley Porter Papers, carbon copies of letters sent; some letters and memos, Folder: 1924–25, H/J Letters sent, Invitations for musicale, 9 November 1924.

HUG 1706.103, carbon copies of letters sent; some letters and memos, Folder: 1925–26, A–Z, Party at Elmwood for Joyce and Beatrice Porter, 4 December 1926.

HUG 1706.104, Letter from William Henry Goodyear to A. Kingsley Porter, 8 November 1909.

HUG 1706.105, Correspondence: 1916–24, from Kingsley Porter to Joseph Breck, from Hôtel De France & Choiseul, 239–241 Rue St Honore, Place Vendome, Paris, 20 February 1919.

HUG 1706.105, Arthur Kingsley Porter Papers, Correspondence, folders not included in main file (1916–24), The Route Deluxe to Italy: SS *Duilio*.

HUG 1706.105, Arthur Kingsley Porter Papers, Correspondence re. Income Tax 1922 (Return).

HUG 1706.105, Arthur Kingsley Porter Papers, Correspondence re. Purchases of Elmwood, letter from Dr Francis L. Burnett, 205 Beacon Street, Boston, MA, 1 February 1923, re. the letting of Elmwood.

HUG 1706.107, Letters and papers re. estate in Donegal, Ireland (Glenveagh); Inishbofin. c. 1930–38; letter to Kingsley from Joseph McCarthy of Falcarragh, Co. Donegal, Ireland, 21 November 1930.

HUG 1706.107, Letters and papers re. estate in Donegal, Ireland (Glenveagh); Inishbofin. c. 1930–38; letter to Kingsley from Edward Dixon of Meenlaragh, Gortahork, Co. Donegal, 13 May 1931.

HUG 1706.110, Family correspondence 1880–99, Correspondence and papers of Porter Family, Folder 1882–83, Letter from Louisa to Timothy H., undated.

HUG 1706.110, Family correspondence 1880–99, Correspondence and papers of Porter Family, Folder 1882–83, Letter from Timothy H. Porter to Blachley Porter, undated.

HUG 1706.110, Family correspondence and papers of Porter Family 1880–99, Letter from Timothy H. to Kingsley, undated.

HUG 1706.110, Family correspondence 1880–99, Letter from Timothy H. to Louise, undated.

HUG 1706.110, Family correspondence and papers of Porter Family 1880–99, Poems written to Kingsley's mother by her husband on her birthdays, 1866–76.

HUG 1706.110, Family correspondence and papers of Porter Family 1885–86, Folder 1892–93, Letter from Timothy H. Porter to Kingsley, 15 July 1886.

HUG 1706.110, Family correspondence and papers of Porter Family 1880–99, Correspondence and papers of Porter Family, 1892–93, Letter from Blachley to Kingsley, 17 April 1892.

HUG 1706.110, Family correspondence and papers of Porter Family 1880–99, Folder 1892–93, Letter from Louis to Kingsley, 9 April 1893.

HUG 1706.114, Correspondence of Arthur Kingsley Porter and Lucy W. Porter, 1911–25; 1911: Before Engagement, Letter from Kingsley to Lucy, undated.

HUG 1706.114, Correspondence of Arthur Kingsley Porter and Lucy W. Porter, 1911–25; 1911: Before Engagement, Letter from Kingsley to Lucy, on headed paper: Hotel Schenley, Pittsburgh, Pennsylvania, undated.

HUG 1706.114, Correspondence of Arthur Kingsley Porter and Lucy W. Porter, 1911–25; 1911: Before Engagement, Letter from Kingsley to Lucy, undated.

HUG 1706.114, Correspondence of Arthur Kingsley Porter and Lucy W. Porter, 1911–25; 1911: Before Engagement, Letter from Kingsley to Lucy, 15 June 1911.

HUG 1706.114, Correspondence of Arthur Kingsley Porter and Lucy W. Porter, 1911–25; 1911: Before Engagement, Letter from Kingsley to Lucy, 24 July 1911.

HUG 1706.114, Correspondence of Arthur Kingsley Porter and Lucy W. Porter, 1911–25; 1911: 1911–12: After engagement, Letter from Lucy to Kingsley, undated.

HUG 1706.114, Correspondence of Arthur Kingsley Porter and Lucy W. Porter, 1911–25; 1911: 1911–12: After engagement, Letter from Lucy to Kingsley, from 346 West 71st, 13 December 1911.

HUG 1706.114, Correspondence of Arthur Kingsley Porter and Lucy W. Porter, 1911–25; 1911–12: After engagement, Letter from Lucy to Kingsley, 26 December 1911.

HUG 1706.114, Correspondence of Arthur Kingsley Porter and Lucy W. Porter, 1911–25; 1911–12: After engagement, Letter from Kingsley to Lucy, on headed paper: Hotel Schenley, Pittsburgh, Pennsylvania, 28 December 1911.

HUG 1706.114, Correspondence of Arthur Kingsley Porter and Lucy W. Porter, 1911–25; 1911–12: After engagement, Letter from Kingsley to Lucy, 13 January 1912.

HUG 1706.114, Correspondence of Arthur Kingsley Porter and Lucy W. Porter, 1911–25; 1911–12: After engagement, Letter from Lucy to Kingsley, May 1912.

HUG 1706.114, Correspondence of Arthur Kingsley Porter and Lucy W. Porter, 1911–25; 1911–12: After engagement, Letter from Lucy to Kingsley, 23 October 1912.

HUG 1706.114, Arthur Kingsley Porter Family Correspondence, Correspondence of A.K. Porter and Lucy W. Porter c. 1914–19, Box 1, Letter from Kingsley to Mrs Wallace, from Florence, 3 February 1913.

HUG 1706.114, Family correspondence, Correspondence of A.K. Porter and Lucy W. Porter c. 1914–19 Letter from Robert Lansing to A. Kingsley Porter, 21 August 1918.

HUG 1706.114, Correspondence of Arthur Kingsley Porter and Lucy W. Porter 1911–25, 1918: Letters from A. Kingsley Porter in Rome to Lucy W. Porter in Paris, from Grand Hôtel de la Cloche, Dijon, 26 October 1918.

HUG 1706.114, Porter Family Correspondence, Correspondence of A.K. Porter and Lucy W. Porter c. 1914–19, Box 1, From Kingsley to Lucy, from Dijon, undated.

HUG 1706.114, Correspondence of Arthur Kingsley Porter and Lucy W. Porter 1911–25, 1918: Letters from A. Kingsley Porter in Rome to Lucy W. Porter in Paris, from Grand Hôtel de L'Europe, Bourg-en-Breuse, 28 October 1918.

HUG 1706.114, Correspondence of Arthur Kingsley Porter and Lucy W. Porter 1911–25, 1918: Letters from Lucy W. Porter in Paris to A. Kingsley Porter, 28 October 1918.

HUG 1706.114, Correspondence of Arthur Kingsley Porter and Lucy W. Porter 1911–25, 1918: Letters from A. Kingsley Porter in Rome to the Ambassador, from Rome Grand Hotel, 31 October 1918.

HUG 1706.114, Correspondence of Arthur Kingsley Porter and Lucy W. Porter 1911–25, 1918: Letters from Lucy W. Porter in Paris to A. Kingsley Porter, 2 November 1918.

HUG 1706.114, Correspondence of Arthur Kingsley Porter and Lucy W. Porter 1911–25, 1918: Letters from A. Kingsley Porter in Rome to Lucy W. Porter in Paris, 2 November 1918.

HUG 1706.114, Correspondence of Arthur Kingsley Porter and Lucy W. Porter 1911–25, 1918: Letters from A. Kingsley Porter in Rome to the Ambassador, from Rome Grand Hotel, 3 November 1918.

HUG 1706.114, Correspondence of Arthur Kingsley Porter and Lucy W. Porter 1911–25, 1918: Letters from A. Kingsley Porter in Rome to the Ambassador, from Rome Grand Hotel, 4 November 1918.

HUG 1706.114, Correspondence of Arthur Kingsley Porter and Lucy W. Porter 1911–25, 1918: Letters from A. Kingsley Porter in Rome to Lucy W. Porter in Paris, Rome Grand Hotel, 5 November 1918.

HUG 1706.114, Correspondence of Arthur Kingsley Porter and Lucy W. Porter 1911–25, 1918: Letters from A. Kingsley Porter in Rome to Lucy W. Porter in Paris, Rome Grand Hotel, 6 November 1918.

HUG 1706.114, Correspondence of Arthur Kingsley Porter and Lucy W. Porter 1911–25, 1918: Letters from A. Kingsley Porter in Rome to Lucy W. Porter in Paris, 7 November 1918.

HUG 1706.114, Correspondence of Arthur Kingsley Porter and Lucy W. Porter 1911–25, 1918: Letters from A. Kingsley Porter in Rome to Lucy W. Porter in Paris, undated.

HUG 1706.114, Correspondence of Arthur Kingsley Porter and Lucy W. Porter 1911–25, 1918: Letters from A. Kingsley Porter in Rome to Lucy W. Porter in Paris, 13 November 1918.

HUG 1706.114, Correspondence of Arthur Kingsley Porter and Lucy W. Porter 1911–25, 1918: Letters from Lucy W. Porter to A. Kingsley Porter, from Hôtel Alexandra, Nice, 18 November 1918.

HUG 1706.114, Correspondence of Arthur Kingsley Porter and Lucy W. Porter 1911–25, 1919: Letters from Lucy W. Porter to Miss Ruth Wallace containing enclosures from others, 27 April 1919.

HUG 1706.115, Family correspondence, Correspondence of A.K. Porter with Louis Porter (his brother) 1916–33; Letter from Kingsley to Louis from 450 West End Avenue, New York, 1 March 1916.

HUG 1706.115, Family correspondence, Correspondence of A.K. Porter with Louis Porter (his brother) 1916–33; 10 November 1928.

HUG 1706.115, Family correspondence, Correspondence of A.K. Porter with Louis Porter (his brother) 1916–33; Letter from Kingsley to Louis, Shepherd's Hotel, Cairo, 18 November 1928.

HUG 1706.115, Family correspondence, Correspondence of A.K. Porter with Louis Porter (his brother) 1916–33; Letter from Kingsley to Louis, 3 April 1929.

HUG 1706.115, Family correspondence, Correspondence of A.K. Porter with Louis Porter (his brother) 1916–33; Letter from Kingsley to Louis, 7 June 1929.

HUG 1706.115, Family correspondence, Correspondence of A.K. Porter with Louis Porter (his brother) 1916–33; 23 June 1929, letter.

HUG 1706.115, Family correspondence, Correspondence of A.K. Porter with Louis Porter (his brother) 1916–33; Letter to Louis from Kingsley, 18 December 1929.

HUG 1706.127, Appointment correspondence of Lucy Porter, Diaries 1919–23; 1927–29; Appointment pads 1918, 1927–33.

HUG 1706.150, Selection of photos from Kingsley and Louis Porter's world tour of 1902.

HUG 1706.185, Kingsley Porter to Bernard Berenson, 9 January 1920.

HUG 1706.185, Kingsley Porter to Bernard Berenson, 14 January 1920.

HUG 1706.185, Kingsley Porter to Bernard Berenson, 11 November 1925.

HUG 1706.185, Kingsley Porter to Bernard Berenson, 25 June 1926.

HUG 1706.185, Kingsley Porter to Bernard Berenson, 19 June 1933.

Kingsley Porter to Edward Forbes and Paul Sachs, 29 August 1929.

Other Archive Sources

Brooklyn Museum Archives, New York, William Henry Goodyear Archival Collection SRG, Correspondence with Arthur Kingsley Porter.

A Cruise To The Orient: Auguste Victoria, Hamburg–American Line (leaflet), 1901.

'Five Hundred Thousand Curses on Cruel John Adair', local Donegal ballad, author unknown.

Glenvairn Castle Museum Archives, Bryn Athyn, PA, Letter from A.K. Porter to Raymond Pitcairn, 24 October 1917.

Glenveagh Castle Archives, Document No. 36 (1–4 August), pp.110–14, *Diary of Visitor in Mrs Porter's Time*.

Glenveagh Castle Archives, Document No. 43, *Gave Lecture at Visitor Centre 1991 on Kingsley Porter: Dr Joseph Wortis*, unpublished, 1991.

Glenveagh Castle Archives, Docment No. 44, *Agreement Kingsley Porter and Daniel Sweeney*, Re. Fence, published, 26 May 1931,

Glenveagh Castle Archives (Donegal), Document No. 31 (22 October 1985), P. Harbison, 'Arthur Kingsley Porter 1883–1933: Résumé of His Life' (unpublished).

Gracious Living in Stamford, Late 19th and 20th Early Centuries, c. 1892 (Stamford Historical Society, c. 1892).

Maryland Historical Trust, Lambdin House, Survey Number T-253.

Missing Person Investigations: Guidelines and Curriculum (California Commission on Peace Officer Standards and Training, December 2011).

Missing Persons Review and Recommendation (Ireland: Garda Inspectorate, March 2009).

National Archives of Ireland, Coroner's Inquest, Co. Donegal, 1933, IC/83/117.

Newberry Library, Inventory of the Waller Family Papers 1803–1938 (bulk 1803–88), Roger and Julie Baskes Department of Special Collections, 60 West Walton Street, Chicago, IL.

Official Register of Harvard University, Containing Report of the President of Harvard College and Reports of Departments for 1923, 1924, 23, 2 (20 January 1926).

Official Register of Harvard University, Containing Report of the President of Harvard College and Reports of Departments for 1925, 1926, 24, 8 (9 March 1927).

Official Register of Harvard University, Containing Report of the President of Harvard College and Reports of Departments for 1932, 1933, 31, 3 (5 February 1934).

The Pond Bureau, Publicity sheet for Æ's lecture tour in the USA, 23 October 1930.

Princeton University Library, Princeton, NJ, Allan Marquand Papers, 1858–1951 (bulk 1878–1950), Correspondence with Arthur Kingsley Porter, 1918–20: Box 17, Folder 38.

Stamford Vital Records, 1875–1906, page: 133: Births 1883 O–P.

United States Department of Immigration and Naturalization Archives, Passport Application of Arthur Kingsley Porter, 8 January 1902.

United States Federal Census 1870.

United States Federal Census 1880.

United States Federal Census 1930.

United States Patents, Oscar T. Earle, 10 January 1865; 9 March 1880; 9 September 1873; 14 June 1870; 9 March 1880.

United States Social Security Death Index.

Yale College Class Book, 1904 (Dorman Lithographing, 1904), http://books.google.com/books?id=nkA4AAAAYAAJ&dq=blake man+quintard+meyer&sitesec=reviews.

Yale University, Obituary Record: Graduates of Yale University, Deceased from June 1900 to June 1910, vol. 1900 to 1910 (New Haven, CT).

Yale University Library, Records of Arthur Twining Hadley as President of Yale University, 1899–1921, letter to Mr Hadley, from A. Kingsley Porter, 450 West End Avenue, New York, 28 January 1916, courtesy of Digital Collections (Image numbers 45040 and 45041), New Haven, CT.

Tape Recordings

Brown, R.F., Oral history interview with Henry Francis Sayles, 28 March 1974 to 11 July 1975, for the Archives of American Art, Smithsonian Institution, Washington, DC, http://www.aaa.si.edu/collections/interviews/oral-history-interview-henry-sayles-francis-13137.

Brown, R.F., Oral history interview with Frederick A. Sweet, 13–14 February 1976, in Sargentville, ME, for the Archives of American Art, Smithsonian Institution, Washington, DC, http://www.aaa.si.edu/collections/interviews/oral-history-interview-frederick-sweet-12866.

Brown, R.F., Oral history interview with S. Morton Vose, 24 July 1986 to 28 April 1987, at his home in Brookline, MA, for the Archives of American Art, Smithsonian Institution, Washington, DC, http://www.aaa.si.edu/collections/interviews/oral-history-interview-s-morton-vose-12367.

Cummings, P., Oral history interview with Fairfield Porter, 6 June 1968, for the Archives of American Art, Smithsonian Institution, Washington DC. http://www.aaa.si.edu/collections/interviews/oral-history-interview-fairfield-porter-12873.

Secondary Sources

Books, Journal Articles and Online Resources
'A. Kingsley Porter 1883–1933', *Bulletin of the Fogg Art Museum*, 3 (November 1933).

Ackermann, J. 'The Visual Arts Collection: Manifold Resources', in L. Todd and M. Banta (eds). *The Invention of Photography and Its Impact of Learning: Photographs from Harvard University and Radcliff College and from the Collection of Harrison D. Horblit* (Cambridge, MA: Harvard University Library, 1989), p.170.

Æ (George Russell), *Æ's Letters to Mínanlábáin* (New York: Macmillan, 1937).

Allen, F.L. *Only Yesterday: An Informal History of the Nineteen Twenties* (New York: Harper & Row, 1989). First published 1931.

American Architects Directory (New York: R.R. Bowker LLC, 1970), 3rd edn.

'Ancestry of Lucy (Bryant Wallace) Porter', http://babcockancestry.com/SS2-o/p106767.htm.

Anderson, M.O. *Adomnán's Life of Columba*, rev. edn (Oxford: Clarendon Press, 1991).

Anderson, W.L. and Little, D.W. 'All's Fair: War and other Causes of Divorce from a Beckerian Perspective', *American Journal of Economics and Sociology*, 58, 4 (October 1999), pp.901–22.

Baudouin, C. *Studies in Psychoanalysis: An Account of Twenty-Seven Concrete Cases Preceded by a Theoretical Exposition* (London: George Allen & Unwin, 1922).

Baudouin, C. *Psychoanalysis and Aesthetics* (London: George Allen & Unwin, 1924).

Beckwich, J. 'Kingsley Porter: Blazing the Trail in Europe', *Apollo* (December 1970), pp.494–7.

Berenson, B. *Aesthetics and History* (New York: Doubleday, 1954).

Berenson, B. and McComb, A.K. *The Selected Letters of Bernard Berenson* (London: Hutchinson, 1965).

Biography of Gail Porter: www.norfolkwalkfh.com

'A Brief Historical Profile of Wallace & Sons', The Lampworks, http://www.thelampworks.com/lw_companies_wallace.htm.

Chauncey, G., Cott, N.F., D'Emilio, J., Freedman, E.B., Holt, T.C., Howard, J., Hunt, L., Jordan, M., Lapovsky, D., Kennedy, E. and Kerber, L.P. 'The Historians' Case Against Gay Discrimination', George Mason University's History News Network (Seattle, WA), pp.1–2, http://hnn.us/articles/1539.html.

Clavin, P. *The Great Depression in Europe 1929–1939* (New York: St Martin's Press, 2000).

Cornebise, A.E. *Soldier-Scholars: Higher Education in the AEF, 1917–1919* (Philadelphia, PA: American Philosophical Society, 1997).

Davenport-Hines, R. *Titanic Lives: Migrants and Millionaires, Conmen and Crew* (London: Harper Press, 2012).

Decies, Lady, *King Lehr* (1935).

Dictionary of American Biography (New York: Charles Scribner's Sons, 1944).

Dictionary of Art Historians, ed. Lee Sorensen (Durham, NC: Duke University), www.dictionaryofarthistorians.org.

Duff, C. *On Celtic Tides* (New York: St Martin's Griffin, 2000).

Dufresne, T. *Against Freud* (Palo Alto, CA: Stanford University Press, 2007).

Emery, E.N. *Romancing the Cathedral: Gothic Architecture in Fin-de-Siècle French Culture* (Albany, NY: New York Press, 2001).

Feehan, J.M. *The Secret Places of Donegal* (Cork: Royal Carbery Books, 1988).

Forbes, E.W. 'Arthur Kingsley Porter (1883–1933)', *Proceedings of the American Academy of Arts and Sciences*, 69, 13 (February 1935), pp.537–41.

Frank, M. *Denman Ross and American Design Theory* (Lebanon, NH: University Press of New England, 2011).

Freud, S. *The Interpretation of Dreams* (New York: Macmillan, 1913).

Greenburg, G. *Manufacturing Depression: The Secret History of a Modern Disease* (New York: Simon & Schuster, 2010).

Grosskurth, P. *Havelock Ellis: A Biography* (London: Allen Lane, 1981).

Hadley, Rollin Van N. (ed.). *The Letters of Bernard Berenson and Isabella Stewart Gardner, 1887–1924: With Correspondence by Mary Berenson* (Boston, MA: Northeastern University Press, 1987).

Haggerty, A. 'Stained Glass and Censorship: The Suppression of Harry Clarke's Geneva Window, 1931', *New Hibernia Review/Iris Eireannach Nua*, 3, 4 (1999).

Hall, S. and Beveridge, B. *Olympic and Titanic: The Truth behind the Conspiracy* (Haverford, PA: Infinity, 2004).

Harmon, M. 'The Era of Inhibitions: Irish Literature 1920–60', in Masaru Sekine (ed.), *Irish Writers and Society at Large* (Totowa, NJ: Barnes & Noble, 1985).

Hart, M. 'Darien: A Brief History' (Darien, CT: Darien Historical Society, 2009), http://www.darienct.gov/content/108/415/423/default.aspx.

Hassig, D. 'He Will Make Alive Your Mortal Bodies: Cluniac Spirituality and the Tomb of Alfonso Ansúrez', *Gesta* (International Centre of Medieval Art, New York), 30, 2 (1991), pp.140–53.

Hearne, M.F. *Romanesque Sculpture: The Revival of Monumental Stone Sculpture in the Eleventh and Twelfth Centuries* (Ithaca, NY: Cornell University Press, 1981).

Hendrickx, S., Friedman, R.F, Cialowicz, K.M. and Chlodnicki, M. (eds). *Egypt at its Origins: Studies in Memory of Barbara Adams* (Louvain, Belgium: Peeters, 2004).

Hornell, J. 'The Curraghs of Ireland', *The Mariner's Mirror: The Quarterly Journal of the Society for Nautical Research* (Greenwich, London), 14, 1 (January, 1938).

Hoyt, D.W. *The Hoyt Family Meeting: Held at Stamford Connecticut, 20–1 June 1866* (Boston, MA: Henry Hoyt, 1866).

'Inishbofin (Co. Donegal)', http://www.irelandbyways.com/top-irish-peninsulas/irelands-northwest/co-donegals- offshore-islands/inishbofin-co-donegal/.

Johnson, R. *Twentieth Century Biographical Dictionary of Notable Americans* (Boston, MA: Biographical Society, 1904).

Johnson, W. (ed.). *The Papers of Adlai Stevenson: Volume 1, Beginnings of Education 1900–1941* (Boston, MA: Little, Brown, 1972).

Kain, R.M. and O'Brien, J.H. *George Russell (Æ)* (Cranbury, NJ: Bucknell University Press, 1976).

Kallen, S.S. *The Roaring Twenties* (Farmington Hills, MI: Greenhaven Press, 2001).

Keyser, R. *History of the First Company Governor's Foot Guard 1771–1901* (Hartford, CT: 1901).

Knox, I. 'The Houses of Steward from 1500' (2003), http://knoxthe donegalroutes.net/.

Koehler, W.P. (ed.). *Medieval Studies in Memory of A. Kingsley Porter* (Cambridge, MA: Harvard University Press, 1939).

Karman, J. *The Collected Letters of Robinson Jeffers, with Selected Letters of Una Jeffers, Volume 2, 1931–1939* (Stanford, CA: Stanford University Press, 2011).

Larner, J. (ed.). *Glenveagh Castle & Gardens* (Donegal: Glenveagh National Park, 2003).

Lentz II, R.E. *W.R. Trivett, Appalachian Pictureman: Photographs of a Bygone Time* (Jefferson, NC: McFarland, 2001)

Lewis, R.W.B. and Lewis, N. *Letters of Edith Wharton* (New York: Scribner, 1988).

Lord, W. *A Night to Remember* (London: Penguin Books, 1976).

Mâle, E. 'L'architecture et la sculpture en Lombardie a l'Epoque Romane', *Gazette des Beaux-Arts* (Paris), 60 (1918).

Mann, J. 'Georgina Goddard King and A. Kingsley Porter Discover the Art of Spain', in R. Kagan (ed.), *Spain in America: The Origins of Hispanism in the United States* (Chicago, IL: University of Illinois Press, 2002), pp.171–91.

Mann, J. 'Romantic Identity, Nationalism, and the Understanding of the Advent of Romanesque Art in Christian Spain', *Gesta*, (International Centre of Medieval Art, New York), 36, 2 (1997), pp.156–64.

Mann, J. *Romanesque Architecture and its Structural Decoration in Christian*

Spain 1000–1200: Exploring Frontiers and Defining Identities (Toronto: University of Toronto Press, 2009).

Mariano, N. *Forty Years with Berenson* (New York: Knopf, 1966).

Marquardt, T. and Jordan, A.A. *Medieval Art and Architecture after the Middle Ages* (Newcastle Upon Tyne: Cambridge Scholars, 2009), p.8.

McComb, K. (ed.). *The Selected Letters of Bernard Berenson* (Boston, MA: Houghton Mifflin, 1964).

McDougal, M.D. *The Letters of 'Norah' on her Tour through Ireland, Being a Series of Letters to the Montreal 'Witness' as Special Correspondent to Ireland* (Montreal: Private subscription, 1882; eBook, Project Gutenberg, 2004).

McMenamin, A. *When We Were Young: Stories and Photographs* (Balleybofey, Co. Donegal: Voice Publications, 2000).

Monroe, H. (ed). *A Magazine of Verse* (543 Cass Street, Chicago, IL), 14, 6 (April–September 1919).

Moralejo, S., 'The Tomb of Alfonso Ansúrez (1093): Its Place and the Role of Sahagún in the Beginnings of Spanish Romanesque Sculpture', in Bernard F. Reilly (ed.), *Santiago, Saint-Denis, and Saint Peter: The Reception of the Roman Liturgy in León-Castille in 1080* (New York: Fordham University Press, 1985).

Newman de Vegvar, C. 'In the Shadow of the Sidhe: Arthur Kingsley Porter's Vision on an Exotic Ireland', *Irish Arts Review Yearbook*, 17 (2001), pp.49–61.

Parks, G.E. (ed.). *Sexennial Record of the Class of 1904* (New Haven, CT: Yale University Press, 1911).

Petro, P. *The Slow Breath of Stone* (London: Fourth Estate, 2005).

Polar Record, 16, 102 (1972), pp.445–53.

Porter, A.K. *Medieval Architecture: Its Origins and Development, with Lists of Monuments and Bibliographies*, 2 vols (New York: Baker & Taylor, 1909; New Haven, CT: Yale University Press, 1912).

Porter, A.K. *Construction of Lombard and Gothic Vaults* (New Haven, CT: Yale University Press, 1911).

Porter, A.K. *Lombard Architecture*, 4 vols (New Haven, CT: Yale University Press, 1917).

Porter, A.K. *Beyond Architecture* (Boston, MA: Marshall Jones, 1918).

Porter, A.K. 'The Rise of Romanesque Sculpture', *American Journal of Archaeology*, 22 (1918), pp.399–427.

Porter, A.K. *The Seven Who Slept* (Boston, MA: Marshall Jones, 1919).

Porter, A.K. *The Sculpture of the West* (Boston, MA: Marshall Jones, 1921).

Porter, A.K. *Romanesque Sculpture of the Pilgrimage Roads*, 10 vols (Boston, MA: Marshall Jones, 1923).

Porter, A.K. 'The Tomb of Doña Sancha and the Romanesque Art of Aragon', *Burlington Magazine* (October 1924).

Porter, A.K. *Spanish Romanesque Sculpture* (Florence: Pantheon, 1928).

Porter, A.K. *An Egyptian Legend in Ireland*, Verlag des Kunstgeschicht-lichen Seminars (Marburg, Germany: Philipps University, 1929).

Porter, A.K. *The Virgin and the Clerk* (Boston, MA: Marshall Jones, 1929).

Porter, A.K. *The Crosses and Culture of Ireland* (New Haven, CT: Yale University Press, 1931).

Porter, A.K. *The Writings of A. Kingsley Porter (1883–1933): A Bibliography*, compiled under the direction of Lucy Kingsley Porter, with an introduction by Lucy Kingsley Porter (Cambridge, MA: Fogg Art Museum 1934).

Porter, A.K. *The Crosses and Culture of Ireland: Five Lectures Delivered at the Metropolitan Museum of Art, New York (February and March 1930)* (New Haven, CT: Yale University Press, 1935).

Porter, A.K. 'Letter to Æ', in Æ (George Russell), *Æ's Letters to Mínanlábáin* (New York: Macmillan, 1937), p.86.

Porter, A.K. *Three Plays* (Portland, ME: Anthoensen Press, 1952).

'Porter, Arthur Kingsley 1883–1933', Worldcat Identities, http://www.worldcat.org/identities/lccn-n50-23212.

Porter, L.K. 'Introduction', in Æ (George Russell), *Æ's Letters to Mínanlábáin* (New York: Macmillan, 1937).

Porter, L.K. *Glenveagh Castle: Visitors' Book: 1931–1937* (1937).

Porter, L.K. 'Introduction', in W.P. Koehler (ed.), *Medieval Studies in Memory of A. Kingsley Porter* (Cambridge, MA: Harvard University Press, 1939).

Porter, L.K. *The Owners of Elmwood: A History & Memoir* (Cambridge, MA: Cambridge Historical Society, 1949).

Preston, D. *Lusitania: An Epic Tragedy* (Berkeley CA: Berkeley Books, 2003).

Reilly, B.F. *Santiago, Saint-Denis, and Saint Peter: The Reception of the Roman Liturgy in León-Castile in 1080* (New York: Fordham University Press, 1985).

Richardson, H. 'Preface', in Françoise Henry, *Studies in Early Christian and Medieval Irish Art, Volume III: Sculpture and Architecture* (London: Pindar Press, 1985).

Richardson, H. 'The Fate of Kingsley Porter', *Donegal Annual*, 45 (1993), p.83–7.

Rootsweb: http://wc.rootsweb.ancestry.com/.

Rudolph, C. (ed.). *A Companion to Medieval Art: Romanesque and Gothic in Northern Europe* (Boston, MA: Blackwell, 2006).

Samuels, E. and Samuels, J.N. *Bernard Berenson: The Making of a Legend* (Cambridge, MA: Belknap Press, 1987).

Shand-Tucco, D. *Ralph Adams Cram: An Architect's Four Quests: Medieval, Modernist, American, Ecumenical* (Amherst, MA: University of Massachusetts Press, 2005).

Shorter, E. and Healy, D. *Shock Therapy: A History of Electroconvulsive Treatment in Mental Illness* (New Brunswick, NJ: Rutgers University Press, 2007).

Stamford Historical Society website: http://www.stamfordhistory.org/.

Sterner, R. *Full Moon Dates Between 1900 and 2100* (Baltimore, MD: Applied Physics Laboratory Laurel, Johns Hopkins University, 2000), http://home.hiwaay.net/~krcool/Astro/moon/fullmoon. htm.

'Una Jeffers Correspondence: The Luhan Letters, Excerpts, 1937', *Robinson Jeffers Newsletter*, 37 (Summer 1993).

'The Ward Names of Cane Hill', The Time Chamber, 2007–11, http://www.thetimechamber.co.uk/Sites/Hospital/Cane%20Hill/WardNames.php

Warren, A. *Becoming What One Is* (Detroit, MI: University of Michigan, 1995).

Whitehill, W.M. *Analecta Biografica: A Handful of New England Portraits* (Brattleboro, VT: Stephen Greene Press, 1969).

Willey, D.A. 'Bathing Facilities of the Modern Steamship – 1913', *Modern Sanitation*, 10, 9 (September, 1913).

Woloch, N. *Women and the American Experience: A Concise History* (New York: McGraw-Hill, 2002).

Wortis, J. *Fragments of an Analysis with Freud* (New York: Simon & Schuster, 1954).

Newspaper Articles

Arcadian Weekly Gazette, 'Bolt Fells Twenty People', 5 August 1895.

The Bridgeport Herald, 11 March 1900, 'Quality not Quantity'.

The Brooklyn Daily Eagle, 27 March 1920, 'Notes of Coming Books'.

The Brooklyn Daily Eagle, 10 July 1933, 'A. Kingsley Porter, Archaeologist, 50, Believed Drowned Is Missing in Stormy Sea off Irish Coast'.

The Brooklyn Daily Eagle, 30 November 1934.

The Chicago Sunday Tribune, 26 May 1912, 'New of the Society World: Personal Notes'.

The Chicago Tribune, 19 February 1903, 'Events in Chicago Society'.

The Chicago Tribune, 2 July 1933.

The Daily Boston Globe, 11 January 1925, 'Table Gossip'.

The Daily Boston Globe, 28 February 1925, 'Harvard Advances Edgell and Morize'.

The Daily Boston Globe, 3 June 1925, 'SS Martha Washington Takes 235 from Boston'.

The Daily Boston Globe, 11 May 1933, 'Old Cambridge Houses Opened in Aid of Architects' Emergency Relief Drive'.

The Daily Boston Globe, 10 July 1933, 'A. Kingsley Porter Is Missing Abroad: Archaeologist Feared Lost in Storm off Ireland'.

The Daily Boston Globe, 11 June 1939, 'New England Art Collectors Show Excellent Taste'.

The Daily Boston Globe, 18 February 1940, 'Medieval Art Exhib Opens at Museum here'.

The Daily Boston Globe, 6 April 1941, 'Reception Planned at Fogg Museum by Pan-American Society of Massachusetts'.

The Daily Boston Globe, 5 September 1943, 'Cambridge Women's War Finance Committee Plans Book and Author War Bond Rally'.

The Daily Boston Globe, 26 January 1944, 'War Time: Society'.

The Daily Boston Globe, 9 April 1944, 'Cambridge Concert'.

The Daily Boston Globe, 25 November 1945, 'Federation to Hold Victory Ball'.

The Daily Boston Globe, 22 May 1949, 'International Student Association Spring Festival at "Elmwood" in Cambridge'.

The Daily Boston Globe, 1 November 1950, 'Society: Flower Portraits'.

The Daily Boston Globe, 12 December 1951, 'Society: Experts to Lecture for Benefit of Mt Auburn Hospital'.

The Daily Boston Globe, 29 June 1957, 'Society: Here from New York'.

The Donegal Democrat, 15 July 1933, 'The Missing Archaeologist'.

The Donegal Vindicator, 7 October 1933, 'Donegal Mystery: Grim Clue to Tragedy, USA Professor'.

The Evening Post (New York), 14 December 1891, 'Died'.

The Hartford Courant, 14 January 1901, 'Timothy H. Porter's Will'.

The Hartford Courant, 13 April 1901, 'Settlement of Estate of Rev. Timothy H. Porter'.

The Harvard Crimson, 13 March 1918, 'French Architecture Lecture at 8.15'.

The Harvard Crimson, 15 March 1918, 'Italian Paintings on Exhibition'.

The Harvard Crimson, 31 January 1924, 'Other Changes in Faculty'.

The Harvard Crimson, 18 March 1930, 'Second Lecture by Porter'.

The Harvard Crimson, 11 July 1933, 'Porter still Unheard of after Violent Storm'.

The Harvard Crimson, 12 December 1935, 'Collections and Critiques'.

The Harvard Crimson, 23 September 1963, Andrew T. Weil, 'Fords Occupy Restored Elmwood: Gerry Lowell Lived in Old Fame House'.

The Harvard Crimson, 14 October 2001, '33 Elmwood'.

The Harvard Crimson, 21 November 2002, A.R. Palcy, 'The Secret Court of 1920'.

Hudson Daily Evening Register (New York), 19 March 1894.

The Irish Independent, 17 August 1931, 'Social and Personal'.

The Irish Independent, 12 October 1934, 'Mrs Kingsley Porter's Valuable Work: A Woman Archaeologist'.

The Irish Independent, 17 August 1936.

The Irish Independent, 28 February 1937, 'Books Received'.

The Irish Independent, 1 October 1941, 'Philadelphia Owner'.

The Irish Press, 10 July 1933, 'Well-Known Professor Drowned in Donegal: Curragh Caught in Thunderstorm'.

The Irish Press, 11 July 1933, 'No Trace of Prof. Porter: Gardai and Islanders Search off Coast'.

The Irish Press, 12 July 1933, 'Donegal Coast Tragedy'.

The Irish Press, 13 July 1933.

The Irish Press, 17 August 1936, 'Three Tragic Deaths: Donegal Inquest US Visitor's Ban on Doctors'.

The Irish Press, 3 July 1937, 'Fatal Collision, Septuagenarian Cyclist's Tragic Death'.

The Irish Times, 17 August 1931, 'Court and Personal'.

The Irish Times, 30 September 1931. 'Royal Society of Antiquaries: Professor Kingsley Porter's Paper'.

The Irish Times, 10 July 1933, 'Bathing Accident in Donegal: Mr J. Kingsley Porter Drowned: From Our Correspondent, Letterkenny'.

The Irish Times, 11 July 1933, 'Late Dr Kingsley Porter: Letterkenny'.

The Irish Times, 15 September 1933, 'Coroner's Tribute'.

The Irish Times, 23 September 1933, 'Inquest without a Body'.

The Irish Times, 6 October 1933, 'The Innisboffin Bones: Guards Find no Trace: From Our Correspondent Letterkenny'.

The Irish Times, 27 October 1980.

The Irish Times, 5 September 2011, G. Moriarty, 'Where Eagles Dare'.

The Leitrim Observer, 7 October 1933, 'Donegal Boy's Find: Bones on Strand Recall Recent Tragedy'.

The New York Evening Post, 21 March 1925.

The New York Evening Post, 23 May 1929, 'Miss Joyce Porter Completes Plans for June Wedding'.

The New York Evening Post, 10 July 1933, 'Searchers Look in Vain for Harvard Archaeologist, Feared Drowned'.

The New York Herald, 13 January 1897, 'Barred Doors to Bridal Couple: But Mr and Mrs Timothy H. Porter Effected an Entrance through a Rear Window: Third Wife on the Stand'.

The Paris Herald, 4 October 1932, 'Two Men Found Shot in Flat here: Suicide Pact Seen'.

The New York Times, 28 December 1861, 'Died'.

The New York Times, 10 November 1870, 'Married'.

The New York Times, 10 January 1891, 'Mr Merritt's Statement: What He Has to Say about the Fayerweather and Hoyt Wills'.

The New York Times, 30 March 1893, 'His Registration Accepted: Pastor McNeille's Dress Suit and Patent Leathers Lose the Day'.

The New York Times, 27 March 1894, 'Charges of Insanity Withdrawn'.

The New York Times, 30 March 1894, 'Porter-Earle'.

The New York Times, 15 July 1894, 'Millionaire Porter Claims Conspiracy'.

The New York Times, 8 January 1895, 'Timothy Porter's Troubles: Answer of the Defendants Against Whom the Aged Bridegroom Brought Suit for $200,000'.

The New York Times, 6 January 1898, 'Porter Conspiracy Quashed'.

The New York Times, 31 October 1902, 'Charges Against a Banknote Company'.

The New York Times, 4 December 1906.

The New York Times, 2 January 1909, 'Among the Authors'.

The New York Times, 17 April 1909.

The New York Times, 9 December 1913, 'Passengers For Europe'.

The New York Times, 5 April 1914, 'Architecture: Important Results of Mr Goodyear's Researchers, by A. Kingsley Porter'.

The New York Times, 31 March 1915, 'Jewels Lost in Fire'.

The New York Times, 4 January 1916, 'Died'.

The New York Times, 28 November 1916, 'Davanzati Art Sale now near $1,000,000'.

The New York Times, 3 December 1916, 'December Social Gayeties'.

The New York Times, 22 July 1917, 'Notable Books in Brief Review: Lombard Architecture'.

The New York Times, 11 November 1917, 'Loan Exhibition of Italian Primitives for War Relief: Art at Home and Abroad'.

The New York Times, 11 November 1917, 'The Week's Free Lectures'.

The New York Times, 19 December 1917, 'Old Italian Table Cover Brings $4,000'.

The New York Times, 26 July 1919, 'Poetry and Drama'.

The New York Times, 25 September 1921, 'Art Course For Children'.

The New York Times, 20 November 1921, 'Art Societies and Individuals'.

The New York Times, 27 November 1921, 'Art Watercolour and Art'.

The New York Times, 12 August 1923, 'A Pilgrimage to the Land of Romanesque Art: New Chronology Established for Medieval Monuments'.

The New York Times, 25 October 1924, 'New York, It's Big Income'.

The New York Times, 15 March 1925, 'John Borden Marries'.

The New York Times, 30 January 1929, 'Six Ships Sale Today for Foreign Ports'.

The New York Times, 21 June 1932, 'Gets Honorary Degree'.

The New York Times, 30 January 1932, 'New York Youth a Suicide in West: Peter K. Stockton, Harvard Sophomore, Shot Himself Jan. 16 in Michigan Hotel'.

The New York Times, 11 January 1933.

The New York Times, 31 January 1933, 'Mrs Waller Borden Wed'.

The New York Times, 4 June 1933, 'A Swedish Art Congress'.

The New York Times, 10 July 1933, 'A. Kingsley Porter Drowned off Ireland: Archaeologist Lost from Boat in Storm'.

The New York Times, 26 September 1933, 'Old Lowell House Is Left to Harvard: Arthur Kingsley Porter's Will Provides for Memorial after Death of Widow'.

The New York Times, 15 August 1936, 'Special to New York Times: Princeton, NJ'.

The New York Times, 20 January 1946, 'L.H. Porter Dead: Noted Lawyer, 71'

The New York Times, 1 July 1946, 'Mrs Louis H. Porter: Widow of Corporation Lawyer a Leader in Stamford Clubs'.

The New York Times, 18 December 1946, 'Stamford School Buys: Daycroft Gets Main House and Part of Porter Acreage'.

The New York Times, 15 October 1952, 'Eleanor B. Wallace'.

The New York Times, 21 September 1962, 'Mrs A. Kingsley Porter Dead: Widow of Harvard Medievalist'.

The New York Times, 7 November 1962, 'Widow of Archaeologist Wills Million to Harvard'.

The New York Tribune, 29 July 1896, 'Fight over the Hoyt Estate Settled'.

The New York Tribune, 14 March 1897, 'Timothy H. Porter Suit Fails'.

The New York Tribune, 28 September 1901, 'Weddings'.

The New York Tribune, 2 December 1901, 'Louis Porter Ill: Was Conspicuous Recently because of Litigation against His Father'.

The New York Tribune, 2 June 1912, 'June Brides A-Plenty'.

The New York Tribune, 1 October 1922.

The People's Press (Donegal), 15 July 1933, 'Donegal Sea Mystery: American Professor Missing: Cause of Death Unknown'.

Philadelphia Inquirer, 21 April 1912, 'Panniers Reign Supreme in Paris Fashion World'.

The Poughkeepsie New York Daily, 10 July 1933, 'Porter Archaeologist Feared Lost in Storm, Dublin, Irish Free State'.

The Rochester Democrat and Chronicle, 10 July 1933, 'Scientist Lost at Sea in Small Boat'.

The Schenectady New York Gazette, 9 July 1933, 'Porter, Noted Archaeologist Reported Lost'.

The Schenectady Gazette (New York), 3 October 1933, 'Believe Bones on an Island May Be Those of Porter: Dublin, Irish Free State'.

The Sun (Baltimore), 4 February 1901, 'Widow of a Millionaire'.

The Sun (New York), 4 October 1891.

The Sun (New York), 11 January 1894, 'Mr Porter's Lovemaking'.

The Sun (New York), 12 January 1894, 'Mr Porter's Love Letters: Some of the Copies that One of the Millionaire's Sons Made'.

The Sun (New York), 30 March 1894, 'Mr Porter Marries Miss Earle:

He Is the Eccentric Millionaire Whose Love Letters Became Public Recently'.

The Sun (New York), 3 January 1901, 'Timothy H. Porter Dead: Well-Known Trustee of the J.B. Hoyt Estate Passes Away'.

The Sun (New York), 16 January 1901. 'Timothy H. Porter's Estate: Contest of the Will Began and Prolonged Litigation Likely'.

The Sun (New York), 17 February 1909.

The Sunday Independent, 16 August 1936, 'Donegal'.

Utica Herald Dispatch, 27 June 1904.

The Washington Times, 18 July 1908, 'American Scholarship'.

Weekly Irish Times, 25 April 1931, 'Dublin Weddings'.

Yale Daily News (New Haven, CT), 19 October 1916, ' "Cupid and Psyche" Will Start Pageant Festivities'.

Yale Daily News (New Haven, CT), 23 January 1917, 'Art Collections at Yale Finest of All Universities', by A. Kingsley Porter of the Yale School of Fine Arts.

Yale Daily News (New Haven, CT), 20 March 1917, 'Corporation Makes Several Important Appointments'.

Index

Adair, Cornelia Wadsworth Ritchie, 153–5, 157

Adair, John George, 155, 162, 229, 236

Adirondacks, New York, *11ill*, 32, *33ill*, 42, 53–4, *54ill*, 153, *155ill*

Æ (George Russell), 10, 153, 156, *172ill*, 233
   The Avatars, 190, 198, 215
   correspondence with Porters, 164, 174, 181, 182, 183, 185, 190, 191, 194–5, 198, 207–8, 234–5
   day of Kingsley's disappearance and, 7, 12, 212, 213, 220, 226, 227
   death of, 235
   at Elmwood Mansion, 167
   at Glenveagh after the disappearance, 213, 214, 215, 216, 219
   illustrations in *Glenveagh Castle: Visitors' Book: 1931-37*, 173
   paintings at Glenveigh, 5, 171–2, *172ill*
   visits to Glenveagh (1931-33), 170–2, 185, 186, 191, 192, 194–5, 236

Aegean Islands, 124–5

Aix-en-Provence, 89

Alba, Duke of, 168

Alfonso Ansúrez, sarcophagus of, 127–30, *128ill*, 168, 198, 229–30

Amalfi Coast, 93

American Art Gallery, New York, 64

Amiens, France, 89

An Clachan, Inishbofin, 165

Anfossi the chauffeur, 76, 78, 84, 93, 94, 97, 100, 102, 112, 114, 131, 138, 141

Ansonia, Connecticut, 48

architecture
   in ancient Rome, 43, 45, 69
   damage in First World War, 67–8, 69–77, 78–9, 80, 81–2, *81ill*, 83, 88

export of monuments to USA, 101–2, 130, 168
French, 40–4, 62–3, 67–8, 78, 80–1, 83–4, 88–9, 95–6, 101–3, 117, 118, 247
Italian, 44, 46, 56, 61–3, 74, 83, 89, 93, 117
Kingsley as expert on, 63–4, 65, 99, 143–4, 246–7
Kingsley's abhorrence of commercial art, 44–5, 65
Kingsley's books on, 42–6, 61–6, 68, 83, 92, 97, 104, 108–9, 113, 116–18, 136, 137, 150
Kingsley's mystical conversion, 40
Mâle criticises Kingsley's theories, 62–3, 65, 118
Moorish designs, 131
Spanish, 63, 96–9, 117, 121–3, 125, 127–30, 131–2, 136, 137, 198, 242, 247
use of grotesque ornament, 62, 89
   see also Gothic architecture; monuments; Romanesque architecture; sculpture

Armagh, Northern Ireland, 168, 173

Armour, Matt, 163

Arneill, James Rae, 152

Astor, Caroline, 55

Astor, John Jacob, 52

Athens, Greece, 114, 115

SS *Auguste Victoria*, 38

Avalon, Burgundy, 78

the Azores, 113–14

Baker, Sergeant, 231

Baker & Taylor of New York, 43

Barcelona, Spain, 97, 132

Bari, throne of San Niccola, Italy, 117

Baudouin, Charles, 147, 148–9, *148ill*
SS *Beatriice*, 145
Bective House, Co. Meath, 137–8, 139
Bellevue Art Training College, France, 79
Berenson, Bernard, 96, 101, *103ill*, 160
    Aesthetics and History, 247
    coins 'Ritzonia' term, 55
    cooling of friendship with Kingsley,
        114–15, 124–5
    I Tatti villa in Florence, 93, 103–5, 106,
        110, 127
    Kingsley's letters to, 63, 91–2, 104, 105,
        125, 126–7, 206
    praises *Lombard Architecture*, 63
    travels with Porters in Europe, 84–5, 89,
        114–15, 133
Berenson, Mary, 84–5, 93, 104, 114, 124–5,
    133
Bernard, George Grey, 101
Bertaux, Madame, 118
Bird, Mrs, 168
Blachley Lodge, Darien, Connecticut, *15ill*,
    16, 21, 26, 29, 31, 36, 37, 38, 152, 239
Bolster, Sheriff, 26, 34
Book of Durrow, 139
Book of Kells, 138, 139
Borden, Ellen (née Waller, later Mrs Adlai
    Stevenson), 53, 124, 134, 137, 160, 170,
    194, 242
Borden, John, 53, 124
Boston, Massachusetts, 167, 238
Bowles, Mrs, 198
Breck, Joseph, 79, 136
Bridgeport, Connecticut, 20–1, 29, 37
Bridgeport Herald, 34–5
British Library, London, 5
British Museum, London, 141–2
The Brooklyn Daily Eagle, 217
Brooklyn Institute of Arts and Science, 45,
    57, 63
Brown, Herbert, 189
Brown, Robert F., 243
Browning School for boys, New York, 32
Bryn Athyn Cathedral, Pennsylvania, 64
Bryn Mawr University, Pennsylvania, 96
Buck, Rev. George H., 53
Burlington Magazine, 123
Byzantine art, 113, 114–15, 124, 125, 137

SS *Cameronia*, 203
Campbell, Alan, 177–81, 182, 183, 184–5,

186–9, 190, 191–2, 204, 209, 226, 227,
    233, 240
    death of, 239
    at Elmwood Mansion, 195–8, 199–203
    feelings towards Kingsley, 196–7, 201
    at Glenveagh Castle, 184–5, 186, 187–9,
        215–16
Canterbury, Kent, 142
Carcassonne, France, 102
Carnegie Institute, Pittsburg, 161
Carpenter, John Alden, 194
Cashel, Rock of, Ireland, 137
Castle Stewart, Co. Tyrone, 170
Catholic Church, Irish, 156, 183
SS *Cedric*, 133, 136, 146, 152
Celtic Revival, 173
Censorship of Publications Act (Ireland,
    1929), 156
Childers, Erskine, 138, 219
Childers, Erskine Hamilton, 138
Childers, Molly (née Osgood), 138, 181, 207,
    219
Christian Science, 235
Cione, Jacopo di, 238
Civil War, Irish, 155, 157
Clark, Miss (of Stamford), 22–5
Clarke, Harry, 156
Clonmacnoise, Co. Offaly, 139, *140ill*
Cluny, Benedictine abbey, France, 117, 246
Cobh, Ireland, 137, 162
Coll, Pat, 10–11, 12, 169–70, 185, 211, 222,
    223
Coll, Tom, 223, 224
Colony Club, New York, 61
St Columba, 162, 164, 176
Columbia University, 42, 48, 91
Commission for Historical Monuments, 67
Como, Italy, 119
Conant, Kenneth, 246
Connor, Mr, 179
Conques, Sainte-Foy abbey church, 95–6
Cormicy Church, France, *81ill*
Coutances Cathedral, Normandy, 40, *41ill*
Cox, A., 220, 235
Crankshaw, Mrs, 170, 181, 191, 218
Cummings, Eugene R., 151
Cuxa, abbey of St Michel , France, 101

Darien, Connecticut, 13, *15ill*, 16, 239
Davanzati Palace auction, New York, 61
Davis, Harry, 167, 194

De Forest, Judge, 30
de Valera, Éamon, 183, 195, 206
Derby, New Haven, 48, 53
Derryveagh Mountains, 3, 153, *154ill*
Dexter, Rose, 159, 197, 218–19
Dixon, Edward, 169
Donaghmore House, Castlefinn, Co.
   Donegal, 139–41
Donegal, County, 139–41, 146, 152–6, 170,
   181, *208ill*
The Donegal Democrat, 218
Dublin, Ireland, 138, 139, 168, 170, 205, 207
SS *Duilio*, 123
Dunraven, Earl of, 171
Durham, Bull, 100, 102
Durrow Abbey, Ireland, 139

Earle, Mabel Hastings, 20–1, 25, 26, 28–9,
   34–5, 36, 37, 121
   ante-nuptial agreement, 29, 31, 37
   'Conspiracy Case' and, 29–31, 33
Earle, Oscar T., 20
Edgell, George, 75
Egypt, 130, 137, 142, 144–6, 152, 161, 173
Eleanor (Lucy's sister), 130
Eliot, T.S., 196
Ellis, Havelock, 147, *178ill*, 196–8, 200–2,
   215–16
   The Dance of Life, 180
   death of, 237
   Kingsley and, 177–81, 182–3, 184, 185,
      186–7, 188, 189–90, 191–2,
      199–200, 204–6, 226, 227
   Lucy and, 232–3, 234, 237, 240
   Sexual Inversion, 177
Elmwood Mansion, Cambridge,
   Massachusetts, 5, 106, 109–13, *109ill*,
   176, 181–2
   Æ stays at, 167
   Alan Campbell at, 195–8, 199–203
   Ellen's wedding at, 194
   Harvard University and, 106, 230, 244
   Kingsley's teaching at, 110–11, 112, 125,
      167–8
   Lucy at (after 1933), 234, 237–9, 240
   Lucy returns to (September 1933), 230
   after Lucy's death, 244
   Porters' social life at, 111, 123, 130,
      133–5, 146, 147, 157, 159, 167, 198,
      202
Eucharistic Congress (Dublin, 1932), 183, 206

Farmington, Connecticut, 48
Ferry, James, 224
Fessenden, Samuel, 28, 29, 30, 37
Fianna Fáil, 183
First World War, 57, 58, 65, 67–8, 69–75,
   80–1, 86–7
   armistice, 75, 78–9
   damage to architecture, 67–8, 69–77,
      78–9, 80, 81–2, *81ill*, 83, 88
Florence, Italy, 93, 103–5, 238
Fogg Art Museum, Harvard, 64–5, 82, *126ill*,
   161, 205, 233, 238
   Kingsley appointed Professor of Fine Arts,
      91–2
   Kingsley's gift of Sahagún sarcophagus
      slab, 127–30, *128ill*, 168, 198, 230
   Kingsley's room at, 111
Forbes, Edward, 75, 91, 96, 108, 111, 152–3,
   161, 205, 219
Fort Royal, Co. Donegal, 170
Freudian psychoanalytic theories, 120–1,
   147–9, 233, 234

Gallagher, Fr, 170, 171, 174, 207
Gardaí, 213, 214, 217, 218, 231
Gartan, Co. Donegal, 162
Garthorne-Hardy, Geoffrey, 172–3
Geneva, Switzerland, 118
The Geneva Window, Harry Clarke, 156
Gerry, Elbridge, 106
Gimbaldo Ibi, 75
Glasgow, University of, 141
Glendalough, Co. Wicklow, 138
Glenn, Superintendent, 231
Glenveagh Castle, Co. Donegal, 3–6, *4ill*,
   154ill, 244–6
   Æ's paintings at, 5, 171–2, *172ill*
   Alan Campbell at, 184–5, 186, 187–9,
      215–16
   Civil War and, 155, 157
   curse on owners of, 162, 229, 236
   erection of deer fence on estate, 168, 179
   gardens, 3, 163, 176, 205
   Glenveagh Castle: Visitors' Book: 1931–37,
      173, 236
   Kingsley plans return to (1930), 160
   after Kingsley's disappearance, 12, 213,
      215–16, 218–19
   library, 5, 171, *171ill*, *172ill*, 175, 215
   Lucy as hostess at, 170, 171, 172–3, 174–6

Lucy at (after 1933), 234, 235–6
Lucy sells (1937), 236–7
mahogany four-poster bed, 5, 175, *175ill*
meaning of name, 153
Porters at (1930), 162–5
Porters at (1931), 168–76, 177–81
Porters at (1932), 184–93
Porters at (1933), 203, 205–8
Porters' purchase of (1929), 156–7
Porters see for first time (1929), 153–6
Glynn, Superintendent, 220
Goodyear, William Henry, 45, 57, 63, 89
Gothic architecture, 42, 43–4, 65
French, 40, *41ill*, 43, 46, 84, 118
Italian, 44, 46, 56, 62, 93
ribbed vault, 46, 62
Great Depression, 158, 160, 195, 209
Greek art, 66, 114–15
Grosskurth, Phyllis, 177, 227
Grove, Lady, 184, 191
Il Guariento (Venetian artist), 61
Guggenheim, Benjamin, 52

Hadley, Arthur Twining, 60
Hamburg-American Line, 38
Hammond, Professor, 115
Harbison, Professor, 242
Harkness Tower, Yale, *59ill*
The Harvard Crimson, 239
Harvard University, 91, 143, *202ill*
A. Kingsley Porter Professorship, 244
attitudes to homosexuality at, 150–1, 152,
182–3, 230
Elmwood Mansion and, 106, 230, 244
fraternity meets over Kingsley, 204
Kingsley appointed William Dorr
Boardman Professor, 124, 125
Kingsley considers resigning, 152–3, 206,
208–9, 228
Kingsley receives reassurances from
Forbes, 205–6, 228
Kingsley's leaves of absence from, 119,
131
Kingsley's return to (January 1933),
192–3, 194
Kingsley's summonses to Lowell House
(1933), 197, 200, 202, 203, 204
Kingsley's teaching at, 108–13, 123–4,
125–30, 133–6, 144, 157, 161, 165,
167–8, 181–2, 195, 199
legacies to in Kingsley's will, 230

Lucy bequeaths papers to, 240
*Medieval Studies in Memory of A. Kingsley
Porter*, 237, 240–1
tributes to Kingsley, 247
see also Fogg Art Museum, Harvard
Havrincourt, Battle of, 69
Healy, D., 227
Heron, Eddie, 229
Herrity, Ned, 231
the Hindenburg Line, Battle of, 69
Hitchcock, Russell, 138, 163–4, 247
Holmes, Mrs, 168
homosexuality, 149–51, 152, 189–90, 237
Havelock Ellis and, 177–81, 182–3, 196,
232, 233, 234
Kingsley-Alan Campbell affair, 177–81,
182, 183, 184–90, 191–2, 195–8,
199–203, 209, 226, 227
Lucy establishes scientific fellowship,
232–3, 234
Horton, Dr, 89, 90
Hoyt, Natalie, 237
the Hoyts of Connecticut, 14–16, 20, 49, 244
battle over J.B. Hoyt's will, 20, 26, 32
Hubert, Monsieur, 68, 69, 70, 74, 78
Huling, Lorraine, 61

Inishbofin island, *8ill*, 168–70, 171, 207,
208ill, *221ill*, 231, 236, *240ill*, 244,
246ill
hut/cottage on, 7–9, 165–7, 169, *169ill*,
170, 176, 185, 209–10, 244, *246ill*
Kingsley's disappearance from, 5, 7–12,
209–11, 215, 216–18, 220–4
Interpol, 214
Iona, island of, 141
Ireland
Catholic Church, 156, 183
Civil War, 155, 157
Co. Donegal, 139–41, 146, 152–6, 170,
181, *208ill*
see also Glenveagh Castle;
Letterkenny; Magheraroarty
Irish Free State, 156, 183, 184
Kingsley's attraction to, 160, 162–3, 165,
173
Kingsley's lectures on, 160–1
Porters' travels in (1928), 136–9
Irish High Crosses, 111, 137, 138, 139, *140ill*,
141, 160–1, 164, 173–4
Egyptian iconography and, 152, 161, 173

The Irish Independent, 237
The Irish Press, 216, 217
The Irish Times, 216, 231

Jaca, San Pedro de, Aragon, 121, 123
Jacob di Cione, 65
James, Alice, 194
Jarves Gallery, Yale, 58
Jeffers, Una, 236
Joyce, James, 156

Kells, Co. Meath, 138
Key, Ellen, 147
King, Georgina Goddard, 96
King's Academy, Stamford, 28
Kleinberger Galleries, New York, 64

La Rochelle, France, 103
Labhraidh Loingseach, relic of, 173
SS *Laconia*, 157
Lafitte-Cyon, Françoise, 237
Lake George, New York, *1ill*, 53–4, *54ill*,
     153, *155ill*
Lane, Dr, 170
Lane, Sir Hugh, 58
Lansing, Robert, 69
Larne, Ireland, 141
Lausanne, Switzerland, 118
Lavery, Sir John, 48
League of Nations, Office of Museums, 230
The Leitrim Observer, 231
León, Spain, 127–8, 198
Letterkenny, Co. Donegal, 184–5, 186, 205,
     207, 208
Loomis, Roger, 115–16, 198
Loop, Henry Augustus, 35
Lounsbury, Governor George E., 34–5
Lowell, Abbott, President of Harvard, 10, 123,
     150–1, 167, 197, 203, 204, 206, 209
Lowell, James Russell, 106
Lucas, Mary, 191
RMS *Lusitania*, sinking of, 58
Lyons Cathedral, 78

Madeira, Island of, 131
A Magazine of Verse, 83
Magheraroarty, Co. Donegal, 7, 8, 165, 169,
     208, 211–12, 218, 220, 223, 224
     Æ waits at pier (8 July 1933), 12, 212,
     220, 226, 227
Mâle, Émile, 62–3, 118

Marble Hill, Co. Donegal, 146, 152–7, 162
Marburg University, 133, 152
Mariano, Nicky, 104, 115, 133, 228–9
Marquant, Allan, 63
Marshall Jones Company, 85, 108
Marshall Jones Company in Boston, 65, 74
SS *Martha Washington*, 124
Martyn, Hazel, 48
Mason, Thomas, 137
Matthews, Dr Frank, 89–90
Maude, Sheila Cornwallis, 168
McCann, Thomas, 236
McCarthy, Joseph, 166–7
McGee, Owen, 7, 8–9, 10–11, 12, 169,
     209–11, 213, 220–2, 224, 227
McGinley, Dr Joseph P., 220, 226
McGinley, James, 223, 224
McIllhenny, Henry, 237, 244–6
McIntyre, Annie, 184–5
McMillan, E., 179
McNeille, Rev. R.G.S., 20–1
Merritt, Frances (née Hoyt), 16, 19, 157
Merritt, Katherine Krom, 19, 28, 218
Merritt, Louisa Hoyt, 19
Merritt, Schuyler, *15ill*, 16, 20, 21, 26, 27, 28,
     29, 32, 34, 37, 157
     at Elmwood Mansion, 134
     Lucy Porter and, 49
     as representative in Congress, 69
Metropolitan Museum of Art, New York, 64,
     79, 108, 136, 160–1
Meyer, Blakeman Quintard, 42
Mills, Agnes, 194
Mínanlábáin post office, 163, 164
Mitchell, Canon, 152
Mitchell, John, 236
Molloy, Mrs, 168
Monte Carlo, 77
Montpellier, France, 96
monuments
     in the Azores, 113–14
     Byzantine, 113, 114–15, 124, 125, 137
     in Egypt, 145, 152
     in England, 142
     export of to USA, 101–2, 130
     Greek, 66
     Irish portal tombs, 137
     Kingsley's study of origins of, 42, 43, 46,
     61–3
     Kingsley's system for dating of, 43, 62,
     116–18

photographing of, 45, 57, 80, 82–3, 84,
    89, 93, 97, 100–1, 116, 121, 174
at Tara Hill, 139
see also architecture; Irish High Crosses;
    sculpture
Moore, Mrs, 191
Morey, Dr C.R., 219
Muckross House, Killarney, 171
Museum of Fine Arts, Boston, 238

Natalina, 69, 94, 97, 100, 102
National Gallery, Dublin, 138
National Museum of Ireland, 237
Neergard, Dr Arthur, 53
New Haven Colony, 13–16
The New York Evening Post, 217
The New York Times, 57, 62, 86, 118, 123, 217
Noroton, Stamford, Connecticut, 5, *15ill*, 16,
    57
Northern Ireland, 168
Nourse, Mrs, 152

O'Donnell, Peadar, 155
Olympia, Greece, 114–15
Osgood, Dr, 138, 147, 159, 200
Osgood, Mrs, 138, 152

Pamplona, Spain, 99
Pan-American Society of Massachusetts, 238
Park, Dr, 202
SS *Patria*, 113
Peltz, William L., 53
The People's Press, 217–18
Perry, Dr Lewis, 167
Philadelphia Museum of Art, 237
photography, 45, 57, 82–3, 89, 100–1, 102,
    108, 116, 121, 174, 247
Pickens, William, 39
Pirie, Mrs Robert S., 194
Pitcairn, Raymond, 64
Plumbley, Louise, 33
Poitiers, France, 103
Pontorson, Church of Notre Dame, *88ill*
Portchester Castle, Hampshire, 142
Porter, Arthur Kingsley, LIFE AND
    CHARACTER
    accepted as expert on architecture, 63–4,
        65, 99, 143–4, 246–7
    acknowledges Lucy's contribution, 136
    appearance of, 38, 94–5
    Bachelor Degree in Fine Arts, 58, 61

bequest to Yale refused, 60, 143
birth, 13, 14, 16
bond with brother Louis, 37–8, 49–50,
    67, 144–5
bouts of serious depression, 144, 146–7,
    149, 177
Alan Campbell affair, 177–81, 182, 183,
    184–90, 191–2, 195–8, 199–203,
    209, 226, 227
character of, 38, 42, 48, 52, 56
childhood, 16, 17–19, 20, 21, 22, 26–8,
    32, *33ill*, 35, 120–1, 149
Christmas 1929 and, 159
collection of Italian artworks, 60, 61, 64,
    65, 238
on commercialism in art, 44–5, 65
cooling of friendship with Berenson,
    114–15, 125
correspondence with Lucy, *18ill*, 48–52,
    51ill, 53, 54, 70–5, *76ill*
courtship of Lucy, 48–50
disillusionment with human race, 86–7,
    95, 99, 125–7
Havelock Ellis and, 177–81, 182–3, 184,
    185, 186–7, 188, 189–90, 191–2,
    199–200, 204–6
engagement and marriage, 50–3
family background, 13–14
father's will and estate, 36, 37
financial losses, 209, 223–4, 228
gifts of monuments to Fogg Art Museum,
    127–30, *128ill*, 168, 198, 230
on Greek art, 66
Harvard University and *see* Fogg Art
    Museum, Harvard; Harvard
    University
hobby of hunting, 16, 38, 150
homosexuality of, 149–51, 152–3,
    177–81, 182–3, 184–90, 191–2,
    195–8, 209, 223, 226, 227
honorary doctorate from William's
    University, 184
honours from Société Française
    d'Archéologie, 46, 65
inner torment, 87, 91–2, 144, 146–7, 149
interest in drama, 19, 61
lack of self-confidence, 91–2
lectures at Fogg Art Museum, 161
letters to Bernard Berenson, 63, 91–2,
    104, 105, 125, 126–7, 206
letters to brother Louis, 92, 144–5, 146,

147, 159
love of nature, 19, 28, 32, 99
love of/need for art, 40, 43–5, 65–6
Lucy as perfect companion, 82–3
Medieval Studies in Memory of A. Kingsley Porter, 237, 240–1
meets Lucy, 47
need for solitude, 82, 87, 92, 95, 164–5
photographs of, *5ill, 11ill, 43ill, 100ill, 126ill, 129ill, 132ill, 135ill, 191ill, 240ill, 248ill*
photography and, 45
propensity for self-deceit, 104, 105, 127
rowing boat *The Swan*, 168–9
seeks European home, 85, 93
shyness of, 38, 48, 52, 58, 63, 92, 104, 105
social awkwardness, 52, 63, 75, 92, 105
student at Yale, 36, 38, 39, *39ill*, 91
study of architecture, 40, 42, 58, 91
summonses to Lowell House (1933), 197, 200, 202, 203, 204
system for dating Romanesque monuments, 116–18
teaches at Yale, 58, 60, 61, 64, 67
teaches in France, 113, 119, 136
teaching ability, 58, 110–11, 112, 144, 246
as visiting professor to Spain, 119–20
wealth of, 44, 110, 123, 144, 158, 193, 209, 228, 243
will of, 60–1, 230, 232–3
William Dorr Boardman Professorship, 124, 125
Porter, Arthur Kingsley, DISAPPEARANCE, 4–5, 7–12, 209–12, 213–25, 226–9, 235–6, 240–1
accident theories, 216–17, 222, 226, 227, 228–9
Coroner's Inquest, 209–11, 219–25, 226, 242
foul play rumours, 229
Lucy and, 7–12, 209–12, 213–16, 217, 218–19, 222, 223–4, 225, 226–8, 235–6, 240–1, 244
mystery theories, 217–18, 224–5
newspaper reports of, 216–18, 231, 235
reported discovery of bones, 231
searches for Kingsley, 7–12, 210–11, 213, 214
sightings of Kingsley, 4, 242
suicide theories, 227, 233
superstitious theories, 229–30

survival theories, 215, 224, 229, 242, 243–4, 247–8
Porter, Arthur Kingsley, TRAVELS
attraction to Ireland, 160, 162–3, 165, 173
in Egypt and Sudan with Lucy (1928-29), 144–6
in Europe with Lucy (1923), 113–19
in Europe with Lucy (1925), 124–5
in Europe with Lucy (1927), 131–3
in France and Spain with Lucy (1920), 94–103
honeymoon and trip to Italy, 53–6, *54ill*
hut on Inishbofin, 7–9, 165–7, 169, *169ill*, 170, 176, 185, 209–10, 244, *246ill*
at I Tatti in Florence with Lucy, 93, 103–5, 106, 110, 127
in Ireland with Lucy (1928), 136–9
in Italy (1908-10), 44, 45, 46
in Italy and France with Lucy (1921), 106–7
in Italy with Lucy (1920), 93–4
love of adventure and travel, 9, 38, 39, 49, 56–7, 98–9, 105, 113, 120–1, 143, 243–4
at Marble Hill with Lucy (1929), 152–7
reluctance to return to USA, 104–6, 127
return to New York (October 1919), 89
return to USA (January 1933), 193, 194
reunited with Lucy at Monte Carlo, 77
in Scotland and England with Lucy (1928), 141–2
in Spain with Lucy (1924), 120, 121–3, *122ill*
theft of case, 125, 137
tour of Normandy (1904), 40
Works of Art Service in France and Italy (1918-19), 67–8, 69–77, 78–85, 88–9
world cruise with Louis, 38–9, 143, 145
see also under Glenveagh Castle
Porter, Arthur Kingsley, WORKS and LECTURES
Beyond Architecture, 64, 65, 150
Columcille Goes (drama), 164
Conchobar's House (drama), 164
The Construction of Lombard and Gothic Vaults, 44, 46
The Crosses and Culture of Ireland, 173
'The Crosses and Culture of Ireland' (lectures, 1930), 160–1
An Egyptian Legend in Ireland (lecture),

152
Lombard Architecture, 61–3
Medieval Architecture: Its Origins and Development, 42–4, 49
Pope Joan (drama), 164
'The Rise of Romanesque Sculpture', 63
Romanesque Sculpture of the Pilgrimage Roads, 68, 83, 92, 97, 104, 108–9, 113, 116–18, 242
The Sculpture of the West (lecture series), 108–9
The Seven Who Slept (drama), 74, 85–6, 87–8, 95, 99, 125
Spanish Romanesque Sculpture (Sorbonne lectures), 97, 136, 137
'The Tomb of Doña Sancha...' (article, 1924), 123
The Virgin and the Clerk (drama), 145, 158, 161
Porter, Beatrice, 57, 61, 112, 130, 146, 152, 159, 198, 234
Porter, Blachley, 16, 17, 19, 20, 25–6, 31–2, 35
Porter, Ellen Marion (née Hatch), 37–8, 57, 159, 239
Porter, Fairfield, 133
Porter, Joseph A., 36
Porter, Joyce, 57, 61, 113, 124, 130, 147, 152, 239
Porter, Louis, 10, 20, 123, 135, 186, 197, 218, 232
    behaviour of father and, 25–6, 27–8
    birth and childhood, 16, 17–19
    bond with brother Kingsley, 37–8, 49–50, 67, 113, 144–5
    children of, 57, 61, 112–13, 124, 135, 146, 147, 152, 159, 239
    'Conspiracy Case' and, 29, 30, 31, 33
    death of, 239
    Elmwood Mansion and, 106
    father's will and estate, 36, 37–8
    fire at home of, 57
    hostility to third Mrs Porter, 29, 30, 31, 33, 35, 37
    ill health, 38, 143
    injured in Arizona, 32
    Kingsley's depression and, 144–5, 146
    Kingsley's letters to, 92, 144–5, 146, 147, 159
    legal career in New York, 36, 57
    world cruise with Kingsley, 38–9, 143, 145

Porter, Louis Hopkins (Junior), 57, 61, 152, 239
Porter, Louise Hoyt, 57, 61, 113, 157, 239
Porter, Lucy (née Bryant Wallace), *5ill*, *100ill*, *129ill*, *132ill*
    acceptance that Kingsley gone forever, 12, 215, 226
    appearance of, 47, 94
    attends Stockholm conference in Kingsley's place, 219
    back injury, 146, 147, 152
    birth of, 48
    character of, 47–8, 50, 56
    charitable work, 64, 67, 124, 237, 238
    at Coroner's Inquest, 209–11, 219–20, 223–4, 225, 226
    correspondence with Kingsley, *18ill*, 48–52, *51ill*, 53, 54, 70–5, *76ill*
    courtship of, 48–50
    death of, 241
    death of Peter Teigen and, 235
    as deserving of co-author status, 116
    diaries, 5, 80, 82, 95, 115, 136
    disappearance of Kingsley, 7–12, 209–12, 213–16, 217, 218–19, 222, 223–4, 225, 226–8, 235–6, 240–1, 244
    early married life, 56–7, 58–60
    Havelock Ellis and, 232–3, 234, 237, 240
    enforced separation from Kingsley (1918), 69–77
    engagement and marriage, 50–3
    establishes scientific fellowship on homosexuality, 232–3, 234
    feelings of apprehension, 94–5
    in France (1918-19), 78–85, 88–9
    Glenveagh Castle and *see under* Glenveagh Castle
    grows weary of travel, 115–16, 120, 142
    honeymoon and trip to Italy, 53–6, *54ill*
    as hostess at Elmwood, 110–13, 123, 124, 130, 133–5, 146, 147, 157, 159, 167, 194, 198, 238
    Inishbofin island and, 169
    introduction to *Medieval Studies*, 237, 240–1
    Kingsley acknowledges contribution of, 136
    on Kingsley and Ireland, 162–3
    Kingsley-Alan Campbell affair and, 179, 180, 183, 184–6, 187–9, 195–8, 199–203, 209, 226

Kingsley's homosexuality and, 149–50,
   177, 179, 180, 184–6, 187–9, 195–8,
   199–203, 209, 226
life at Elmwood (after 1933), 234, 237–9,
   240
love of art, 47, 82–3, 138
meets Kingsley, 47
operation to remove cyst, 89–90
as perfect companion for Kingsley, 82–3
relocation to France (1918), 67–8, 69, 143
returns to Elmwood (September 1933),
   230
reunited with Kingsley at Monte Carlo,
   77
sister Ruth, 10, 53, 82, 83, 102, 104, 130,
   137, 152, 159
sisters of, 112, 130, 146, 147, 152, 174,
   194, 206
social calender, 52, 58, 66–7, 112, 133–5,
   146, 147, 157, 165, 167–8
social skills, 47, 75
times spent alone (1929-30), 159–60, 161,
   162, 165
Austin Warren on, 238
will of, 60–1, 232, 244
Æ's Letters to Mínanlábáin, 211–12, 235–6
Glenveagh Castle: Visitors' Book: 1931-37,
   173, 236
The Owners of Elmwood: A History and
   Memoir, 239
The Writings of A. Kingsley Porter (1883-
   1933): A Bibliography, 233
see also under Porter, Arthur Kingsley,
   TRAVELS
Porter, Maria Louisa (née Hoyt), 14–17, 19,
   35
death of, 20, 21, 35, 120, 149
estate of, 21, 28, 36–7
Porter, Timothy Hopkins (Timothy H.), 14,
   15ill, 16–17, 19–20, 21, 32
battle over J.B. Hoyt's will, 20, 26, 32
'Conspiracy Case' and, 29–31, 33–4
correspondence with young women,
   21–6, 27
death of, 36
marriage to Miss Earle, 28–9, 30–1, 33,
   34–5, 36
Probate case over sanity of, 26–8
will and estate of, 36–7
Post, Chandler, 75, 111, 134, 159, 194
Prentice, Judge, 33–4

Princeton University, 67, 136
   Art Museum, 63
Prohibition in USA, 105, 150
psychoanalysis, 120–1, 147–9
Pusey Library, Harvard University, 5

Raphoe, Bishop of, 188
Reims Cathedral, 70ill
religion, 13, 78, 156, 161, 179
Rice, George T., 168
Rice, Mrs, 218
Ritch, Thomas, 20, 21, 26, 27, 29, 32, 34, 37
'Ritzonia', 55–6
Robinson, Mrs, 198
SS Roman, 131
Romanesque architecture, 85, 89, 93, 95, 97,
   99, 107, 143
   Kingsley's system for dating of, 43, 62,
      116–18
   Mâle criticises Kingsley's theories, 62–3,
      65, 118
   Spanish, 63, 121–3, 125, 127–30, 131–2,
      136, 247
   use of grotesque ornament, 62, 89
Rome, ancient, 45, 69, 74
Ronda, Spain, 131–2
Roosevelt, President F.D., 198
Ross, Denman, 104, 108, 147, 167, 247
Royal Dublin Society (RDS), 139
Royal Society of Antiquarians, 173

Sachs, Paul J., 108, 111, 112, 152–3, 160
Saha, 229
Sahagún sarcophagus slab, 127–30, 128ill,
   168, 198, 229–30
Santander, Spain, 98ill
Santiago de Compostela, Spain, 63, 85, 94,
   95, 96, 97–8, 106, 108–9
Saranac Lake, New York, 32, 33ill
Schock, Constable, 26, 34
sculpture, 65, 97, 98, 99, 168
   The Adorning Angel, 238
   in the Azores, 113–14
   from Emelia-Romagna region, 62
   Greek, 66, 115
   hidden during war, 88
   Irish influences, 117, 137
   Italian Romanesque, 119
   lions of Aix-en-Provence, 89
   Moorish influence in Spain, 117–18
   photographing of, 57, 98, 100–1, 116, 121

pilgrimage route to Santiago de
   Compostela and, 63, 85, 94, 95–8,
   106, 108–9, 117
sarcophagus of Alfonso Ansúrez, 127–30,
   128ill, 168, 198, 229–30
sarcophagus of Doña Sancha,, 123
Spanish Romanesque, 63, 117–18, 121–3,
   127–30, 132, 136, 137, 198, 242, 247
see also architecture; monuments
Second World War, 238
Senlis, France, 82, 83, 84, 88
Seville, Spain, 132
Shaw, George Bernard, 156
Shelbourne Hotel, Dublin, 138, 168, 205
Shelley, Percy Bysshe, 141
Shorter, E., 227
Sienna, Italy, 93–4
Silos, Santo Domingo de, Spain, 117, 242
Simone da Bologna, 65
Siwanoy Indian tribe, 13
Société Française d'Archéologie, 46, 65
Soissons Cathedral, Picardy, 84
Sorbonne University, Paris, 113, 119, 136
Soutter, Agnes K., 14
Soutter & Company, New York, 14
Spengler, Oswald, 180
stained-glass, medieval, 65
Stevenson, Adlai, 242
Stewart, Lady, 170
Stockholm, 219
Stockton, P.K., 182–3
Stoddard, Rudolph, 189
The Sun, New York, 27, 44
superstition, 229–30
Sweeney, General Joseph, 155
Sweet, Frederick, A., 111–12

Tara Hill, Co. Meath, 139
Teigen, Peter, 136, 137, 235
Thomas, Hugh James, 235
RMS *Titanic*, sinking of, 52–3
Tommaso di Cristoforo Fini, 61
Tory archipelago, 163, 165
Tory Island, 165, 218
Trinity College Dublin, 138, 139

Union Trust Company of New Haven, 37
United States of America (USA)
   conservatism of in 1920s, 105–6, 143,
   150–1
   early puritans, 13
   late nineteenth-century immigration, 15
   prosperity in 1920s, 105
   settlement of the west, 99

Vassar College, New York, 15
Veagh, Lough, 153
Vézelay, France, 85
Volpi, Professor Elia, 64
Vose, Morton, 111, 242–3

Waldman, Milton, 181
Wall Street Crash (1929), 158
Wallace, Ellen (née Bryant) , 48, 134
Wallace, Thomas, 48, 60
Waller, Elizabeth (née Bryant Wallace), 48, 53,
   83
Waller, James B., 48, 53, 83
Walls, Franklin J., 53
Warren, Austin, 133–4, 238
Warren Point, Northern Ireland, 168
Washington Times, 44
Wharton, Edith, 55
Whitehill, Walter Muir, 166, 246–7
Wilcox, Cyril, 151
William's University, Williamstown,
   Massachusetts, 184
Winslow, Dr, 203
Woodland Cemetery, Connecticut, 5, 36, 244,
   245ill
Woolsey Hall, Yale, 61
Wortis, Dr Joseph, 233, 234

Yale University, New Haven, 14, 36, 38, 39,
   39ill, 48, 58, *59ill*, 61, 91
   refuses Kingsley's bequest, 60, 143
Yeats, William Butler, 139, 180